Joel Harrison and Neil Ridley are at the forefront of providing expertise and innovation in the drinks world. From whisky to gin, cognac to cocktails, the duo has a wealth of knowledge to share. As well as writing for a number of different publications around the world, such as the *Telegraph* and *World of Fine Wine*, they also appear regularly on TV and act as judges for the prestigious International Wine and Spirit Competition (IWSC) awards. Their last book, *Distilled*, won the Fortnum & Mason Drink Book of the Year award in 2015.

Joel and Neil approach the drinks world with an irreverent, independently minded spirit. They can be found at www.WorldsBestSpirits.com or on social media @WorldOfSpirits.

STRAIGHT UP

To our friends and families,
who have supported us
incredibly throughout the
research for this book.

An Hachette UK Company
www.hachette.co.uk

First published in Great Britain in 2017 by Mitchell Beazley,
a division of Octopus Publishing Group Ltd, Carmelite House,
50 Victoria Embankment, London EC4Y 0DZ
www.octopusbooks.co.uk
www.octopusbooksusa.com

Distributed in the US by Hachette Book Group, 1290 Avenue
of the Americas, 4th and 5th Floors, New York, NY 10104

Distributed in Canada by Canadian Manda Group, 664 Annette
St., Toronto, Ontario, Canada M6S 2C8

ISBN 978-1-78472-273-9

A CIP catalogue record for this book is available from the
British Library.

Printed and bound in China.

10 9 8 7 6 5 4 3 2 1

Group Publishing Director: Denise Bates
Creative Director: Jonathan Christie
Senior Editor: Leanne Bryan
Editor: Abi Waters
Picture Research Manager: Giulia Hetherington
Picture Library Manager: Jen Veall
Senior Production Controller: Allison Gonsalves

MORE THAN >550< BARS

STRAIGHT UP

The insiders' guide to the world's most interesting bars and drinking experiences

MITCHELL BEAZLEY

Joel Harrison & Neil Ridley

CONTENTS*

FOREWORD*

BY RYAN CHETIYAWARDANA

I've been fortunate to know Joel and Neil for a number of years. We were brought together by some mutual friends and the knowledge that we shared – a love of music, whisky and fine drinks – and I've been very happy that we've been able to indulge in these passions in numerous locations around the world. It was through this insight that we shared a love of wonderful bars and that there is so much that goes into making the world's best venues – be it a bar, a restaurant or a recording studio – and so often it's the people at the heart of them. Whenever you travel, I suggest food and drink as a window into a culture, and crucially I'll suggest taking recommendations from the bar staff in these venues.

The beauty of *Straight Up* is that it taps into the experience of Joel and Neil – two of the industry's best travelled Bon Vivants. They can cast a critical eye over proceedings, but they've also taken the ingenious step of asking the various professionals they've met on their travels to make their own suggestions. Not only does this offer such gems as where to enjoy a fabulous whisky if that's your thing, or suggesting a tour of a city, it crucially casts the spotlight on the individual offerings of a certain venue; be it a White Lady shaken by Hidetsugo Ueno at Bar High Five, or an Old Fashioned on tap in Sydney's The Baxter Inn.

Of course, venues will ebb and flow, and there's a danger in the expectations that can come with visiting anything ranked as "the world's best". But hopefully you'll understand the difficulty of any ranking, look beyond these accolades and simply be able to enjoy someone's labour of love. Even as bartenders move on (it's worth following your favourites though!), the best venues still maintain their magic, and the essence of their offering, even though they will evolve with the new talent that makes their mark. This book tracks both the bartenders and the venues, leaving you equipped with everything you need to have a great time, wherever in the world you may be.

Much like the voyeuristic glimpses of the rich and famous from our youth (*Through the Keyhole* to MTV's *Cribs*), this wonderful book also offers a look into what many of the world's best bartenders drink, and where they go to drink it. Although these nuggets are useful beyond a curiosity, they also offer a glimpse into the best offerings around town. And these glimpses are exactly what makes the world's greatest bars so...great. It demonstrates the details that make them special, as well as the warmth that comes with knowing the people behind the bar. Of course, this book will help you find the amazing venues that are changing the world one drink at a time, but hopefully it will also introduce you to the fantastic, creative and passionate people who have taken to this diverse industry.

Dive in, and let Joel and Neil guide you into great experiences wherever you are. *Straight Up* is an essential companion for newbies and connoisseurs alike!

WELCOME*

BY JOEL HARRISON & NEIL RIDLEY

A word often used, but rarely acted out. A throwaway greeting at a check-in desk, or printed on a doormat. But what does "welcome" really mean? It means a warm smile on arrival, attentive staff and attention to detail. It means home-from-home, a place to let your hair down and relax. It means to be wanted, appreciated and accepted.

And this is what this book is all about. It is a book inspired by smiles and soundtracked by laughter, with a backdrop of the clinking of glasses and the chitter-chatter of conversation. It is a book rooted in hospitality, where the house pours are conviviality and cordiality.

In this book we aim to take good cheer and amplify it.

"Nobody goes to a bar for a drink. You go for the experience."
— JARED BROWN, DRINKS HISTORIAN & MASTER DISTILLER, SIPSMITH GIN

Over the past decade working as professional drinks writers, we have been fortunate enough to travel the world, experiencing drinking cultures far and wide. In that time, we have sipped cocktails and downed beers in places that have made us feel totally at home, despite being thousands of miles away. We have met incredible people who have dedicated their lives to the art of hospitality – the bartenders themselves who are

at the beating heart of any great bar – and we have shared spirits with those who own, make and promote some of the best-known drinks in the world.

Here, we add our own experiences to those of over 100 industry professionals, distilling the world of drinking down into this book; curating a list of over 550 tried-and-tested venues from all corners of the earth* where you'll be truly welcomed, where you'll feel simply at home.

So, welcome. In the truest sense of the word. We hope to see you at the bar of some of these establishments, and if you visit, let us know on Twitter or Instagram @WorldOfSpirits Cheers!

It is a book inspired by smiles and soundtracked by laughter, with a backdrop of the clinking of glasses and the chitter-chatter of conversation.

Before anyone says we missed an entire continent... If you fancy heading to arguably the world's remotest bar, make it the tiny **Faraday bar at the Vernadsky Research Station on the Antarctic Peninsula. Built by the British and now owned by Ukraine, it has just seven seats, where you can enjoy shots of home-distilled vodka, wine and beer for around $3. As experiences go, this has to be one of the most extreme, but surely one of the most life-changing. Now, to ask for ice, or not...*

HOW THIS BOOK WORKS*

While *Straight Up* is not an exhaustive list of wunder bars around the globe, what we hope it provides you with is an indispensable guide to some of the most memorable experiences when it comes to drinking in a bar. Here, you'll find everything from some of the world's classiest hotel bars; the most dynamic and innovative molecular mixology labs; the most rock'n'roll divebars; the most fabulously overblown tiki joints; whisky and gin paradises; rendezvous for rum; wonderful wine bars and brew pubs, whose selection of beer simply boggles the mind.

But don't just take our word for it, trust our contributors. We've pulled together a crack team of over 100 of the finest and most well-seasoned palates from around the globe – full details and biographies of whom you can peruse on pages 282–3. Bartenders; bar owners; distillers; brewers; drinks writers; brand ambassadors; and a few other friends, who we trust implicitly with our drinks orders – simply because they have racked up the air miles exploring the most vibrant city drinking cultures and hidden gems for a snifter.

You'll find each continent has been mapped out, and within these sections, over 500 different bars have been fully reviewed, each with their best attributes explained. Alongside the review you'll find the following information:

The Bar In Three Words:

The bar's attitude and atmosphere, simplified. May sometimes run to four...

They Say:

We asked each and every one of our able-palated contributors to sum up their experience at the bar in a sentence and here they tell it like it is.

We Say:

Many of the bars within the book were also our personal favourites too, so here you'll find our own thoughts on what makes them so great.

The Drink To Try:

Where applicable, we've tried to detail one of the main highlights of what to try when you're visiting. Some bars are famous, for example, for their Martinis so surely it would be madness not to try one, wouldn't it! As a lot of the bars refresh their menus regularly, it isn't possible to do this with every outlet, and some of the very best are the type of place where we wholeheartedly suggest asking the bartender for their wildest suggestions.

Price Rating:

A one-to-five scale. It's almost impossible to base this on the type of bar, so we've looked at an average of over 550 different menus from around the globe. Clearly some countries have much higher prices than others, so we've taken this into consideration dependent on where the bar is based and what it offers. You'll find humble pubs clocking in at one star alongside cheap tiki joints, right through to meticulously crafted Japanese cocktails and also sophisticated hotel bars that naturally come with a higher rating. One thing's for sure though, the *experience* in each place we've listed here is most definitely five stars!

The StarTenders

Peppered throughout each continent are one-to-one interviews with the StarTenders. These truly gifted individuals represent the very best that the drinks industry has served up, and each one has their own story to tell about their personal favourite places to drink around the world – crucially, where they relax, drink in hand, when they're off duty. We even talked a good few of them into revealing the recipes for some of their greatest cocktails for you to try making at home.

Their wisdom has enabled this guide to come together and we're incredibly proud to have shared a drink with a good number of them. We encourage you to do the same! Alongside them are a few other features, entitled *"A Drink With..."* and here you'll find other people and places that we think are well worth their own focus: breweries and brewers; cocktail paraphernalia emporiums; trend-setting restaurateurs and chefs; distillers; drinks historians; and convention founders. Alongside all our brilliant contributors, they have given *Straight Up* some of the tastiest titbits of where to drink and what to try.

City Guides:

Across *Straight Up* we'll be focusing on key cities, putting the spotlight on some of the real hidden gems to visit, as suggested by, and indeed some of them written by, the best people possible: the folks who live there. We've singled out Athens, Hong Kong, London, Toronto, Havana, New York, Berlin, Cape Town, Sydney, Dublin, Edinburgh and San Francisco, alongside some truly memorable bar crawl suggestions from our StarTenders in Tel Aviv, Moscow, Helsinki, Mexico City, Barcelona, Singapore, Paris and Lima...phew!

All right. You with us? Fancy a drink? We certainly do...let's go. As Kingsley Amis (roughly) once said: "We'll get the first round, after that, you're on your own."

THE ONE(S) THAT GOT AWAY*

CASITA, LONDON

In the process of compiling this book, we realized that there's bound to be a few places that, between putting down our empty cocktail glass, writing a review and the lengthy publishing process, have probably given up the ghost and become the stuff of spirits legend; gone but not forgotten, leaving behind a wake of lasting memories, hangovers and crusty bourbon bottles. Equally, there have been some new openings (Swift – see page 49, Three Sheets, Scout and others in London; Black Tail, The Lø and more in New York...you get the picture) to fill those left by the dearly departed.

The sad fact is that no matter how much passion there is to succeed, sometimes other things, like life, get in the way and it is indeed better to burn out brightly, than to simply fade away. With that in mind we'd like you to raise a glass to one such fallen gem, **Casita** in London's Shoreditch. This tiny Central/South American-themed place was, perhaps, the ultimate Bartender's Bar, certainly in East London anyway. It was also a regular for us; somewhere to pop in for a welcoming shot of Tequila Con Verdita, which actually felt like it was doing you a favour on the way down. You'd always stay that little bit longer than you intended; it would always make you late in some way, but wherever you needed to be after, you'd usually arrive with a smile. When the bar's owner, Will Foster, took the difficult decision to close the place after a decade,

The sad thing is that in the time it has taken to write, design and publish this book, a few more of our chosen favourites from around the globe may well have gone the same way as dear Casita.

a huge number of people were sad to see a masterclass in homespun hospitality disappear from the London landscape.

The story isn't all doom and gloom however. In the cellars underneath the bar, from the ashes of Casita, has sprung **Found** (which you can read about on page 33) and there are plans to turn the space that Casita once occupied into another bar, with some of the old team at the helm.

The sad thing is that in the time it has taken to write, design and publish this book, a few more of our chosen favourites from around the globe may well have gone the same way as dear Casita – a fact of life and one that is unfortunately inevitable, given the financial and social challenges faced by bar owners.

No matter what may happen though, let's all take the opportunity to toast that one place that is special in our hearts, wherever it once lay; whatever its fate and with whomever you shared a memory and a decent drink...we salute you. *Salut!*

● REYKJAVIK *page 114*

● BERGEN *page 112*

pages 110–11 OSLO ●

page 105 GOTHENBURG ●

● CRAIGELLACHIE *page 63*
● ABERDEEN *pages 62–3*

pages 64–5 ISLAY ●
● EDINBURGH *pages 56–60*
● GLASGOW *pages 61–2*

pages 106–7 COPENHAGEN

page 51 LIVERPOOL ●
● MANCHESTER *pages 50–1*

pages 92–3 HAMBURG ●

pages 66–9 DUBLIN ●

page 51 BIRMINGHAM ●

pages 86–9 BERL
● AMSTERDAM *pages 98–101*

pages 54–5 BRISTOL ●

LONDON *pages 18–49* ANTWERP *page 102*

page 55 LYME REGIS ●

page 92 ERFURT ●

● BRIGHTON *page 54*

pages 102–3 BRUSSELS

● FRANKFURT *page 93*

page 92 NUREMBERG ●

pages 72–9 PARIS ●

pages 90–1 MUNICH ●

page 97 ZURICH ●

page 123 MILAN ●

● BORDEAUX *page 79*

page 123 VE

pages 122–3 ROI

● BARCELONA *pages 80–3*

page 83 MADRID ●

● CÓRDOBA *page 85*

page 85 JEREZ ●

14

EUROPE*

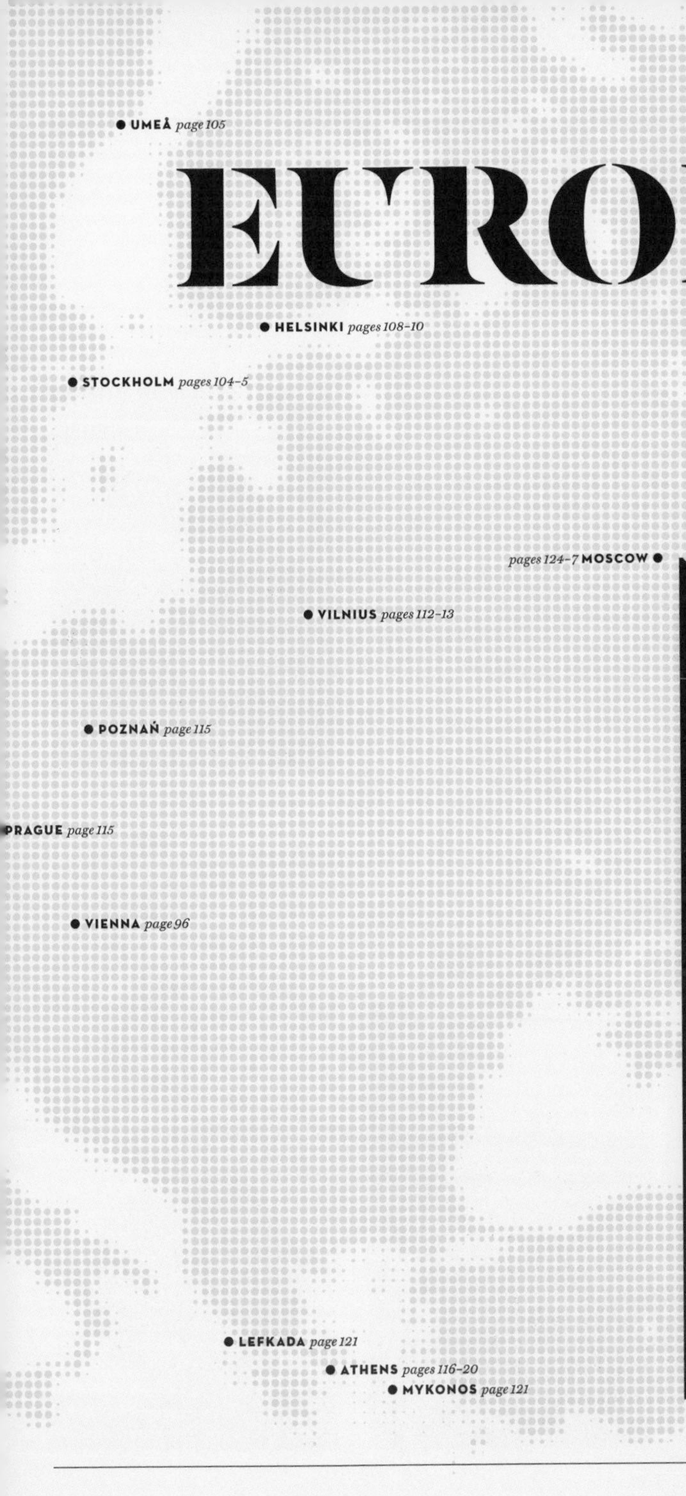

● UMEÅ *page 105*

● HELSINKI *pages 108–10*

● STOCKHOLM *pages 104–5*

pages 124–7 MOSCOW ●

● VILNIUS *pages 112–13*

● POZNAŇ *page 115*

●PRAGUE *page 115*

● VIENNA *page 96*

● LEFKADA *page 121*

● ATHENS *pages 116–20*

● MYKONOS *page 121*

Countries

INTRO*

urope is a place that is currently undergoing enormous change, from both a political and a cultural point of view. When it comes to the bar scene, it's unlikely you'll find any other continent that offers as much diversity, in styles of drink, creativity in cocktail craft and service. In many respects, anyone who lives in Europe is very spoiled when it comes to the sheer wealth of great bars, all but a few hours' flight away.

Starting with London, a powerhouse of truly brilliant establishments, which has caused ripples of trends to permeate outward. From the scene stealing, game-changing attitudes toward innovation and unusual ingredients, served up in the East End of the city, to the outstanding, timeless elegance of the capital's very best hotel bars, London's influence on the global cocktail scene cannot be underestimated. Because of this,

you'll find a mighty fine list of incredible London bars over the next few pages.

It's also worth pointing out the rich history of Edinburgh's influence on the cocktail scene (see pages 56–9), where a number of the world's best bartenders started their apprenticeships. Many of the bars we've included continue to be highly lauded as world class.

From here, it's on to Paris. A renaissance of the French cocktail scene has been spearheaded by a few select bars over the past five years, bringing genuine artistry into the drinks creations, backdropped by the historical chic that the city is well known for.

When it comes to the bar scene, it's unlikely you'll find any other continent that offers as much diversity, in styles of drink, creativity in cocktail craft and service.

Berlin, too, is a city rich in cocktail culture and currently boasts several stone-cold not-to-be-missed classics.

Scaling the northernmost point in Europe with Reykjavik, travelling all the way down through Scandinavia, Spain, Italy and eventually arriving 5,000 kilometres (3,100 miles) southward in Athens, we've planned quite the cocktail journey for you.

LONDON*

L ondon has acted as the destination for some of the world's greatest bartenders, many setting up shop there, to give the city a genuine melting pot of flavours and drinking experiences. Because of this, the sheer wealth of new bar openings is tricky to capture at any given moment: turn around for a second and suddenly a new destination (such as the excellent Swift in Soho or Untitled in Dalston, to the east of the city) opens its doors and proves why it is essential to make London one of your ultimate must-visits. Be it a tiny dive bar (see Crobar on page 31) or a divine hotel bar martini experience (Connaught Bar on page 30), you'll need to give yourself plenty of time to get around so many landmark drinking experiences.

THE BAR WITH NO NAME AKA 69 COLEBROOKE ROW →

Have you ever thought about turning your front room into a cocktail bar? Well, that's kind of what 69 Colebrooke Row is like, a simple place hidden away off the main streets of North London's Islington area. Colebrooke Row was a revelation when it was opened in June 2009 by Tony Conigliaro (see opposite) and pioneered molecular mixology techniques that have changed the face of cocktail-making in the 21st century. Just one room houses a few seats and a cocktail list with some "must-try" items, such as the Prairie Oyster, which is served oyster-style, to be consumed in one go. Such was the innovation of the cocktails at this bar that Tony C, as he is known in the business, now has a drinks development company called The Drink Factory.
✖
69 Colebrooke Row, London N1 8AA +44 (0)7540 528 593 www.69colebrookerow.com
✖
IN THREE WORDS:
Education, Education, Education.
THE DRINK TO TRY:
Prairie Oyster.

WE SAY:
Now listed as a London classic, the techniques developed here are now seen in bars around the world.
THEY SAY:
"Discovering 69 was a small revelation for me...still serving some of the world's most creative, yet simple drinks."
— **REMY SAVAGE, PARIS**
"The drinks are outstanding."
— **KELSEY RAMAGE, CANADA**
PRICE RATING: ✳✳✳

FOCUS*

STARTENDER
TONY CONIGLIARO, UK

As pioneers come, Tony Conigliaro is perhaps one of the most well-known and progressive mixers of drinks in the business. Since 2009, when he opened The Bar With No Name (aka 69 Colebrooke Row), he has continued to push boundaries in flavour. Alongside his newly opened Bar Termini (see page 49), which specializes in the classic Negroni cocktail, Tony's Drink Factory lab (thedrinkfactory.com) is a playground for his inspiration, where he collaborates with chefs, chocolatiers and perfumers.

Where do you drink when you're off duty?
I go to the pub as I don't want to think of work. **The French House** in Soho (frenchhousesoho.com) is my favourite and I've been going there for years.

Your favourite drink of all time?
A Martini...5:1 ratio of old school gin and old school vermouth and garnished with a twist.

Where is your favourite city in the world to go drinking in and why?
Tokyo has a great energy right now. I look forward to every visit because of the attention to detail.

What do you think is the most underrated cocktail of all time and why?
It would be the Army and Navy. It's just such an amazing drink.

Tell us a secret about making the perfect Negroni...
Our Negronis are "cooked" sous vide at a low temperature. This gentle heat stimulates the breakdown of aromatic compounds within the liquid, creating a result that is almost identical to a bottle-aged cocktail, but with more integrated flavours and an added silkiness.

What would you say is one of the most important "signature serves" that you've come up with?
Launched at 69 Colebrooke Row in 2012, the Terroir has become iconic. A playful take on terroir in wine, we have blended distillations of clay, flint and lichen to explore the effect of the environment in flavour. Our Terroir harnesses and explores the mineral qualities of the earth to create a play on the terroir of wine without the wine itself.

TONY'S TOP BARS:

✖
Bar Trench, Tokyo (see page 136) *"Go there to see Rogerio!" (but if you can't, go to page 135 for an interview with this StarTender).*

✖
The Seven Jokers, Athens (+30 21 0321 9225) *because you will have a hilarious night.*

✖
Midnight Rambler, Dallas (see page 235) *It has the best music policy ever and (bartenders) Chad and Christy are great.*

✖
L'Entrée Des Artistes, Paris (lentreedesartistespigalle. com) *This has the most humble drinks makers making easily the best drinks in town.*

FEATURE*

A DAY DRINKING IN LONDON

Sometimes it's hard to see the wood for the trees, especially if you actually live in the forest, so when it comes to London, one could say there are a lot of very flavoursome trees to choose from. Writing as residents of this city, it's sometimes easy to overlook the finer points of a day out drinking here, particularly as the city is split into so many distinct regions and styles of places to enjoy.

A lunchtime pint has become a preoccupation for those in love with London's glorious pub scene and starting out on this path has to be a visit to the **Cittie Of Yorke** ⬇ (samuelsmithsbrewery.co.uk) on High Holborn. In fact, relating to the wood analogy above, this place certainly (tree)tops the bill. Cavernous in size, the Cittie Of Yorke is panelled from floor to ceiling in wonderfully vintage dark wood, setting the tone for a perfect place to enjoy a pint of Sam Smith's Sovereign Bitter. It is gloriously free from the mass-market beer brands that surround us on a daily basis and sets the tone for a city drenched in liquid history.

From here, amble your way down toward Maiden

Lane, where you'll find **Rules** (rules.co.uk), London's oldest restaurant, established in 1798. The main theme here is hearty, British fare (think steamed suet steak and kidney puddings) cooked to perfection and washed down with one of the house cocktails, like The Rules (gin, Dubonnet and vintage *crémant*) or a silver tankard of ale.

Tipplers looking for a "swift one" post-lunch could visit **The Whisky Exchange** shop (thewhiskyexchange.com) on Bedford Street, which will result in some light education for your palates on any spirit you care to mention; you'll no doubt leave with several clinking bags of unusual spirits to enjoy at a later date.

From here, you have a choice of directions your libacious day could take you:

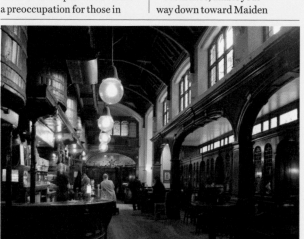

A:

Head into Soho, making sure you visit the swift Italian-themed brilliance of **Bar Termini** (see page 49) for a little Negroni, with an essential visit to **Gerry's Wine and Spirits** (gerrys.uk.com) on Old Compton Street, to stock up on numerous weird and wonderful cocktail bitters.

B:

Head west to Chiswick for a tour of the Fuller's **Griffin Brewery** (fullers.co.uk) for a glimpse into British beer-making history, with several tasty stops at its **Hock Cellars** on the way. Or...

C:

Head in the opposite direction to the **East London Liquor Company** (see page 32), arguably one of London's most exciting and progressive micro distilleries, who have an award-winning craft gin, vodka and, incredibly, London's first rye whisky slowly maturing away.

By this time, London's vibrant early evening starts to kick in and you'll most likely need some food. Head to **Cafe Pacifico ⏶** (see page 26) for a Tommy's Margarita and some generously filled tacos before making London's inspiring cocktail scene a must-see with Shoreditch your first port of call. Head over to **Happiness Forgets** (see page 36) before it starts to fill up, followed by a swift walk to **Found** (see page 33), one of our new favourite haunts.

If you choose to stay in the central area, no visit to London's cocktail scene is complete without a Martini, and two

of the finest exponents of this classic, Agostino Perrone at **The Connaught Bar** (see page 30) and Alessandro Palazzi at **Dukes** (see page 32), are both highly recommended.

With a broad spectrum of choice on offer, it's impossible to become tired of the sheer number of great places to drink in the capital.

At the end of the night (or is that early the next morning?), you may well find yourself partying

the night away at the **Crobar** in Soho (see page 31). If you do, we might well see you in there.

LONDON*

AMERICAN BAR

American Bar is a term that you can encounter across the world in many hotels, and basically means "cocktail bar" coming from the days when the great bartenders, and really the inventors of the cocktail, were fantastic American showmen such as the legendary Jerry Thomas. These chaps and chapesses were not exclusively American, however. In the early part of the 20th century a certain Harry Craddock, born in the sleepy, leafy town of Stroud, Gloucestershire, headed off to America to learn the great art of making cocktails. After becoming an American citizen, he ended up back in his native United Kingdom during Prohibition where he joined the American Bar at the Savoy, in 1920.

After a successful decade behind the stick, Craddock published a cocktail book, *The Savoy Cocktail Book*, which today stands not only as one of the greatest drinks books

ever produced, but includes some drinks, such as the Corpse Reviver #2, which have become staples of many drinks menus around the world.

Today, under the guidance of Erik Lorincz, the bar thrives, echoing the days of the early 1900s when glitz and glamour were the order of the day, and cocktails were as much entertainment as the theatre (of which the Savoy also boasts one of London's finest).

✖

Savoy Hotel, Strand, London WC2R 0EU +44 (0)20 7836 4343 fairmont.com

✖

IN THREE WORDS:
Taste The Past.

THE DRINK TO TRY:
You have to go for a Craddock classic, such as a White Lady.

THEY SAY:
"An all-time favourite of mine, great."
— STEPHAN BERG, GERMANY
"There simply is no equal."
— MICHAEL VACHON, USA
"It's exceptional and unrivalled."
— REBEKKAH DOOLEY, UK
"Classic drinks with modern touch in overwhelming ambiance."
— MARIAN BEKE, SLOVAKIA
PRICE RATING: ✖✖✖✖✖

BEAUFORT BAR

This may sound slightly sycophantic, but the Savoy Hotel can boast not one but two entries in this book (rather like The Connaught Hotel, see page 28 and 30). This is simply down to the reason that both its bars, the American Bar (see left) and the Beaufort Bar are so significantly different in style, but equally awesome, that no listing is complete without having them in tandem. Walking in through the grand entrance to the hotel, down the steps past the tables of tea-taking folk, is quite a sight in itself, but entering the vast, high-ceilinged Beaufort Bar is something else altogether. As rooms go, it's *very* impressive. Dark, rich and opulent, it serves to demonstrate how the concept of the hotel bar has survived every cocktail trend, by simply being at the top of its game, from the exemplary service to the attention to detail in each drink. As prices go, the Beaufort isn't cheap, but you won't feel out of pocket at any point, as the experience is utterly world class. Start your evening with a glass of Champagne and then work your way into the complex Tunnel Book Menu, which is broken down into distinct areas, paying homage to the various celebrities who called the hotel their second home – including Marilyn Monroe, Alfred Hitchcock and Fred Astaire. Come the Apocalypse, when all other cocktail bars have long since departed this earth in a charred haze of mezcal and Islay whisky, the Beaufort Bar will still be standing tall like a mighty oak; a haven of panache in one of London's most iconic and splendid dining locations.

✖

Savoy Hotel, Strand, London
WC2R 0EU +44 (0)20 7836 4343
fairmont.com

✖

IN THREE WORDS:
Timeless, Unbridled Elegance.

THE DRINK TO TRY:
The Fred Astaire-inspired Under The Stars, with its complex bourbon notes.

THEY SAY:
"A beautiful classic hotel with a new bar crew doing their job exceptionally well!"
— MARIAN BEKE, SLOVAKIA
PRICE RATING: ✱✱✱✱✱

BLACK ROCK ↗

Embracing the trend toward the modern appreciation of whisky, this distilled drink is very much the focus here – quite literally, as the small basement venue is mostly taken up by a huge table made from a half tree trunk, which runs the entire length of the room. Herein lies the secret of Black Rock. As well as the well-stocked cabinets of whisky (arranged into styles from light/heavy, rather than by region or alphabetically) the trunk has two channels cut into it, each one holding a different, constantly evolving "living" whisky – a house

blend and a sweetened liqueur style offering – both of which are superb. The Scottish-themed bites top off what is arguably London's best place to explore whisky without A: needing to take a qualification or B: a bank loan to explore some real gems.

✖

9 Christopher St, London
EC2A 2BS +44(0)20 7247 4580
Blackrock.bar

✖

IN THREE WORDS:
Wood Maketh Whisky.

THE DRINK TO TRY:
The Talisker Mizuwari is probably the best outside of Tokyo.

WE SAY:
Friendly, knowledgeable staff and a ton of great juice. Dive in and get your palate wet.

PRICE RATING: ✱✱

BLIND PIG

Situated on Poland Street (home to the legendary Milk And Honey, see page 40) the Blind Pig makes its home (or sty?) above the trendy eatery and sister venue the Social Eating House. Climb up the stairs bathed in neon light glow and you'll find yourself in one of the trendiest spots in this part of town. With the decor and bartenders inspired by old school craft workshops, the cocktails are simply wonderful. Owned by top chef Jason Atherton, expect to find mini baskets of popcorn and other fun elements attached to your drink, but it is what is in the glass that counts. Try the Slap 'n' Pickle, or for a bit of fun their Skittles-washed vodka!

✖

58 Poland Street, London
W1F 7NR +44 (0)20 7993 3251
socialeatinghouse.com

✖

IN THREE WORDS:
Childlike Cocktail Fun.

THE DRINK TO TRY:
Slap 'n' Pickle for the pickle lovers out there.

WE SAY:
Simply a wonderful night out of fun, experience and, above all, utter creativity.

PRICE RATING: ✱✱✱

FEATURE*

A DRINK WITH...
JARED BROWN

If experience is wine, then Jared Brown's stories are vintage Champagne. He is one of the founders of the Sipsmith Gin Distillery (sipsmith.com) which, when it was started in 2009, was the first copper pot still distillery to open in London in 189 years. Jared is not just a Master Distiller, but also a celebrated drinks historian and award-winning drinks communicator. His experiences around the world allow him to legitimately be called a Bon Viveur.

"When I go into a bar, the first thing I look for is the greeting. It tells me also how the service is going to be. For me, this is the single most important element in service in a bar.

Back in the day, in New York, I was a starving hotel school student and I could either afford to take the train to school, or walk the 50 blocks so I could eat that day. I would save up and at the end of the month I'd have an extra $20. I'd put on a suit and tie and walk into the bar at the Four Seasons restaurant (now known as the **Ty Bar**

When I go into a bar, the first thing I look for is the greeting. It tells me also how the service is going to be. For me, this is the single most important element in service in a bar.

at the **Four Seasons Hotel,** fourseasons.com) and have one Martini. I would be treated with as much respect and welcome as the billionaires sitting in there. They knew I was just a student and this was my only suit and tie, and that I was only going to have one, but I was treated just as well.

Nobody goes to a bar for a drink. You go for the experience.

When it comes to my top bar experience, then simply walking into **El Floridita** in Havana (see page 274) will always be a favourite. My wife and I were in there once, and we asked the bartender to make whatever he felt like making, which is when we discovered the Jai Alai, a cocktail lost around the world but invented in Cuba in the early 20th century, made up of gin, sweet vermouth, in a rocks glass, topped with soda and a lemon wedge. A wonderful drink that actually predates the Negroni.

Going into **Bar High Five** in Tokyo (see page 133) is always an incredible experience. There, it is about watching technical perfection, or as near as you can get to it. The bartenders taste every drink using spoons, forcing a slurp, so they are really tasted properly, against the pretence of tasting through a straw.

There is a bar up in the Shiga Highlands in Japan that I loved for one reason only: the sign on the sliding glass door as you entered that simply said, "Please keep door closed or monkeys will come in". I remember sitting in the bar, having a beer and looking out seeing disappointed monkeys because we'd read the sign.

Another great bar experience has to be **The Drifter** ➜ by **The Green Door Tavern** in Chicago (thedrifterchicago.com). It's not been long since this bar was discovered, in the literal sense. The Green Door Tavern is an old Chicago establishment; lots of curios on the walls, trying to be a bit of a pub. One afternoon, a very old man came in, went downstairs and came back up to ask what happened to the downstairs bar. They told him they didn't have one, but he was adamant that they did. So they went downstairs, the old man put his hand on the wall and said, 'There is a door behind this wall, there is a bar here'.

The old man got so worked up, he punched a hole in the wall with his stick. One of the staff shone a torch through the hole and they saw a door. It turns out that behind the door was a Prohibition-era burlesque bar completely intact, bottles still behind the bar; the hand-painted burlesque posters still hanging; the stage in place; a few dirty glasses on the bar.

It had sat unmoved, untouched, undiscovered when they found it. They fixed it up slightly and brought in burlesque acts that fit the room. You walk into a time warp. And the drinks are good! So to me, how can this not be ranked as one of the best bars in the world?

Another great experience is the **Paradiso** (paradiso.cat), a pastrami sandwich shop [in Barcelona], where you walk through the wooden refrigerator and you're into this stunning speakeasy bar. But then you go into the men's toilet and you pull down the soap dispenser, and there is a red button behind it. You press that and this whole wall with sink swings out of the way and you're in a speakeasy within a speakeasy!

When I'm not travelling and am back at home in the Cotswolds, my locals are **The Kingham Plough** (thekinghamplough.co.uk) and the **The Golden Ball** in Lower Swell (thegoldenballinn.com). Also **The Slaughters Manor House** (slaughtersmanor.co.uk), which is a short walk through the woods from my house. When you order a cocktail, the first thing they do is to chill a glass; this should be the first thing anyone does when a cocktail is ordered!"

LONDON*

B.Y.O.C. ↓

Imagine for a second that you wanted your very own private cocktail experience. Where would you choose? Yes, you could effectively hire any of the bars in here (for a fairly hefty price tag, we imagine) but would it really give you that truly memorable experience? Probably not as much as B.Y.O.C. in Soho. Here, and in the three other boutique bars that bear the name B.Y.O.C., (Bring Your Own Cocktail), you'll get a personalized bartender for the evening and a space to play: all you need to provide are

the spirits and the friends to enjoy them. Coupled with a few "storecupboard ingredients" of their own, they can work from whatever you decide to bring along spirits wise.

✖

21 Great Windmill Street, London W1D 7LB +44 (0)203 441 2424 byoc.co.uk

✖

IN THREE WORDS:
Bring, Create, Smile.

THEY SAY:
"Give the bartenders any type of unusual ingredient, they'll always manage to make something great out of it!"
—RAISSA DE HAAS, HOLLAND

WE SAY:
A superbly fun concept, that really feels personal and entertaining.

PRICE RATING: ✱✱
(based on a fixed per-head price)

CAFE PACIFICO

A legendary name, should you be a fan of Mexican cuisine, Cafe Pacifico (along with its now sadly closed spiritual cousins El Nivel and La Perla) has been very much the leading light in bringing a little bit of a *sonrisa* to the capital since 1982. We've never met a person who doesn't smile when they see a freshly made tortilla, bursting at the seams with gloriously colourful

salsa, guacamole and steaming chicken strips. The extra-wide smiles then seem to arrive once the Margaritas come out. Here you'll find pitchers of the drink, which are seemingly bottomless, depending on who you are drinking with and smiling at – all made with a genuine panache from Ocho Blanco and Reposado tequila, beautifully balanced, honeyed agave nectar and fresh lemon. The list then simply explodes into life with more signature Margaritas (vanilla and pomegranate) and soon, you'll forget you're in central London at all, whisked off to a destination where dancing in the street is mandatory, still smiling from ear to ear.

✖

5 Langley Street, London WC2H 9JA +44 (0)20 7379 7728 cafe-pacifico.com

✖

IN THREE WORDS:
Smile! It's Tequila.

THEY SAY:
"Pablo 'Papi' Hurtado [legendary Columbian bartender, now based in Philadelphia] took me there the first time, then I ended up working there for almost five years. I still go in."
—JON ANDERS, NORWAY
"An absolute inspiration."
—MEGS DEMEULENAERE, UK

PRICE RATING: ✱✱

CALLOOH CALLAY ↑

Inspired by Lewis Carroll's *Jabberwocky*, Callooh Callay takes its name from a poem about total nonsense. Unsurprisingly, the vibe the team have created here truly lives up to its surrealist imagery. From the Narnia-esque wardrobe, which guests can enter and find themselves in a wonderfully cool environment, through to their more exclusive, mirrored back bar upstairs (which can often boast a different menu to the main bar), the bar feels like walking into another world. And then there's the drinks menu, the design of which changes regularly and has won design awards. Enter...and be prepared for the unexpected.

✖
65 Rivington Street, London
EC2A 3AY +44(0)20 7739 4781
calloohcallaybar.com
✖

IN THREE WORDS:
Beware The Jabberwocky.

WE SAY:
One of East London's classic cocktail venues.

PRICE RATING: ✱✱✱

CEVICHE

If there was ever proof needed that the hospitality business is really part of the entertainment industry, then look no further than this book: written by two former record executives turned award-winning drinks writers, it also features an interview with the chaps at Noble Rot (see page 38), one of whom is the former MD of Island Records, and add to this Soho's Ceviche, owned and run by Martin Morales (see page 279), himself a former record company executive.

With a passion for all things Peruvian, Martin distilled the experiences of his childhood in Lima to open his restaurant Ceviche, and introduce London to one of the finest cocktails in the world: the Pisco Sour. Martin built this Soho haunt on great cooking and excellently executed Pisco Sours, sourcing the best possible spirit for his cocktails, as well as infusing pisco with different herbs, spices and fruits to give a wide kaleidoscope of flavours for his bar team to play with. The bar hosts Pisco masterclasses and the whole bar team have become unofficial Pisco priests, singing the praises of this spirit.

✖
17 Frith Street, London W1D 4RG
+44(0)20 7292 2040
cevicheuk.com
✖

IN THREE WORDS:
Pisco A GoGo.

THE DRINK TO TRY:
It has to be the Pisco Sour.

WE SAY:
Make sure you stay for food, too.

PRICE RATING: ✱✱✱

CLARIDGE'S

Claridge's is often referred to as "the first hotel in London". Its long and illustrious history has made it a place to be seen, and if you hang around the reception long enough, you'll undoubtedly bump into someone famous.

The hotel boasts two bars, the main Claridge's bar and the Fumoir bar; the latter is small and intimate, with cocktails from a curated collection of mainly dark spirits, served in a Lalique-inspired setting. The former is twice the size, lighter and perfect for an afternoon drink. It even has its own door onto the street, allowing discreet access for those falling between Mayfair's members' clubs, top restaurants and high-end shops and in need of a mid-afternoon Negroni.

Brilliantly managed, this is hospitality at its best.
✖
Claridge's Hotel, Brook Street,
Mayfair, London W1K 4HR +44
(0)20 7629 8860 claridges.co.uk
✖

IN THREE WORDS:
London's First Hotel.

THE DRINK TO TRY:
The Brook Street, their take on a Martinez.

WE SAY:
Very well-curated drinks, from the back bar to the cocktail list. A Mayfair must.

PRICE RATING: ✱✱✱✱

FOCUS*

STARTENDER
AGOSTINO "AGO" PERRONE

Ago Perrone needs little introduction when it comes to cocktails delivered with a panache like no other. His playground is The Connaught Bar at The Connaught hotel in Mayfair, a place which oozes sophistication and a generous nod to the golden cocktail era of the 1920s. Ago and his team have reached a level of mastery that has seen The Connaught Bar crowned with multiple awards over the last few years.

Where is your favourite city in the world to go drinking in?
It would be easy to say London or New York...however, when I was in Athens recently I thought it was great; the vibe and mix of local and exotic cultures.
What do you look for in a bar, as a sign of true greatness?
The smile on people's faces – both the staff and the clients.
Where do you drink when you're off duty?
I love the cabinet in my own living room, my bartender knows me better than I do! Yes, I like to mix a cocktail or two for myself.

I am Italian and what is better than the Negroni... perfect for any occasion, it has spirit to lift, sweetness to relax and spicy to cure!

Your favourite drink of all time...
I am Italian and what is better than the Negroni... perfect for any occasion, it has spirit to lift, sweetness to relax and spicy to cure!
Describe The Connaught Bar in 3 words.
Cocktails, Service, Personality.

✖
AGO'S MULATA DAISY

This drink really sums up the
skill and attention to detail
practised by Ago and his team.
Despite bringing together some
unusual ingredients, it feels
like a classic drink, which
harks back to the golden age
of cocktails in the 1920s.

40ml light aged rum
20ml freshly squeezed lime juice
1 bar spoon of caster sugar
½ bar spoon of fennel seeds
20ml Crème de Cacao Brown
10ml Galliano l'Autentico

Put all the ingredients, except the
Galliano, into a shaker filled with
ice and shake. Pour the Galliano
into a Champagne coupe rimmed
with cacao powder and double
strain the rest of the drink from
the shaker over the top.

AGO'S TOP FIVE BARS AROUND THE WORLD:

✖
**Bar Hemingway at The Ritz,
Paris (ritzparis.com)** ↑
*A wonderful environment – one
that makes you travel in time.
You really feel as though you are
in a Hemingway novel.*

✖
**The Blue Bar at The Berkeley,
London (the-berkeley.co.uk)**
*One of the most exciting openings
of 2016 with great drinks and a
very cool vibe.*

✖
**La Capilla, Tequila, Mexico
(see page 270)** *Owner Don
Javier is the Buddha of
bartenders! A good bar will
always make you feel at home…
Don Javier certainly has the
natural skills to make time freeze
and ensure you enjoy sipping
Tequila in good company of
locals and visitors.*

✖
**Nottingham Forest, Milan
(nottingham-forest.com)** *The
bartender/owner Dario Comini
is a pioneer in modern mixology
and the scientific approach to
cocktails. He is a good friend
and truly an inspiration in our
profession.*

✖
**Oriole Bar, London
(see page 43)** *A good blend of
creative colonial cocktails, live
music and wonderful decor in
a spacious place; makes you
truly feel as though you are on
a different planet.*

LONDON*

THE COBURG BAR

The first of two appearances for The Connaught hotel in the book (see this page). This one is equally worthy of attention. You could say The Coburg is a little like the bookish brother of the flamboyant showman; quietly getting on with its craft in a beautifully lit, colourful, comfortable setting at the heart of the hotel. For years The Coburg was the place to meet and greet enlightened drinking buddies. Here you would find craft gin distillers sharing their new wares with the bar staff, while in the corner, folk would be chatting about vintage Armagnac. For us, it was – and still is – one of London's best destination bars. Just don't shout about it too loudly, otherwise we'll never be able to get a seat.

✖

Carlos Place, London W1K 2AL
+44(0)20 7499 7070
the-connaught.co.uk

✖

IN THREE WORDS:
Contented, Comfortable Style.

THE DRINK TO TRY:
The house Whisky Sour.

WE SAY:
Snuggle into the hugely comfortable armchairs. Order a Whisky Sour. Pull out your copy of Hemingway's Old Man And The Sea from your bag. Lose a few hours. Repeat.

PRICE RATING: ✶✶✶✶

THE CONNAUGHT BAR

Undoubtedly, one of the most highly regarded destination bars in London, The Connaught Bar in Mayfair, headed up by the charismatic Agostino "Ago" Perrone (see page 28) and his team, seems to land awards on a never-ending basis for its style, service and cocktails. The Connaught has always trod a perfectly balanced

The Connaught has always trod a perfectly balanced line between inspiration and reinvention of the classics...

line between inspiration and reinvention of the classics, as well as staying abreast of the most modern trends and steering away from the gimmickry that has consumed a few of its competitors.

The Martini trolley, which effortlessly glides to your table, delivers silky smooth chilled gin or vodka perfection. Each one is given a bespoke treatment for you by way of half a dozen or so different infusions, including lavender, cardamom, vanilla, liquorice and grapefruit. The result is not only theatrical, but effortless, timeless and above all else...peerless. Extraordinary.

✖

Carlos Place, London W1K 2AL
+44(0)20 7499 7070
the-connaught.co.uk

✖

IN THREE WORDS:
Theatre Of Elegance.

THE DRINK TO TRY:
Either a bespoke Martini, or the Bloody Mary: a reinvention of the classic, using a sublime celery foam.

THEY SAY:
"Everything in this bar is absolutely seamless every time I go."
– KELSEY RAMAGE, CANADA

WE SAY:
One of the ultimate destination bars in the world.

PRICE RATING: ✶✶✶✶✶

THE CROBAR ↑

There is one hell of a band assembling in the afterlife: Hendrix on guitar; Lemmy on bass; Bonham on drums. Think of the noise this lot would make, and you've got the vibe of The Crobar. Describing themselves as a "bourbon, beer and rock bar", they know what they do, and they do it well. Located in London's Soho, this place comes to life long after other bars have closed. As a result, you'll find the most diverse collection of people at any bar in London, post-midnight with the fallout from Soho's clubs melting in with off-duty bartenders, band members and those just not ready to go home. Don't expect table service or fancy cocktails. Do expect to keep on drinking. To have to shout. And to probably lose your shoes. That's the sort of thing that happens here. Welcome to The Crobar.

✖
17 Manette Street, London W1D 4AS +44(0)20 7439 0831 crobar.co.uk

✖
IN THREE WORDS:
ROCK. AND. ROLL.
THE DRINK TO TRY:
Bourbon and Coke. Happy hour from 4pm each day.
THEY SAY:
"Metal (which I love), beer (which I love) and late night (which I love)."
- **RYAN CHETIYAWARDANA, AKA MR LYAN, UK**
WE SAY:
Like the 1960s, if you remember being there you've not had enough fun.
PRICE RATING: ✱

DANDELYAN

When the current cocktail revolution in London started to roll, it divided a city. In the West End, around Soho and Mayfair, hotels led the charge with white-coated bartenders with cocktail trollies. In the East End, the hipster movement took hold, converting old shops, warehouses, even barges, into bars. This divide has been bridged by the brilliant DandeLyan. The brainchild of Mr Lyan, aka Ryan Chetiyawardana (see page 6), and his team, it is a hotel bar with hints of hipster.

Geographically situated between the West End and the East End in London, it finds its home in the trendy Mondrian hotel. With waiting staff clad not in all white, nor in dark black, but a stylish, almost Nordic grey, the cocktails deliver East London creativity with West End style. Simply a must on the cocktail trail of England's capital city.

✖
Mondrian, 20 Upper Ground, London SE1 9PD
+44 (0)20 3747 1063
(morganshotelgroup.com)

✖
IN THREE WORDS:
East Meets West.
THE DRINK TO TRY:
Concrete Sazerac.
THEY SAY:
"Hotel bars shouldn't be this good! Heaven."
— **JANE PARKINSON, UK**
WE SAY:
A must visit for a complete London drinking experience.
PRICE RATING: ✱✱✱✱

LONDON*

DUKES BAR ↓

If we had our way, every great bar in the world would have its own unique theme tune to hum while you sipped and savoured their delicacies. If Dukes had a theme tune, it would be Monty Norman's "James Bond Theme", as this discreet hotel bar nestled in the back streets of St James's has suave spy written all over it. Dukes is supposedly the location where Ian Fleming developed some of his most memorable characters, and the cocktail list

reflects the Bond connections sympathetically: from the zesty double punch of the classic Vesper, through to the 89 Jermyn Street, a Martini based around Bond's favourite fragrance, "89".

The real highlight is the drinks trolley, where Alessandro Palazzi crafts his takes on the classics by using an array of frozen spirits and zero dilution. Powerful, charismatic and charming, the drinks should be issued with a licence to kill, given their potency.

✖
Dukes, 35 St James's Place, London SW1A 1NY +44 (0)20 7491 4840 dukeshotel.com
✖

IN THREE WORDS:
Kiss Kiss Bang-bang.
THE DRINK TO TRY:
The Martinez.

THEY SAY:
"I love Martinis – and Alessandro makes monstrous glasses of perfection!"
— **ALEX DAVIES, UK**
"No purer or more elementary pleasure."
— **ALLEN KATZ, NEW YORK**
WE SAY:
White-coated perfection. Every drink feels like stepping into the pages of a Bond novel. Order a gin Martini, sit there and picture yourself as a spy.
PRICE RATING: ✱✱✱✱

EAST LONDON LIQUOR COMPANY

The resurgence of London's craft distillery scene may not be at quite the same level of, say, New York, but quietly, over the past five years, several key operations have cropped up, each one offering a unique take on flavour and spirit personality. Of these, by far and away our favourite is East London Liquor Company, located near Victoria Park in East London. Alex Wolpert and his head distiller Tom Hills have created a distilling playground. The gins are a perfect base for the range of great cocktails the distillery bar can whip up for you. It's the sort of place where you want to bring a newspaper, grab a Negroni and catch up on life, away from the strains of central London chaos.

Alongside the bar and micro distillery is an Italian-themed restaurant and craft spirits bottle shop...so everything one needs to lead a very happy existence.

✖
Unit GF1, Bow Wharf, 221 Grove Road, London E3 5SN
+44 (0)20 3011 0980
eastlondonliquorcompany.com
✖

IN THREE WORDS:
Distilling Paradise Found.

THE DRINK TO TRY:
Anything using the distillery's "standard" gin – it's anything but standard.

WE SAY:
London's hottest micro distillery, with a gem of a bar attached. Book in to have a tour and enjoy some of the best gin in London.

PRICE RATING: ✱✱

FOUND

As we mentioned at the start of this book, there's a bar that we class "the one that got away". For many in the drinks business, Casita was the ultimate "bartenders' bar"; a destination loved by so many for its honesty and no bulls*** ethos. When it closed in 2016, we cried into our Tequila con Verditas and desperately hoped that somewhere else would pick up the baton of inspired, convivial drinking. Little did we know that such a place already existed – literally in Casita's basement. Founded by Casita's long-standing bartender Oskar Klimaszewski, Found opened in September 2015. Like Casita, the menu is a simple, solid list of a dozen or so drinks, centred around gin, Tequila and mezcal.

✖
5 Ravey Street, London EC2A 4QW foundthebar.com
✖

IN THREE WORDS:
Found Our Home.

THE DRINK TO TRY:
Tommy Goes To Thailand.

WE SAY:
Found brings together all our favourite things into one tiny space: shots of Tequila, great bartending, a big-hearted host and a finely tuned menu.

PRICE RATING: ✱✱

FRANK'S CAFE ↑

Peckham, Southeast London, was home to the BBC's best loved wheeler-dealer, Del Boy Trotter, whose yellow three-wheeled Reliant Regal van became an iconic statement of rags-to-riches, despite adversity. But should Del Boy drive around Peckham today he would see how much it has changed. Gastro pubs now fill the high street, along with boutiques, artisanal bakeries and...estate agents. Should Del Boy decide to park up on the 10th floor of the Peckham multi-storey carpark, he'd get the fright of his life. Since 2008, the carpark has hosted Frank's

Cafe – a rooftop bar/diner with a twist. Incorporating visual arts, architecture and sculpture, Frank's is a living, breathing art project. The cocktail menu is built around Campari, but over the years, "Frank's Campari Bar" has evolved into something much more, with gourmet-level street food, making it one of the destinations of the summer.

✖
10th Floor, Peckham Multi-Storey Carpark, 95a Rye Lane, London SE15 4ST frankscafe.org.uk
✖

IN THREE WORDS:
Luvley Jubbly, Rodders.

THE DRINK TO TRY:
The Boulevardier.

WE SAY:
Visit on a summer's evening and watch the city skyline, Negroni in hand, while muttering to yourself as Del Boy would have done: "This time next year, Rodney, we'll be millionaires..."

PRICE RATING: ✱

FOCUS*

STARTENDER
ALASTAIR BURGESS

Ali Burgess knows a few things about awards. His first bar, Happiness Forgets (see page 36) in East London's Hoxton Square, has featured consistently in the World's 50 Best Bars list since 2012. Another buzzy East End outlet, Original Sin (originalsin. bar) has followed, along with a bistro, Petit Pois (petitpoisbistro. com), all of which should keep the affable Mr Burgess busy. Check his instagram feed @AliLovesADrink and you'll find him off somewhere exotic, always on the lookout for his next awesome flavour discovery.

Where do you drink when you're off duty?
Sager + Wilde, Hackney Road, London (see page 47). I really love wine and it's a place where I can completely relax and not worry about how the drink will come out or how good it will be. Right now, I am also a huge fan of Joyeux Bordel (joyeuxbordel.com) and DandeLyan in London (see page 31).
Your favourite drink of all time...

What's your favourite pair of shoes?? I pretty much mainly drink Daiquiris, Old Fashioneds and/or Americanos.
Where is your favourite city in the world to go drinking?
It's not a city – it's a neighbourhood, and that is East London. You have around six or seven world-class bars within walking distance of each other and a few more a five-minute cab ride away. Plus, it has a plethora of amazing restaurants, all of which are so varied. You're well catered for across the board.
What do you look for in a bar, as a sign of true greatness?
You can't package greatness. It comes with time and patience, and it's different for everyone. I look for great people first and foremost. It's all about attitude. A bar is a place where people come to spend their free time, so it'd better be great. Time is the most precious commodity – you can't buy it, you're not getting any extra – so guests/customers must be treated with respect, even if they might not deserve it sometimes.
Give us one of your signature drinks from Happiness Forgets...
One of our bestselling drinks is the Perfect Storm. It's a twist on the classic Dark and Stormy, but the prune and honey make it a more exciting variant.

THE PERFECT STORM

50ml Skipper dark rum
5ml Vieille Prune plum brandy
20ml fresh lemon juice
15ml honey syrup (2 parts honey to 1 part water)
15ml fresh ginger juice (2 parts ginger to 1 part caster sugar)
ginger ale, to top up

Shake the ingredients together. Pour over ice. Top up with ginger ale and garnish with lemon.

LONDON*

THE GIBSON, LONDON

Given the East End's fondness for all things retro, you could be forgiven for missing The Gibson and its turn-of-the-last-century finery as you trundle down Old Street. But venture inside and the bar's unique mandate of Classic Drinks Reimagined is crystal clear. The Gibson was set up by rising industry stars Marian Beke and Rusty Cerven and central to their fiendish plot is The Gibson cocktail ↓.

The lines of vintage shakers, beautiful distressed mirror tables and other period bar accoutrements give a timeless feel, as does that signature cocktail, which comes served in

silver Martini flutes, complete with homemade pickled onions.

By creating The Gibson, Beke and Cerven have unquestionably raised the heart rate of London's cocktail movement by several beats. Everything flows perfectly and, despite the outlandish nature of some of the drinks, the skill that is on display here is absolutely undeniable.

✖
44 Old Street, London EC1V 9AQ
thegibsonbar.london
✖

IN THREE WORDS:
Uncompromising Classical Complexity.
THE DRINK TO TRY:
The Electric Earl.
THEY SAY:
"A cosy bar serving cocktails with exotic flavours and great complexity."
— EDDIE NARA, HONG KONG
WE SAY:
Despite its historical leanings, The Gibson is a beacon of truly modern innovation.
PRICE RATING: ✳✳✳

GORDON'S WINE BAR

Gordon's is the original stalwart of London's subterranean drinking culture. It is housed in the low, stone-arched cellars of Kipling House, once the home of Samuel Pepys and the spot in which Rudyard Kipling

once lived and worked, writing several of his best-known works. Arguably London's oldest wine bar, little has changed in Gordon's decor since it was established in 1890. From a wine perspective, it is lacking pretence or pomposity, with a list that focuses on personality over region. Its only flaw is its popularity: for a seat in the cellars, you have to arrive before 4pm – better still, eat lunch there and see in the rest of the evening with a few beakers of oloroso sherry.

✖
47 Villiers Street, London WC2N 6NE +44 (0)20 7930 1408 gordonswinebar.com
✖

IN THREE WORDS:
The Ultimate Vintage.
THE DRINK TO TRY:
The casks of amontillado, fino and oloroso sherries (ordered by the schooner, or beaker).
THEY SAY:
"A priceless atmosphere in such an historic part of London. Its charm never fails to impress."
— TOM ASKE, UK
PRICE RATING: ✳✳

LONDON*

HAPPINESS FORGETS

Shoreditch could well be a vision of either heaven or hell, depending on your outlook in life. This once neglected area of East London is now home to some of London's most progressive bars and restaurants, as well as being a shining beacon of all things techy, specie and start-up in the Brave New World of 3D printing and AI. It just so happens that in the basement of no. 8–9 Hoxton Square, the aptly named Happiness Forgets is a perfect antidote for the savvy business-minded madness that is fast consuming the area. Simple yet beautiful drinks make Happiness Forgets outstanding in almost every respect: from the service, the knowledge and the concepts to the liquid creations themselves. Owner Ali Burgess (see page 34) has given the place a genuine soul, where the ethos is Great Cocktails, No Wallies. It takes some of the best bars years to develop the natural, hospitable feel that Happiness Forgets has achieved in their first few years.

✖
8–9 Hoxton Square, London
N1 6NU happinessforgets.com
✖

IN THREE WORDS:
Don't Be a Wally.

THE DRINK TO TRY:
Start your journey with an Aviation and finish with a Journalist: both gin-based classics, beautifully done.

THEY SAY:
"One of the most amazing places...simple drinks, very tasty, good atmosphere, good service and great technique."
— **MARC ALVAREZ SAFONT, SPAIN**
"Ticks all the boxes. I wish all local bars were like this."
— **ALEX KAMMERLING, UK**

PRICE RATING: ✖ ✖ ✖

LOUNGE BOHEMIA ↗

Being a maverick in any field is likely to garner as much criticism as it does praise and Lounge Bohemia is no stranger to both. The brainchild of Czech mixologist Paul Tvaroh is something of an enigma; a website with only a mobile number as point of contact and a draconian "appointment only – no suits, no office wear" door policy ensures only those truly in the know get to sample the bar's hospitality. The bar has enjoyed this level of exclusivity for about a decade now, and yet it still

feels fresh and exciting. Paul has created an intimate, yet creative environment with sensational molecular (or "manipulative" as he likes to puts it) cocktail creations bursting with fresh ideas and flavours. He often creates cocktails based on flavours that work well together in food and he relies heavily on his sense of smell. "This is one of the reasons why we have such a huge range of in-house infusions," he explains, "from things like mace blades, poppy seed, digestive biscuits and leather. Mostly because I find standard spirits and liquors don't enable me to make the flavour combinations I want to create."

✖
1e Great Eastern Street, London
EC2A 3EJ loungebohemia.com
*by appointment only

✖

IN THREE WORDS:
Maverick to The Max.

THE DRINK TO TRY:
The Sgt Pepper: A heady mix of pepper-infused vodka, lemon juice and elderflower.

THEY SAY:
"A great small spot, hidden and run by a great owner, where you leave with a great experience and sense of hospitality."
— MARIAN BEKE, SLOVAKIA

PRICE RATING: ✴✴✴✴

LOVES COMPANY

Situated across the street from the Nightjar (see page 43), this is truly a bartender hangout. It isn't just the great cocktails that make this place the toast of the town, it is also their fantastic spread of toasted sandwiches on their bespoke and unique toastie menu, for which they take the same creative approach to flavours that they do with their cocktails. You can order a toasted sandwich snack to accompany your drink, with names such as Crustin Bieber, Play That Funghi Music and Jamon Eileen. There is a similarly playful attitude toward their cocktails,

with a good mix of classic and extreme experiments in their apothecary section, where their own blends and infusions are created and often used in their main cocktails. With this level of creativity, you can really see why this place is so highly recommended.

✖
1 Imperial Hall, 104–122 City Road, London EC1V 2NR
+44 (0)20 7253 3777

✖

IN THREE WORDS:
Butter Me Up!

THE DRINK TO TRY:
The Wraparound.

WE SAY:
A great place to go mid-cocktail crawl in East London to line your stomach and keep hydrated.

PRICE RATING: ✴✴✴

MARK'S BAR ⬇

When you name your bar, using your own name could be a sign of either arrogance or confidence. In regard to Mark's Bar, the latter is the case. The Mark in question is Mark Hix, highly celebrated English chef and proprietor of several restaurants around the UK, with his Hix in Soho playing

home to this highly innovative bar. To be precise, Mark's Bar is a collaborative effort across several of Hix's restaurants, also bringing in the considerable skills and flair of veteran bartender Nick Strangeway. The eccentric feel is apparent as soon as you descend the stairs into the joint. Taxidermy, carboys filled with maturing cocktails and shelves of eclectic bartending paraphernalia all give you confidence that you will be served a highly memorable drink – largely speaking with a British feel to the ingredients. Gin is one of the key spirits here, so take a recommendation or simply go with one of the classics.

✖
66–70 Brewer Street, London W1F 9UP +44 (0)20 7292 3518
hixrestaurants.co.uk

✖

IN THREE WORDS:
Soho's Subterranean Splendour.

THE DRINK TO TRY:
Tom And Jerez.

THEY SAY:
"This is my local never-fail-to-enjoy-myself-here bar. Boom."
— JANE PARKINSON, UK

WE SAY:
An essential pre-steak night sojourn in Soho.

PRICE RATING: ✴✴✴

FEATURE*

A DRINK WITH...
MARK ANDREW & DAN KEELING

Londons Lamb's Conduit Street is that rarest of things: a London location that maintains a Dickensian air of bygone time; home to some of the city's best-known and most fashionable independent retailers, it could have been the inspiration for J K Rowling's Diagon Alley. And one of the newest residents could be straight out of the pages of Harry Potter, too.

Noble Rot wine bar and restaurant ↓ is the brainchild of Mark Andrew, a former wine buyer for a Kensington-based vintners, and Dan Keeling, a successful music business executive who now finds himself more concerned with tasting notes over musical notes.

The pair met when Dan was the managing director of Island Records, whose HQ happened to be next door to the shop Mark was working in at the time.

"Yeah, it was through my job in Kensington where I met Dan, who was just starting his journey into wine. I'd started to host some wine tastings, just so I could learn about wine, and Dan, whose office was next door, started coming along," explains Mark.

"We bonded over a love of wine, the same wine writers, music and other bits of culture and became good friends."

In 2013 the pair decided to start a wine publication, looking at the topic through a lens focused also on contemporary culture and the creative arts, and *Noble Rot*, the magazine, was born.

"We started *Noble Rot* in 2013 by writing most of it ourselves and laying it out on Mark's ancient laptop," explains Dan.

"We started the magazine because there was nothing out there that spoke about wine with humour and context in a similar way to what other favourite publications did about their subjects. (The pair cite electronic music magazine *Jockey Slut* and the football magazine *The Blizzard* as influences on their DIY approach.) We want to contextualize wine with reference to food and pop culture rather than present it in the singular way that most wine magazines tend to."

It was, according to the founders, somewhat of a struggle, with just 1,000 copies of the first issue distributed around the drinking haunts and wine shops of London. "Some shops wouldn't even let us give copies to them," Mark muses.

After working hard to bring contemporary wine content to the curious consumer through their magazine ("I still think of us as a fanzine rather than a magazine...we aren't trying to present ourselves as 'experts', but as fans trying to introduce other

challenges of turning it into a place that reflects their ideals and makes it one of the best drinking establishments in the town?

"It's the people. Every day, the people, the staff," Mark explains.

"From the kitchen forward, we have a great team here. The best bars in the world don't have to be the most expensive. Alcohol helps, but there is alcohol in a lot of places, and that alcohol can be interchangeable, but what is not interchangeable and not replicable is how the venue makes you feel."

"You've hit the jackpot when you find a place that makes you feel comfortable, that you want to return to...and if it happens to have the best wine list, or the best cocktails, and knows exactly what they're doing, then you have the Holy Grail."

Noble Rot isn't a revolution in wine, it's an evolution: a venue rooted in the past, with a well curated, contemporary-yet-classic wine list, a welcoming atmosphere and founders who just want you to have a good time.

Like the sound of Noble Rot? Also try out the Clown Bar, Paris's slick, sophisticated gastro-wine haven (clown-bar-paris. com); Stockholm's Burgundy (see Tweed, page 105) for an outrageously comprehensive cellar of vintages; and London's Sager + Wilde (see page 47) for a broad and innovative approach to both wine and cocktails.

people to the beauty of great wine," says Dan), their passion evolved into wanting to open a drinking haunt that reflected the vibe of their publication.

"Inspiration hit when we went on a trip to the Jura in eastern France to cover the region for the fourth issue of the magazine," Dan remembers.

"After an aborted idea to open a Burgundy-focused bar – our favourite wine region – we decided to open a broader Noble Rot bar, which can reflect all the wines that we love to write about in the magazine."

And before long the magazine was manifest in bar form, with the personality and

characteristics that attracted readers to the periodical woven into the fabric of the establishment.

"The vibe of this place is incredible", says Mark.

"It has 300 years of history, it's been a wine bar since 1973 and it was a grocer's before that. All of humankind has gone through this building. You can tell it just has a warmth and a vibe to the building. It was clearly a place that brought a lot of joy to a lot of people and we have just helped to roll that on for a new generation."

It is all well and good taking over a venue that has housed a wine bar since the middle of the last century, but what are the

LONDON*

MARKSMAN

London is famed for its traditional public houses. Yet despite being the beating heart, the soul of the people, from the working classes through to those with fat wallets, the UK pub culture is in decline. With pubs under the threat of rising rents, rising beer costs and the falling price of ale in supermarkets, it is always pleasing to uncover a gem of a traditional drinking haunt, and Marksman is one of those.

Styled now as a public house and dining room, this fantastic East End boozer, which serves the very best of local beers, ales, lagers and ciders, is located less than a 10-minute walk from Hoxton station.

With a dining room featuring guest slots from some of the best-known chefs around, the whole place has a funky-fresh feel and, like The Running Horse (see page 47), is a great London pub, reborn, reimagined and reawakened for a new generation of drinker.

✖
254 Hackney Road, London E2 7SJ +44 (0)20 7739 7393 marksmanpublichouse.com
✖
IN THREE WORDS:
Hits The Bullseye.
THE DRINK TO TRY:
Always default to a local ale.
WE SAY:
Eat, drink and be merry.
PRICE RATING: ✱✱✱

MERCHANT HOUSE

With the recent explosion of craft, small batch and artisan gins, there are a few bars in London that focus on stocking a large number of the juniper-juice spirit. Many will simply cram their list with as many gins as they can find, but one which curates their menu, thinks hard about their serves and understands what gin should be right for the person drinking there that night is Merchant House of Bow Lane.

With a heavy focus on gin, Merchant House has excelled at offering, to those who want to find it, something unusual yet flavoursome. Housed in a small downstairs bar in the City, there is no better place to uncover a world of great British gins (and some from abroad too). Such has been the success of the place that Merchant House now has a second outlet on London's famous Fleet Street, with a focus on Scotch, and Irish whiskey, boasting over 500 different bottles. Not only do the two venues offer great cocktails with their chosen spirit of focus, but both do "bespoke spirit masterclasses" where you can "taste your way through the belligerent histories and painstaking craftsmanship behind every bottle".

✖
Merchant House of Bow Lane: 13 Well Court, Off Bow Lane, London EC4M 9DN +44 (0)20 7332 0044 Merchant House of Fleet Street: 8 Bride Court, London EC4Y 8DU merchanthouselondon.com
✖
IN THREE WORDS:
Specialists Being Special.
THE DRINK TO TRY:
Gin in Bow Lane, Whiskey in Fleet Street.
WE SAY:
A wonderful array of bottles, not just collected but curated.
PRICE RATING: ✱✱✱

MILK & HONEY

Numerous bars have come and gone since Milk & Honey first opened in 2002. A trailblazer like no other, many of the best bartenders, brand ambassadors and industry folk have passed

4

through its doors, and it has much to be praised for. Spread across three floors, despite its size it is not an easy place to find. At the southern end of Poland Street, look for an unmarked door which has a small gap in it to allow people to see out.

Non-members are welcome by reservation only before 11am, and there is a strict set of house rules (even if some of them seem in jest), such as the ideal that "Gentlemen will not introduce themselves to ladies. Ladies, feel free to start a conversation or ask the bartender to introduce you. If a man you don't know speaks to you, please lift your chin slightly and ignore him."

When it comes to the drinks, the list is fantastic, with a vintage twist. The Cobblers, Fizzers and Fixers section will surprise and delight, while the Fresh & Up is a great place to kick-start your cocktail experience. MLKHNY, as this place often calls itself, is part of London's drinking history despite not yet being 20 years old.

✕
61 Poland Street, London W1F 7NU +44 (0)20 7065 6800 mlkhny.com
✕
IN THREE WORDS:
The Land Of….
THE DRINK TO TRY:
Japanese Fizz, which will give your evening a kick-start.
THEY SAY:
"I would read about it in magazines and I just wanted to experience it."
— ALASTAIR BURGESS, UK
WE SAY:
Not a member? Book in for a seat. If you are a member – good work!
PRICE RATING: ✱✱✱✱

MOTHER KELLY'S

Just along from another of the entries in this book, Sager + Wilde (see page 47), is Mother Kelly's, a New York-inspired bottle shop and taproom. If you're into your beer, you're in for a real treat here. Nineteen taps are lined up along the concrete wall, devoted to the finest beers available, which are complemented by six huge fridges that are bulging at the hinges. There is every style of beer imaginable in this joint and, as they say, "We don't have a kitchen as it would have taken up too much beer space". However, they do serve delicious sharing boards and even have street food from around London over the weekends. With an ever-changing beer menu, this is one place to keep visiting time and again.

✕
251 Paradise Row, London E2 9LE +44 (0)20 7012 1244 motherkellys.co.uk
✕
IN THREE WORDS:
Beer To Eternity.
THEY SAY:
"It's a taproom and bottle shop that has an amazing selection of beers and some good spirits. Beer is something that I've learned a lot about from drinking there."
— MARCIS DZELZAINIS, FRANCE
WE SAY:
Hop down and you won't beer-lieve your eyes at the selection.
PRICE RATING: ✱✱

MR FOGG'S RESIDENCE

Close your eyes and think about that brilliant Jules Verne novel *Around the World in 80 Days*,

the story of a quintessentially British gent (ironically originally written in French) who left St James's members' haunt The Reform Club on a fantastical adventure in order to win a £20,000 wager with a fellow club member. Now think about where Phileas Fogg might live post-adventure: wood-panelled, decked out with vintage maps, taxidermy, silver-top canes, top hats, bird cages and hip flasks. Keep this image in your head and turn it into a bar, and you've got yourself Mr Fogg's Residence – a Mayfair bar near Berkeley Square, which is far from being a simple theme bar, maintaining a high standard of cocktails and atmosphere. It also has a sister bar called Mr Fogg's Tavern in Covent Garden.

✕
15 Bruton Lane, London W1J 6JD +44 (0)20 7036 0608 mr-foggs.com
✕
IN THREE WORDS:
A Passepartout Photo.
THE DRINK TO TRY:
Book in for the Tipsy Tea, their take on High Tea.
THEY SAY:
"Delicate and quirky drinks!"
— CSIGÓ KRISZTIÁN, HUNGARY
WE SAY:
If Around London in 80 Drinks has been your wager, then start and finish here.
PRICE RATING: ✱✱✱

FOCUS*

STARTENDER
PETER DORELLI ON THE "THEATRE" OF THE BAR

Peter Dorelli is a legend of the bartending world who has more than a few theatrical tricks up the sleeve of his spotlessly clean white bartending jacket. Since he began his bartending career back in the early 1960s, eventually becoming head bartender at the American Bar at The Savoy for over 20 years, Dorelli has always maintained the underlying qualities that every star bartender must possess: an ability to listen, to tell stories and to make a great drink with a twinkle in one's eye.

What does the term "theatre" behind the bar mean to you?
For me, it means everything because the bar is and should be a place for theatrical performance with the bartenders as actors presenting to their audience – the customers.

What has history taught us about bringing it into the 21st century?
Historically, a lot of great shows were performed behind the bar. This artistry has been somewhat forgotten – the technique of throwing [mixing drinks by passing the liquid between two tins, with progressively greater distance on each "throw"] is something that should possibly be reintroduced on a greater scale and is extremely complementary to the cocktail itself. Also neglected today are blazers [flaming cocktails] (provided they are allowed of course!). They all add to audience appeal.

Where can bar theatre go in the future? Where would you like to see it heading?
I see it becoming more customer friendly with more interaction and a greater show of bartender personality. We have to take a step back to when bartenders were great communicators, listeners, generous hearted and a source of knowledge. There needs to be less of the mixologist and more customer awareness to bring back the art of making each visit to the bar something memorable and special.

PETER'S TOP FIVE FAVOURITES, WHICH PERFECTLY CAPTURE THE "THEATRE" OF THE BAR:

✖
The Connaught Bar, London (see page 30) *Because it has a great atmosphere, it has an amazing team and the cocktail presentations are just brilliant.*

✖
The American Bar, Savoy Hotel, London (see page 22) *They live up to their motto, "For excellence we strive."*

✖
The Jerry Thomas Project, Rome (see page 122) *The exuberance of youth in the atmosphere, the cocktail creations and the team.*

✖
Delicatessen, Moscow (see page 124) *A wonderful place where you can relax and the cocktails are an imaginative twist on the classics.*

✖
Schumann's, Munich (see page 91) *It's all that you expect from a bar. Great atmosphere, professional team, great cocktails and exceptional food.*

LONDON*

NIGHTJAR

When East London was still full of bars best avoided, NightJar decided that it was the perfect place to serve cocktails with flare. They should be praised for this. Part of the early pace-setters in the rejuvenation of East London, the team here have developed a strong style, which can almost be described as "Baroque", due to the overly creative garnishes that bring together floral designs of such flair; they look as if they've been taken directly from a Caravaggio still life.

The menu is split between pre-Prohibition, Prohibition, postwar and signature serves. From the signature serves, try the Breakfast of Champions served in a smoking black egg.

Marked by a small brass plaque adorned with a picture of a bird, NightJar is one of those hidden, basement bars that evoke a bygone era. And when the jazz band starts to play, you'll be transported to a time when cocktails were hidden, but fun and flare were always on show.

✖
129 City Road, London EC1V 1JB
+44 (0)20 7253 4101
barnightjar.com
✖

IN THREE WORDS:
The Greatest Experiment.
THEY SAY:
"Creativity in everything they do."
— **ARIS CHATZIANTONIOU, GREECE**
WE SAY:
A wonderful bar that became, and remains, an instant classic.
PRICE RATING: ✷✷✷✷

ORIOLE

The second bar by the team behind London's NightJar (see left) this takes many of the same cues, such as the fantastic selection of cocktails soundtracked to live jazz music. Described as an "underground cabinet of curiosities", the place is a hive for the unusual, and the cocktails are no exception. Their Fernworthy cocktail ↗ fuses Plymouth Gin with a Tasmanian pepper infusion, radish, voatsiperifery (pepper) and beetroot eau de vie, topped up with Champagne and finished with borage honey; outstanding.
✖
East Poultry Avenue, Smithfield Market, London EC1A 9LH +44 (0)20 3457 8099 oriolebar.com
✖

IN THREE WORDS:
Curiouser And Curiouser.
THE DRINK TO TRY:
Carpathian Swizzle, which includes mistletoe.
THEY SAY:
"Amazing...great drinks."
— **MARC ALVAREZ, SPAIN**
WE SAY:
One great bar is an achievement; two is outstanding.
PRICE RATING: ✷✷✷✷

LONDON*

P. FRANCO

This place is a mix of a wine bar with food and other delights available. Yet another East London eatery that has world-class drinking opportunities to boot, it offers natural wines, a bar, bottle shop, seasonal food and rotating chef residency all at a price comparable to the cost of a London Underground Day Travel Card. Note: no reservations.

Expect to be surrounded by the coolest of the cool, don't dress up, and trust the menu to deliver exceptional food. You can even take away the bottle of wine you had with your meal, from their very own bottle shop, or visit their sister site Noble Fine Liquor on the funky Broadway Market.

✕

107 Lower Clapton Road, London E5 0NP +44 (0)20 8533 4660 franco.co.uk

✕

IN THREE WORDS:
Effortless, Natural, Wonderful.
THEY SAY:
"I'll walk 30 mins in 3 degree, shitty miserable London winter

weather just to get the chance to enjoy this place."
— **IAIN GRIFFITH, AUSTRALIA**
WE SAY:
Go with an open mind, and simply enjoy.
PRICE RATING: ✱ ✱

PEG + PATRIOT ↓

As part of the Town Hall Hotel, Peg + Patriot offers guests and visitors alike the chance to try some of London's most creative concoctions. Far from offering Bed & Breakfast, the hotel offers a B&B of another kind: Bed & Beverage, with those taking up the package given a room for the night plus four bottled cocktails by the team at the bar.

The ultra-creative menu brings together ingredients not often seen on a cocktail list, with the current incarnation featuring "seasonal soda", "oyster shell" and "char" and some cocktails garnished with bacon. Yes, bacon. What's not to love?

One of the most stylish bars in London, P+P gives anyone who has time to explore the menu a real journey of flavour. Oh, and the bar snacks...make sure you order some, even if you are heading to the sublime Typing Room restaurant next door.

✕

Patriot Square, London E2 9NF +44 (0)20 8709 4528 talentedmrfox.com

✕

IN THREE WORDS:
Brilliantly Creative Cocktails.
THE DRINK TO TRY:
The Naked Sazerac.
THEY SAY:
"If you haven't been – you need to go!"
— **MONICA BERG, NORWAY**
WE SAY:
Bringing style to London town.
PRICE RATING: ✱ ✱ ✱

FOCUS*

STARTENDER
ALEX KRATENA

As former head bartender of the London Artesian, Alex Kratena is widely credited for reinventing the traditional five-star hotel bar experience, making it relevant for 21st century tastes and sensibilities. Attention to detail, playful presentation and exceptional approach to service are all hallmarks of Alex's unique approach to bartending. His new venture P(our) (pourdrink.org) sees him bringing together a collective of top bartenders from around the world, to discuss how to make the industry an even more highly respected place to work.

When do you first remember being in a bar and thinking, "This is the career for me"?
You know, I never had that moment! I got into the hospitality business as a young lad at 16 because I needed some money. As a lot of young people do, I ended up working in a bar and restaurant. It was never my choice, never my dream. I just fell into it! It was a natural progression. The thing that helped me is that I've always had a good relationship with being positive about my surroundings and exploring things, and I must admit I enjoy drinking too, so that helped. I've had a long journey.

What makes a great bar?
Anyone can provide a great service, but at the end of the day it is about how it makes you feel. A great bar doesn't always need to be something amazing. In the Czech Republic, I really enjoy going to the pub where the waiters are so rude, to the extent that it is actually funny! They almost act it out. It doesn't always need to be something glamorous.

Which continents do you like to go drinking in and what type of places do you like to go to?
I love drinking in Europe. I think it has a huge amount of great bars and, because it is where I come from, it is very close to my heart. Anywhere from Greece to Germany. Drinking in the Nordics can be great fun, too. I've had some amazing drinks in restaurants around the world. I was recently in Buenos Aires and I had a really simple vermouth cocktail that was just an incredible drink. And at **Maido** in Lima, Peru (maido.pe) I had a drink that was just fermented cacao pulp, which is an experience I'd never had before, but it was brilliant. I had a moment with that drink.

You're famed for your creative serves. Is this an important part of creating a great bar?
To an extent, but it shouldn't be over the top. It plays a part but it shouldn't be all smoke and mirrors. If you look at London's **White Lyan** [Ryan Chetiyawardana's bar, which has now become Super Lyan: superlyan.com], it's very minimalistic, but the drinks have absolutely the same entertainment value. Things need to make sense. The moment it becomes a gimmick, you should stop doing it.

LONDON*

PUNCH ROOM AT THE LONDON EDITION

London's Oxford Street is either the thing of dreams or the stuff of nightmares, depending on how much you like shopping. You might want to brave the masses out looking for a bargain just to find the sanctuary that is the London Edition Hotel. On entering you'll be faced with a lobby that is part posh hotel, part *Cheers*, complete with pool table, bar and reception area. But don't stop there. Continue in and you'll find, hidden away at the back of the hotel, the bijou Punch Room, evoking the Members' Clubs that can be found down the road in Mayfair and St James's.

Punch Room lives up to its name with a menu comprised mostly, but not exclusively, of sharing drinks. When ordered by a group (and yes, thankfully two people count as a group), the sharing cocktail is delivered in a vintage punch bowl with a ladle and glassware, ready to serve yourself.

Punches aren't just any old leftovers thrown in a bowl like they might have been at those college parties from years ago. No, Sir. They are beautifully constructed, ancient recipes, often taking days to make (ask the bar staff for the story of the Milk Punch, which must be prepared in advance), and this is what makes the Punch Room such a unique place to go drinking. You'll be bowl-ed over.

✖

The London Edition Hotel, 10 Berners Street, London W1T 3NP +44 (0)20 7908 7949 editionhotels.com

✖

IN THREE WORDS:
Sharing Is Caring.

THE DRINK TO TRY:
The Milk Punch – don't let the name put you off. It is sublime.

WE SAY:
Book in advance and try to go in a small group of three or four to get the best out of it.

PRICE RATING: ✱✱✱

THE RED LION

The Red Lion is, apparently, the most popular public house name in England and within two streets of this joint in St James's, there is another pub of the same name, so it must be true! As classic London boozers go, this place is a must. A health

and safety nightmare (honestly, try getting to the gents' toilet after a couple of ales, or worse still a couple of Martinis at Dukes Bar, see page 32), this is everything that a great British drinking haunt should be. With guest ales, and whiskies from London's oldest wine and spirits merchants (Berry Bros. & Rudd) just around the corner, it's a curious mix of old money; politicians doing deals over warm ales; cigar enthusiasts who have just been to J J Fox to sit in Churchill's chair and smoke a Monty; and those simply looking to relax after a hard day's work before heading home. Pop in – you never know whom you might meet.

✖

23 Crown Passage, London SW1Y 6PP +44 (0)20 7930 4141

✖

IN THREE WORDS:
Mind The Stairs!

THE DRINK TO TRY:
Go for one of the Berry Bros. & Rudd whiskies behind the bar, left there by Doug, the spirits buyer at BB&R.

WE SAY:
Enjoy it: pubs like this are sadly a dying breed.

PRICE RATING: ✱

THE RUNNING HORSE / THE WHIP

Hidden in the streets of Mayfair, Fitzrovia and St James's in Central London are the great pubs of London town. Fighting against the tide of rising rents, or simply landlords who see flats where drinking dens should be, a few key ones hold on.

One such establishment has undergone a reinvention over the past few years. The Running Horse was established in 1738, and is the oldest public house and kitchen in Mayfair. The rejuvenation of this small but historic venue has been a collaboration between James Chase, of the Chase distillery, and Dominic Jacobs, former bar director at Sketch (which three Michelin starred chef Pierre Gagnaire calls home in London). It opened its revamped doors in 2013.

Not only does The Running Horse serve fab ales and wonderful wines, alongside great pub fare (the chopped burger is a win), but the upstairs is home to The Whip, a small cocktail joint where all drinks are the same price and the service is fantastic.

✖

50 Davies Street, London W1K 5JE +44 (0)20 7493 1275 therunninghorsemayfair.co.uk

✖

IN THREE WORDS:
First Past the Post.

WE SAY:
The oldest pub in Mayfair is a grand old dame, not a knackered old mare.

PRICE RATING: ✳✳✳

SAGER + WILDE ↓

Housed in a railway arch near Bethnal Green tube station, this place is a hipster eatery and cocktail haven, with a sister wine bar just a mile or so away. The venue mixes great wines, bottled beers and exceptional cocktails with their blend of Scandi-style dining (try the Pig's Ear), bringing what seems like a little bit of Denmark to East London. The cocktail list showcases two styles of milk punch, a Rose Petal Ramos and a garden Martini garnished with pea shoots. This place is all about freshness and seasonality, which is reflected brilliantly in their drinks.

A refreshing place to visit for both palate and soul – you're bound to leave happy. With food and drink like this, the next stop on the tube from here shouldn't be Mile End, but Smile, Friend.

✖

Arch 250, Paradise Row, London E2 9LE +44 (0)20 7613 0478 sagerandwilde.com

✖

IN THREE WORDS:
Fresh And Wild.

THEY SAY:
"I'm a huge fan…what's not to love?"

— **JANE PARKINSON, UK**

"My favourite wine bar and hangout when I'm home in London."

— **MONICA BERG, NORWAY**

PRICE RATING: ✳✳✳

SATAN'S WHISKERS

Satan's Whiskers is one of those bars that looks like it shouldn't be there, nor should you want to be inside it. The reality is a bar where the interior is bordello-ish, with stuffed animals, great mood lighting and comfortable chairs, even at the bar. The cocktails are anything but hellish – the menu features a mix of traditional cocktails, short drinks and long drinks, all served with a homely feel. Quite right too, as this place styles itself as a neighbourhood cocktail bar. Be brave and enter Satan's Whiskers for a truly brilliant night out.

✖

343 Cambridge Heath Road, London E2 9RA +44 (0)20 7739 8362

✖

IN THREE WORDS:
Won't Back Down.

THE DRINK TO TRY:
The Blue Bird or indeed a Satan's Whiskers.

WE SAY:
Don't be put off by the dive bar looks, this place utterly rocks.

PRICE RATING: ✳✳✳

LONDON*

THE SOUTHAMPTON ARMS ↓

Many bars will have a focus, especially when it comes to spirits. Goodness knows, there are a few of them in this very book! There are not many that can boast that they specialize in ale and cider, especially ones from "small independent UK breweries". As a result, they can make their own rules, serve what they like, and generally welcome you into their world, where you are certain to try an ale or cider that you haven't before. As this

is a small independent joint, be aware that they don't take bookings. And they are very insistent on that. In fact, on their sparse website it advises you not to call up and ask if they can "put little reserved signs on the tables so me and my mates can turn up when we feel like it and insist that existing customers move somewhere else so we can sit down", which is fair play and makes me want to be one of the existing customers who now isn't being moved for someone else.

✖

139 Highgate Road, London NW5 1LE +44 (0)7958 780073 thesouthamptonarms.co.uk

✖

IN THREE WORDS:
Honest, Independent, Clever.

THE DRINK TO TRY:
Go for an interesting cider, maybe even a scrumpy.

THEY SAY:
"This is the best pub in London for me, hands down."
— **THOMAS ASKE, UK**

WE SAY:
Don't try calling this place for a booking! Just turn up and leave merry!

PRICE RATING: ✱✱✱

THE SUN TAVERN

Whisky bars can take on an unusually different array of guises: the high-end hotel style (see The Craigellachie, page 63); the US dive-style (see The Crobar, page 31) and the traditional pub vibe (see The Bon Accord, page 61). Sitting somewhere between all of these is The Sun Tavern. It can do high-end with aplomb; that it nails wonderfully conceived mixed drinks and has a list of Irish whiskeys is absolutely staggering (special props for the menu itself, which has won awards for its insightfulness). It can do dive and traditional too, in that it's an East End boozer, with great beers, rock'n'roll on the stereo and shots of poitín should you want to go down that route. In fact, there's very little that The Sun Tavern can't do – including maintaining the smile on your face from the moment you first arrive to the time you decide to head home.

✖
441 Bethnal Green Road, London E2 0AN +44 (0)20 7739 4097 thesuntavern.co.uk
✖

IN THREE WORDS:
Sunny Side Up.
THEY SAY:
"Irish whiskey, rock'n'roll, tasty beer... can't fault it."
— IAIN GRIFFITHS, AUSTRALIA
PRICE RATING: ✳✳

SWIFT ↗

Wander around the gentrifying streets of Soho and you'll witness the disappearance of arguably one of the capital's most colourful areas. Fortunately though, for every few chain stores and swanky apartment blocks there are some genuine new gems, which still evoke the spirit of Soho's hedonistic yet convivial charm. One of the latest is Swift, which is spread over two levels, each one offering something completely different. The bar is the brainchild of husband and wife super-team Bobby Hiddleston and Mia Johansson, and their combined passion is on display in every drink. Head upstairs and have a wonderfully light aperitif-style sherry and tonic, and after this has woken up your taste buds, pop downstairs for one of the best whiskey lists in London and a perfectly weighted menu of big flavoured classic-influenced cocktails.

✖
12 Old Compton Street, London W1D 4TQ +44 (0)20 7437 7820 barswift.com
✖

IN THREE WORDS:
Flight Of Fancy.

DRINK TO TRY:
The Irish Coffee. How Swift brings together the simplicity of Jameson Irish whiskey, thick cold cream and sweetened coffee is nothing short of miraculous!
WE SAY:
An outstanding addition to Soho.
PRICE RATING: ✳✳✳

BAR TERMINI

The resurgence of the Negroni is not an unexpected turn. But the way it shifts and evolves to accommodate the changing palates of legions of new fans is the most surprising thing about this undisputed classic, which brings together three simple ingredients: gin, sweet vermouth and Campari, each possessing its own huge personality. By rights, the Negroni should be a shouty mess, given the personality and temperament of said ingredients, but it is a thing of elegance and refinement.

Termini embraces the simplicity of the Negroni, but also moves it in a different direction. The menu is largely built around the drink, but also doubles as a wicked espresso bar. This is not a "destination bar" in the traditional sense, more a drop-in/drop-out joint, harking back to the Italian cafés that populated Soho in the 1960s.

For devotees of the Negroni, Bar Termini is a must-try destination. It feels slightly transient, rather like a bar in a station; a place to meet before moving on to a final destination. As a welcome starting point though, it's just the ticket.

✖
7 Old Compton Street, London W1D 5JE +44 (0)7860 945018 bar-termini.com
✖

IN THREE WORDS:
Italian Aperitivo, Pronto!
THE DRINK TO TRY:
Robusto Negroni.
THEY SAY:
"So very simple but spot on."
— ANDY SHANNON, UK
WE SAY:
Termini has invented pop-in-pop-out sippin' Negroni heaven... you're very, very naughty.
PRICE RATING: ✳✳✳

MANCHESTER, BIRMINGHAM & LIVERPOOL*

CRAZY PEDRO'S

Pizzas. Mezcal. Tequila. A tiny tiki dive bar in the basement. Rum. What's not to like? Indeed, when you have several of life's greatest pleasures effectively all under one roof, you needn't stray too far – and herein lies the appeal of Crazy Pedro's. Claiming Manchester's largest collection of agave spirits, this superb pizza parlour/bar has worked hard to source some real gems and clearly knows its stuff. The cocktails are all well crafted and you can soak up any excesses with a delicious slab of

cheesy delight. What's more, The Liars Club, (theliarsclub.co.uk), which you'll find down below, is a perfectly contained explosion of tiki colour, with a late licence and formidable list of rums and quirky punches. You'll never moan about the Manchester weather again, once you make this your local.

✖
55–57 Bridge Street, Manchester M3 3BQ +44 (0)161 359 3000 crazypedros.co.uk
✖
IN THREE WORDS:
Crazily Good Drinks.
THEY SAY:
"Pizza and mezcal, a great combination."
— JON ANDES BORCHGREVINK, NORWAY
PRICE RATING: ✶ ✶

MOJO ✍

Manchester, now the second biggest city in the UK, is treating its drinkers well. A host of great new bars are bolstering the city's charge to become the best night out outside of London. Leading the charge is Mojo, a New York style loft bar in Deansgate with a heavy nod toward hard liquor and rock 'n' roll. The cocktails served here befit their setting. Classics mostly; their Piña Colada, Hurricane and Long Island Ice Tea are served with

> **Manchester, now the second biggest city in the UK, is treating its drinkers well. A host of great new bars are bolstering the city's charge to become the best night out outside of London.**

as much rock 'n' roll attitude as their twist on the standard classics (try the Cider Car) and come very well priced, too. Mojo has established itself as a must-visit bar, née party venue, in a city known for nurturing good times. In fact, it's proving so popular that there are sister outlets in Leeds and Liverpool (*mojobar.co.uk*). The future of Manchester is bright, and bars such as Mojo will turn this city into the party hub of the UK, so don't miss out.
✖
59 Bridge Street, Manchester M3 3BQ +44 (0)845 611 8643 mojobar.co.uk
✖

THE EDGBASTON

As boutique hotels go, The Edgbaston in Birmingham has to be one of the smallest, but arguably most perfectly formed, with just six bedrooms, each one delivering a timeless Victorian elegance. However, it is the cocktail lounge – or three of them to be precise – that has been turning heads right across the industry since the hotel opened two and a half years ago. Slick table service gives the whole place an elegance harking back to the Art Deco age of drinking. Keep an eye out for the masterclasses from luminaries of the drinks industry, who seldom travel outside of London when imparting their wisdom to a UK audience, but clearly see The Edgbaston as something very special indeed.

✖
18 Highfield Road, Edgbaston, Birmingham B15 3DU
+44 (0)121 454 5212
theedgbaston.co.uk
✖
IN THREE WORDS:
Brilliant Brummy Boutique.
WE SAY:
The effort from the whole bar team is clear to see.
PRICE RATING: ✸✸✸✸

THE SMUGGLERS COVE ↑

Head to the recently refurbished Albert Docks in Liverpool and you might think that you've entered the set of *Pirates Of The Caribbean*, especially when you swing through the doors of The Smugglers Cove, one of Liverpool's newest and most exciting bars. No, this isn't a pirate-themed bar, but it certainly takes its influence from the era of tall ships, export on the high seas and, of course, rum. The bar itself is absolutely cavernous, which mirrors the extensive rum list – that's doing it a disservice as it's an actual book all about the history of rum, which is peppered with a phenomenal selection predominantly from the Caribbean, but with a hearty selection from Guyana, Mauritius, Nicaragua, Venezuela and the UK. It's so comprehensive that you would be hard-pressed to find this level of passion and sheer volume of the spirit anywhere else in the world, and this reason alone makes The Smugglers Cove an essential place to visit, me hearties...

✖
Britannia Pavillion
Albert Dock, Liverpool
L3 4AD +44 (0)151 703 6555
thesmugglerscove.uk.com
✖
IN THREE WORDS:
Rum Old Time.
WE SAY:
Taking rum education to the next level, The Smugglers Cove has nailed its intentions firmly to the mast and set sail for your palates.
PRICE RATING: ✸✸

FOCUS*

STARTENDER
JAMES BOWKER

J ames is one of a new breed of hugely innovative bartenders from the UK, continuously pushing the boundaries of new flavours in mixed drinks, but also championing the golden age of bar service, which he masterfully applies at his current residence, The Edgbaston Hotel in Birmingham (see page 51).

Where do you drink when you're off duty?
Anywhere with good wine or beer! I've recently taken quite a liking to **Cheval Blanc** (chevalblancbar.co.uk), an excellent local wine bar, and **Peel and Stone** (peelandstone.co.uk) in Birmingham. Both are small (I love intimate social spaces) and simple, caring first and foremost about their hospitality and the drinks they are providing.
Your favourite drink of all time?
Cold water on a hot day. Or a Sherry Cobbler. Or a beer. Or, best of all, a drink chosen by a bartender I trust. Tough decisions taste bad.
What is your favourite city in the world to go drinking in?
London. It's always evolving and it's finally learning not to take

itself too seriously. Most serious cocktail cities I've visited are a touch on the arrogant side. Some "amazing" bars have shown me horrific service, but that's never happened to me in London.

What do you think is the most underrated cocktail of all time and why?
Both Sherry Cobblers and Delicious Sours could do with more press. It's no coincidence I've already mentioned Sherry Cobblers because they are so simple and yet so perfect... they manage to be uniquely refreshing without being overly strong, so you feel no guilt in ordering several one after another. Surely, that is the true test of greatness in a cocktail?

Delicious Sours, well, for the sheer audacity of the name [a take on the traditional "sour", but using Calvados and peach liqueur] and also because they are a rare example of balancing rich and sour so well.

James makes us one of his signature drinks:
✖
THE O SOLE MIO

35ml Tanqueray No. 10
20ml fresh lemon juice
20ml Briottet Rhubarb Liqueur
15ml raspberry cordial
(1:1 sugar syrup, infused
with fresh raspberries –
we use a sous vide, but you
can do it on the hob)

3ml Mozart White Chocolate
Liqueur (1 teaspoon if
making at home)
4 dashes homemade
"Ice Cream" Bitters
candy floss and chocolate
flakes, to garnish

Chill a Champagne flute or, if you have one, a glass designed to look like an ice-cream cone! Add all the ingredients to a shaker. Shake it all up, strain it into your chilled glass and garnish with a ball of candy floss to represent the ice cream. Then, add flakes of chocolate and enjoy!

JAMES'S TOP FIVE BARS FROM AROUND THE WORLD:

✖
The Artesian, The Langham Hotel, London →
(artesian-bar.co.uk)
While still open and still excellent, this bar is currently rediscovering its identity with a brand new, talented team. This bar took the traditional five-star hotel bar and turned it on its head.

✖
The Savoy, London – both bars!
(see page 22)
It is, for me, impossible to choose between the American Bar and the Beaufort Bar. What makes them great is that every detail is so carefully considered.

✖
La Venencia, Madrid
(see page 83)
This one isn't a cocktail bar. It's also incredibly cheap. What you get for your money is exquisite sherry chosen by the proprietor,

paired with simple and delicious tapas. It captured for me a way of life that modern bartenders far too often overlook: honest simplicity. La Venencia has a charm that is almost unbeatable, comparable (although utterly different) to the most quaint of British pubs!

✖
Peg + Patriot, London
(see page 44)
What makes them great is that no ingredient is ever off the

table. Nothing is too weird, or impractical. In a simple drink, they will capture something very special.

✖
Dead Rabbit, New York
(see page 212)
I suspect, fairly strongly, that this is a bar that many people will agree is a game-changer. In what way has it changed the game, you might ask? Well, it hasn't. Rather, it has taken three very different types of game (pub, lounge and party) and done them better than anybody else, all under one roof.

BRIGHTON, BRISTOL & LYME REGIS*

THE COCKTAIL SHACK

Known as London By The Sea, Brighton has always been a trend-setting city. Whether you're staying in one of the many local boutique hotels, or simply heading down on a train from The Big Smoke for a quick bit of fun, you can't go too wrong with a drink at The Cocktail Shack. Hidden in the walls of Regency Square (look out for the pink door of the Artist Residence hotel) the bar is made from driftwood salvaged from the local pier. The cocktails are just as creative with brilliant names, such as Lest We Fernet, where a pound from each drink goes to the Royal British Legion. A conscience as well as cocktails. Fantastic!

✖

34 Regency Square, Brighton BN1 2FJ +44 (0)1273 321196 cocktailshackbrighton.co.uk

✖

IN THREE WORDS:
Seaside Spirits Shaken.
THE DRINK TO TRY:
Cachaca in The Rye.

THEY SAY:
"A brilliant drinking den in Brighton."
— HELEN CHESSHIRE, UK
WE SAY:
Drift away with a corking cocktail.
PRICE RATING: ✱✱

HAUSBAR

Opened in June 2006 by Aurelius Braunbarth, Hausbar has brought a genuine injection of Berlin-esque class and style to the bar scene in Bristol. Auri grew up in a Michelin-starred kitchen, where his father worked as a chef, and soon realized that although he loved cooking, he'd much rather be running a bar. His experiences in various German establishments including Harry's NY bar gave him a sense of how his own bar should look and feel.

Hausbar has a minimal lounge style decor, with a classic 1930s simplicity at its heart. The extensive cocktail list is made up of 95 per cent classic cocktails but, as Auri points out, "You'll see it says 'no foam and no jelly' on the house list – I'm not a fan of drinks you have to eat!"

✖

52 Upper Belgrave Road, Bristol BS8 2XP +44 (0)117 946 6081 hausbar.co.uk

✖

Hidden away on Unity Street in Bristol is a place designed to be missed: Red Light. Spot the red light, pick up a phone and call down to the best-dressed bartenders in Bristol.

IN THREE WORDS:
South-Western Class.
WE SAY:
A genuine hidden gem in the Bristol drinks scene.
PRICE RATING: ✱✱✱

RED LIGHT →

Hidden on Bristol's Unity Street is a place designed to be missed. Spot the red light, pick up a phone and call down to the best-dressed bartenders. The bar calls itself an "adult drinking den", but is really an Art Deco hangout. The cocktails are wittily grouped into playful adult areas ("foreplay" etc.) and come sensibly priced.

✖
1 Unity Street, Bristol BS1 5HH
+44 (0)117 929 1453
redlightbristol.xxx
✖

IN THREE WORDS:
XXX

THE DRINK TO TRY:
Anything using Jinzu, a Japanese influenced gin, created by bartender Dee Davies.

WE SAY:
A red-hot bar team makes this venue unmissable.

PRICE RATING: ✱✱

HIX OYSTER & FISH HOUSE →

Okay, so this is a restaurant good and proper. Well, sort of! It is home from home for chef Mark Hix, who hales from Dorset. Situated high on the cliffs above Lyme Regis with a view down the stunning bay and the Jurassic coast, it is a light and informal place to eat the freshest of the fresh seafood. The menu changes daily according to what is available at the market. Couple this with locally foraged ingredients and you've got yourself the foundations of a great drinking experience.

Hix's drinks menu here is not quite as eclectic as at Mark's Bar in Soho (see page 37), but focuses on the local, with five different Black Cow Vodka Martinis (the locally produced vodka, made from milk), a comprehensive list of local cider and perry, three of Hix's own beers (try his Oyster ale) and some banging cocktails such as the Dorset Donkey (his local take on a Moscow Mule)... and this is before you get to his selection of British gin and tonics, or indeed the wines.

✖
Cobb Road, Lyme Regis DT7 3JP
+44 (0)1297 446910
hixrestaurants.co.uk
✖

IN THREE WORDS:
Best Of British.

THE DRINK TO TRY:
The Smokey Black Cow Vodka Martini with smoked salmon.

WE SAY:
The bar with the best view in all of England.

PRICE RATING: ✱✱✱✱

EDINBURGH*

Edinburgh is one of the leading cities in the world cocktail scene, playing host to some cool, accessible and forward-thinking bars. Most of these are forged in the traditional speakeasy-style joint; the reward for those who manage to find these oft-hidden venues is great cocktails and great atmosphere. Over the last decade, a number of high-profile bartenders have served their apprenticeships in hallowed Edinburgh basements, going on to open up award-winning bars of their own around the world. One thing's for sure, the city's influence on drinking culture isn't over yet.

BON VIVANT ↑

Arriving at Bon Vivant after the witching hour is always an experience. The capacious bar and restaurant are full of private little corners where you can peruse the drinks menu, under the watchful eye of the resident bon vivant, Stuart McClusky. The whiskies on offer are dazzling, with many of them making their way into vibrant takes on classic cocktails, punches and mixed drinks. The bar also hosts regular tastings from some of the industry's most entertaining players.

✖
55 Thistle Street, Edinburgh
EH2 1DY +44 (0)131 225 3275
bonvivantedinburgh.co.uk

✖
IN THREE WORDS:
Raconteurs Of Flavour.
THE DRINK TO TRY:
El Mas Loco.
WE SAY:
The length of the menu is perfect, as is the willingness to come up with something surprising in a flash.
PRICE RATING: ✶✶

FEATURE*

A DAY DRINKING IN...
EDINBURGH

It is remarkable how such a small city can punch above its weight when it comes to fantastic drinking joints...

A classic stop-off for tourists visiting the UK (and even more so since the Harry Potter phenomenon took hold, rooted in the surrounds of this ancient city), it is now a key place to visit for those folk looking to drink some of the best cocktails in the world.

It is remarkable how such a small city can punch above its weight when it comes to fantastic drinking joints, with the Scottish capital establishing itself as one of the best cities in the world regarding cocktails.

Sure, this city has brilliant whisky bars as you would hope for from the capital of a country

that produces such a visceral and vibrant spirit, utterly rooted in the local land, culture and history. If you're visiting and you really want to learn more about their local liquor, head to the **Scotch Whisky Experience** ↓ (scotchwhiskyexperience.co.uk) up by the castle. Here you can take a virtual tour of Scotland and its distilleries without so much as getting your galoshes

damp. (It is in a number of different languages too.) There is also a great bar to enjoy a dram or two, as well as a bite to eat.

If visiting the Experience has whetted your appetite for a wee dram, then head to **Whiski** (see page 59) or for a fully immersive experience try the **Scotch Malt Whisky Society** (smws.com), a members-only bar that will, if you ask nicely, let you come in for a drink.

The SWMS is located on Queen Street, which will put you in the perfect location as it is walking distance to **The Lucky Liquor Co** (see page 59), **Bramble** (see page 58), **Bon Vivant** (see opposite), **Panda And Sons** (see page 59) and **Hoot The Redeemer** (see page 58), a remarkable concentration of world class bars all within walking distance of each other, and a fact that makes Edinburgh such a unique city to go drinking in. You'd be wise to hit a taxi to **The Last Word Saloon** (see page 59) after visiting even just two of these bars, which is a perfect place to end your night.

EDINBURGH*

BRAMBLE

Descend the stairs of one of Edinburgh's most celebrated cocktail bars and prepare to be amazed. Bramble might not be the biggest, most lavish joint in town, but the quality of cocktails lovingly produced means that this gem has now reached the ears (and palates) of drinks enthusiasts around the globe. Mike Aikman and his team have put together a revolving drinks list, which perfectly showcases their enthusiasm for mixing the known with the unknown.

✖
16A Queen Street, Edinburgh
EH2 1JE +44 (0)131 226 6343
bramblebar.co.uk
✖

IN THREE WORDS:
Fruity Basement Frolic.

THE DRINK TO TRY:
The Bramble or a Bronson,
whose ingredients list defies
categorization.

THEY SAY:
"Killer tunes, amazing, honest
and warm service and world
class cocktails...it's simply the

product of passion from some
of the best in the business."
— RYAN CHETIYAWARDANA,
AKA MR LYAN, UK

WE SAY:
The original masters in the
Edinburgh bar scene with
exceptionally crafted drinks.

PRICE RATING: ✷✷

HOOT THE REDEEMER ↓

As bars go, this one is quite a creative place. Head down to the hidden entrance on Hanover Street where you'll encounter a fortune-telling coin-op machine that looks as if it came straight from the set of the Tom Hanks classic move *Big*. Hidden behind the door is an homage to 1950s America: alcoholic slushy drinks, their own brand of ice-cream pimped up with booze. The

place even has pages from racy novels pasted to the toilet walls, making this a real drinking den not to be missed. Their ethos, "we aren't a serious bar but we take having fun and making sure you have fun very seriously. Dive in and make your wish!" becomes abundantly clear the longer you're inside.

✖
7 Hanover Street, Edinburgh
EH2 1DJ +44 (0)131 220 0310
hoottheredeemer.com
✖

IN THREE WORDS:
1950s Retro Fun.

THE DRINK TO TRY:
Jungle Bird Slushie, which is a
take on a rum punch.

WE SAY:
Make your wish when going in
and live like it's the 1950s!

PRICE RATING: ✷✷

THE LAST WORD SALOON

The Last Word is indeed "Saloon", which sums up this wee Edinburgh cocktail bar perfectly. Set slightly away from the main part of the city, this basement bar with a simple Americana vibe wears the word saloon well. The bar's lineage is clear, with sister venues The Lucky Liquor Co (see below) and Bramble (see opposite) all flowing from the creative cocktail mind of Mike Aikman and his team of top mixologists, with small signatures, such as bottled cocktails and steel ageing. As far as Edinburgh goes, this is one of the top places for a cocktail and, despite being slightly off the beaten track, should be a "must visit" on any trip to the Scottish capital.

✖
*44 St Stephen Street, Edinburgh
EH3 5AL +44 (0)131 225 9009
lastwordsaloon.com*
✖
IN THREE WORDS:
Last Word First.
THE DRINK TO TRY:
*The Last Word Revisited is
gin-based deliciousness.*
WE SAY:
*Don't leave this till last, get there
early and enjoy!*
PRICE RATING: ✹✹

THE LUCKY LIQUOR CO

Situated on Queen Street, one of Edinburgh's most iconic locations, The Lucky Liquor Co is one of a bouquet of booze boutiques that adorn the city and is unmissable, with its large neon sign proclaiming simply "liquor".

Across two floors, you'll find incredible drinks in an American diner style environment. The chequered floor upstairs sets the scene for a laid-back drinking experience. Downstairs you'll find a pool table, perfect for hanging out with one of their brilliant cocktails. You can even see some of their experiments in cabinets around, or staff working on new creations behind the bar as you sip on a lush libation.

✖
*39A Queen Street, Edinburgh
EH2 3NH +44 (0)131 226 3976
luckyliquorco.com*
✖
IN THREE WORDS:
Lucky, Lucky You!
THE DRINK TO TRY:
*Banana Clipper with Cutty
Sark Prohibition and their own
housemade Sassafras liqueur.*
THEY SAY:
*"This bar is so incredibly
creative...easy, unpretentious
and a lot of fun."*
— **KELSEY RAMAGE, CANADA**
WE SAY:
*A definitive pitstop to any
drinking adventure in
Scotland's capital.*
PRICE RATING: ✹✹

PANDA & SONS

Hidden under what seems like a disused barbershop on Queen Street is a cool basement bar. The cocktail list shows off a fantastic level of creativity, with some inspired titles (the Juan Direction) and a whole section of classics dedicated to a fictional family of panda bears. Sounds odd, but embrace the madness and you'll discover some incredible drinks.

✖
*79 Queen Street, Edinburgh
EH2 4NF +44 (0)131 220 0443
pandaandsons.com*
✖
IN THREE WORDS:
Cocktails With Claws.
THE DRINK TO TRY:
Smokey and the Pandito.
WE SAY:
A must on an Edinburgh night out.
PRICE RATING: ✹✹

WHISKI

The starting point for any malt enthusiast parachuted into Edinburgh, Whiski has won countless awards for its dedication to the spirit. Its central location means the place is always buzzing. A well thought-out menu of around 270 whiskies, including a comprehensive selection of Lowland whiskies as well as some rare gems and a host of whisky-themed "alternative" classic cocktails.

✖
*119 High Street, Edinburgh
EH1 1SG +44 (0)131 556 3095
whiskibar.co.uk*
✖
IN THREE WORDS:
Does Beer Too!
WE SAY:
*Whiski has wisdom, knowledge
and enthusiasm and does Scotch
whisky a real favour.*
PRICE RATING: ✹✹

FEATURE*

A DRINK WITH...
KIERAN MIDDLETON

Kieran Middleton is the brewer and business development manager for Bellfield Brewery, based in Edinburgh.

Has the world of craft beer become a bit of a minefield for the consumer?

Yes. It can be a bit of a minefield, though I'd recommend sticking to the simple formula of mostly drinking the style you like and experimenting when you fancy (and feel brave) into the twisted world of Sours and exotic combinations.

When you're not drinking beer, what do you drink?

I love the development of all things produced in small batches by Scottish artisan producers: Scottish malt whisky, small batch gins with interesting botanicals – and I love a bit of Pinot Noir.

Beer in cocktails – good or bad? Any examples either way?

I would think that the heavily fruit-inspired and aged oaky beers would all be worth experimenting with. You never know where the next great taste experience will come from, so mix away.

KIERAN'S TOP FIVE CRAFT ALE HAVENS

✖
Bad Martha, Martha's Vineyard MA (badmarthabeer.com)
A small but very well considered, timber framed, brewhouse bar directly in front of a large glass window looking though to all the action of the brewery.

✖
Warpigs, Copenhagen (warpigs.dk)
A Mikkeller bar in an old converted slaughterhouse, unashamedly raw and industrial. The main features are the products: Texas-style barbecue food and 22 taps of Mikkeller's finest beers.

✖
Covenhoven, Brooklyn, New York (covenhovennyc.com)
Simple, chilled, unpretentious and with a great little beer garden. Numerous local and inter-state beers are on tap complemented by a wall of refrigerators, packed with beers from all over the world.

✖
Staggs Bar, Musselburgh, Edinburgh (staggsbar.com)
The beer is why you're here. The bar has been in the family for generations and, unlike many modern craft bars, the beer is the star, treated with reverence and celebrity. As always the star of the show is Oakham Ales Green Devil at 6%; you can very easily have too many of this pale and intensely hoppy beauty.

✖
Brel Bar, Glasgow (brelbar.com)
What a treat. A multitude of spaces inside including a mezzanine and conservatory. But the real star is outside, a great beer garden with heated patio and the circular winding seating of the solarium – Glasgow's best "sitooterie". Beyond the physical surroundings there is a solid foundation of good taste in both food and beer selection. All in all you tend to leave with a warm fuzzy feeling, hoping it won't be too long till you return.

GLASGOW✶

THE BON ACCORD

Rather like The Pot Still (see page 62), The Bon Accord has gone about its business of delivering one of the finest selections of whiskies that Glasgow has to offer for over 15 years now and owner Paul McDonagh can pride himself on a job well done. This isn't a glitzy, glamorous whisky bar that has cottoned on to the idea that whisky is seemingly suddenly very cool – it's a cracking pub that also happens to have a constantly revolving list of incredible whiskies (around 400 Scotch malt whiskies at the time of writing). The service and passion for whisky here are heart-warming; a genuine love for the spirit and they will make even the least inclined to a wee drop feel welcome. If only you could bottle such enthusiasm.

✖

*153 North Street, Glasgow
G3 7DA +44 (0)141 248 4427
bonaccordpub.com*

✖

IN THREE WORDS:
C'est Très Bon!

WE SAY:
Top shelf bottles, along with a genuine top shelf service and knowledge.
PRICE RATING: ✱

THE FINNIESTON

Edinburgh may well be one of the cities leading the global charge in the world of cocktails (see page 56), but her well-known neighbour, Glasgow, is not to be left out. Boasting one of the best drinking experiences in the UK (a night out in Glasgow is a must for all you night owls out there), there are some exceptional bars in Glasgow's ultra-cool West End and Merchant City, from converted churches to typical Scottish boozers. One of the very best is The Finnieston, where you can pair some amazing seafood with great libations, such as their house special, The Finnieston Club Cocktail , which is "inspired by Glaswegian cocktail culture and the legendary club cocktails of a bygone era". No night out in Glasgow is complete without a cocktail stop-off here.

✖

*1125 Argyle Street, Glasgow
G3 8ND +44 (0)141 222 2884
thefinniestonbar.com*

✖

IN THREE WORDS:
Seafood And Cocktails.

THE DRINK TO TRY:
Arsenic & Lace.
THEY SAY:
"Probably my fav place for cocktails in the city."
— **GEORGIE BELL, UK**
WE SAY:
The perfect place to start your evening, with great food and cocktails.
PRICE RATING: ✱ ✱ ✱

GLASGOW, ABERDEEN & CRAIGELLACHIE*

THE POT STILL ↓

Whisky, whisky, whisky – in one compact public house. Glasgow's Pot Still is a shining light on Hope Street; a venue that has become a destination for almost every weary whisky connoisseur travelling on to the outer reaches of Scotland – and the distilleries who make the stuff. The interior is still that of a classic Victorian pub: dark wooden alcoves are lined with every conceivable bottle of whisky (over 700) that you could think of: single malts

from across Scotland sit next to all manner of blends and a smattering of world whiskies (the Dutch Zuidam single malt is excellent). All this before we mention the simple pleasure of a plate of pie and beans.

✖
154 Hope Street, Glasgow G2 2TH +44 (0)141 333 0980 thepotstill.co.uk
✖
IN THREE WORDS:
Still Utterly Remarkable.
THEY SAY:
"Quite simply, an amazing whisky range."
— SARUNAS KARALIUS, LITHUANIA
"Big Frank, Guinness and an amazing selection of whiskies – really enough said!"
— RYAN CHETIYAWARDANA, AKA MR LYAN, UK
PRICE RATING: ✴

THE GRILL ↑

Some bars are hidden away behind fridge doors, or through telephone boxes in hot dog shops, some shine brightly from roof tops advertising their wares for miles around. Others, such as The Grill in Aberdeen, hide in plain sight, masked by fogged out windows and elderly facades, yet hiding behind is a great drinking experience: one you'll find by simply pushing the door and walking in. Established in 1870 as a restaurant on Aberdeen's main street (complete with "billiards table and electric lighting"), The Grill is pretty much unchanged from this time with unusual oxidized-bronze fascia panels and scrollwork on the exterior still in place today; it feels very traditional both from the outside and the inside. Yet this bar is really the heart and soul of drinking in Aberdeen, with a fantastically warm atmosphere, a great selection of ales and an even better list of whiskies. They even feature their own bottlings from time to time.

✖

213 Union Street, Aberdeen
AB11 6BA +44 (0)1224 573530
thegrillaberdeen.co.uk

✖

IN THREE WORDS:
Whisky Whisky Whisky.
WE SAY:
Push the door and feel the welcome atmosphere.
PRICE RATING: ✳✳

THE TIPPLING HOUSE

Aberdeen is a city where the days can be exceptionally long in the summer, and very short in winter. For both of these, The Tippling House is the ideal location to while away the long days, or long nights. Described as a "subterranean late-night

tavern serving boutique spirits, hand-crafted cocktails, fine Scottish ales and inspired casual dining", they meet these criteria with aplomb. The cocktails here draw influence from the well-stocked back bar, but use ingredients with a twist. Add fantastic food to this awesome cocktail list, and you can kick off any night in Aberdeen in style with a visit here.

✖

4 Belmont Street, Aberdeen
AB10 1JE thetipplinghouse.com

✖

IN THREE WORDS:
Simply The Don.
THE DRINK TO TRY:
The LaFayette's Cup.
WE SAY:
Oil be damned, this place is great.
PRICE RATING: ✳✳✳

THE CRAIGELLACHIE HOTEL ↓

The Speyside region of Scotland is arguably the jewel in the crown of the country when it comes to whisky, including the world famous Macallan, Glenlivet and Glenfiddich brands. Nestled between these producers lies The Craigellachie Hotel, a historic landmark for any whisky fan making the trip to the region. In 2013 the place received a huge refurbishment, with an emphasis on returning the splendour back to Speyside and the result is superb. With its roaring log fires, relaxed atmosphere and two bars – the Copper Dog, which doubles as a bistro, and the Quaich Bar, a luxuriously wood and leather panelled room, boasting over 900 whiskies from around the world – The Craigellachie does whisky like no other establishment in the region.

✖

Victoria Street, Speyside
AB38 9SR +44 (0)1340 881 204
craigellachiehotel.co.uk

✖

IN THREE WORDS:
Whisky's Winter Warmer.
THE DRINK TO TRY:
The flights of different whiskies from around the region.
WE SAY:
Head there in January and watch the snow falling outside, as you sip a glorious selection of single malts by a roaring fire.
PRICE RATING: ✳✳✳✳

ISLAY✶

LOCHINDAAL HOTEL →

Located in the pretty village of Port Charlotte, on the western side of the island, this hotel is a mainstay of local drinking culture. At some of the more newly renovated establishments you might find a group of bearded Scandinavian whisky enthusiasts or fresh-faced journalists on a press trip, propping up the bar, but here you'll find the locals, quietly sipping on a beer from Islay Ales, paired with a dram of the local good stuff. The collection of whiskies is an ever-changing feast, and the landlord constantly builds on his rare and unusual selection.

✖

11 Main Street, Port Charlotte, Isle of Islay +44 (0)1496 850202 lochindaalhotel.co.uk

✖

IN THREE WORDS:
Ileach's Local Libations.
THE DRINK TO TRY:
Ask for a flight of local whisky.
THEY SAY:
"Unpretentious, but always surreal fun."
— DAVE BROOM, UK

"You can get a pour of Port Ellen or some obscure festival bottling."
—LIZA WEISSTUCH, USA
WE SAY:
Speak to everyone and you'll always hear amazing stories about the island.
PRICE RATING: ✶

PORT CHARLOTTE HOTEL

Classic bars are often located in classic locations, and this hotel on the Isle of Islay is no exception. Sitting proudly in the charming conservation village of Port Charlotte, this coastal hotel has amazing views of the sea and surrounding countryside. The village was built in 1828 by Walter Frederick Campbell, the Laird of Islay at the time and named after his mother, Lady Charlotte. It quickly became a hub for fishermen and visitors alike. The Port Charlotte Hotel was originally built as three

cottages in 1829 before being converted into a hotel. It is in one of these former cottages that their excellent bar is housed. Warm and welcoming, it boasts one of the best selections of whisky on the island, and always has great ales on tap to discover. If you're lucky, you'll be there on a night with live music and the place can erupt before closing, when many people migrate over to the Lochindaal (see left). With just 10 bedrooms, the hotel is small but the attention to detail is excellent, from the fantastic bar to the superb local food.

✖

Port Charlotte, Isle of Islay PA48 7TU +44 (0)1496 850360 portcharlottehotel.com

✖

IN THREE WORDS:
Smoky Paradise Island.
THE DRINK TO TRY:
Any of the local ales and of course a glass of Islay whisky.
WE SAY:
A great place to stay and a wonderful place to drink with sea views and fab food.
PRICE RATING: ✶✶

FEATURE*

A GUIDE TO DRINKING ON ISLAY

D on't be fooled. The Isle of Islay might seem small on a map, but in reality it is a pretty big place. And much like the island, the whisky for which it is famous is a big tasting product, too. If you are familiar with whisky, you'll have seen the word "Islay" on many a label. It is a byword for "smoky", or "peated", a process whereby the local peat (think of it as squidgy coal) is dried, and burned, with the heat and smoke drying out the barley used in the local single malt whisky production. The result is a whisky with a flavour that is directly born of the terroir, and as such makes the island a must-visit for those who love smoky Scotch.

When it comes to drinking on Islay, you can't do better than to start with the whisky distilleries. All eight of them accept visitors and it is advisable to book in advance. Kick off with the "Kildalton distilleries" on the south-east of the island: **Ardbeg**, **Lagavulin** and **Laphroaig** are all within walking distance of each other. With their coastal setting, you can sit down and enjoy a dram at each, and if

you start at the most southerly, Laphroaig, and work north, you can finish with a bowl of soup and a much earned dram in the **Old Kiln Cafe** at Ardbeg before jumping in a taxi back to the elegant and contemporary **Islay Hotel** in Port Ellen.

In the middle of the island lies Bowmore, home to a distillery of the same name ↑. You don't need to do a tour here to nip in and enjoy a glass of whisky while relaxing in a big leather armchair, open fire roaring, gazing out over the loch and across to Bruichladdich. Opposite the distillery sits **The Harbour Inn** (bowmore.com), their front saloon bar yet another great place to grab a dram, or a bite to eat.

En route to Port Charlotte, on the coastal road to the west, you'll be welcomed to visit the **Islay Ales** brewery (islayales.co.uk). A small operation, their beers have become the stuff of legend and

provide the perfect counterpoint for the local whisky.

Before arriving in Port Charlotte, the **Bruichladdich Distillery** (bruichladdich.com) is a must-see, as their whisky is a little more delicate than others produced on the island. Their distillery is also home to The Botanist gin, which is made using locally foraged botanicals and is the perfect arrival drink at the **Port Charlotte Hotel**, a wonderful destination – the rooms are comfortable, the food excellent and the bar well stocked. It is also a short stumble home after a good few beers at the **Lochindaal Hotel** bar (see opposite).

DUBLIN*

BOWE'S ↓

As traditional as they come, **Bowe's** imbues a sense of Irish hospitality into the wonderful surroundings of a traditional Victorian-style Irish boozer. From the panelling and leather and dark wood back bar to the simple beer offerings, you'll immediately feel at home pulling up a stool, waiting the regulation 119.5 seconds for the perfect pint of Guinness and settling down to read your guidebook about how to spend your afternoon in

Dublin. (Don't come here if you're looking for a multitude of craft ales, try Against The Grain for that – galwaybaybrewery.com.) With so many classic Victorian pubs closing and being renovated into apartments or gastro-bars, it's heart-warming to know that some people still value the importance of history and the absolute cultural charm that they bring – and Bowe's is a perfect reflection of this. A true emerald of the city.

✖

31 Fleet Street, Dublin 2
+353 (1)671 4038 bowespub.com
✖

IN THREE WORDS:
Emerald Of Dublin.
THE DRINK TO TRY:
A pint of Guinness!
WE SAY:
Traditional, hospitable and everything you want from an Irish pub in the centre of Dublin.
PRICE RATING: ✖✖

L. MULLIGAN GROCER

With the huge resurgence in Irish whiskey on a global scale – especially from a premium single pot still-style perspective, there are more and more bars collating incredible collections to try, and none more so than L. Mulligan Grocer. Here, the team have taken the concept further than most, treating guests to a

selection that numbers over 140 whiskies from all over the world, split into flavour profile: spicy rich, smoky and fruity. Here's where the fun starts and your whiskey may have an alternative serve available – incorporating different foods (sometimes ice-cream, candy floss or popsicles) as well as different beers, Kombucha tea and locally roasted coffee. It's something you may want to explore if whiskey has previously been an alien – and challenging – concept, but the purists out there needn't worry; there's still a selection of rare Irish whiskeys you can savour with a simple dash of water on the side.

✖

18 Stoneybatter, Dublin 7
+353 (1)670 9889
lmulligangrocer.com
✖

IN THREE WORDS:
Progressive Irish Charm.
WE SAY:
A charming and novel approach to whiskey education delivered by a passionate bar team.
PRICE RATING: ✖✖✖

FOCUS*

STARTENDER
AARON HAYDEN

As one of the chaps behind the success of Dublin's latest buzz restaurant/bar, Peruke & Periwig (peruke.ie), we thought Aaron Hayden would be ideally placed to take us through why Dublin is a city on the move when it comes to brilliantly bonkers drinks. As drinks concepts go, Aaron and his team have really started a revolution and the rest of Dublin will need to play catch up.

What has been the ethos behind Peruke & Periwig? What sets it apart from other bars in Dublin and where does the name come from?
It used to be a wig shop and both words are interchangeable words for wigs or styles of wigs, in different languages. So we run a wig-shop theme bar! I inherited the bar and the attitude from others; it wasn't just about setting up a cocktail bar for bartenders or being elitists about it, i.e. telling customers what a cocktail should be. Instead we try to create the cocktails for everyone, truly try to be customer focused and ensure everyone has an experience they want to talk about.

Can you give us a "signature serve" from the menu and take us through making it?
One that springs to mind is the "In The Navy", named from a Village People song – our menu is music themed. It's a twist on a Navy Grog, technically one of the oldest cocktails. Ours brings together grapefruit juice, lemon, caramel and whiskey or aged rum. It also includes Peychaud bitters and Disaronno liqueur. It's shaken and served over ice in a rocks glass.

Where do you drink when you're off duty?
MVP (mvpdublin.com), a neighbourhood bar that can do beer or craft cocktails, with a good crew.

What's your favourite drink of all time?
Anything from the Sour family: a Whiskey-Sour or Margarita.

What is your favourite city in the world to go drinking in?
At this point most international cities have a growing dynamic bar culture, so you can always find a good spot in most places.

AARON'S FAVOURITE PLACES TO DRINK AROUND THE WORLD:

✖ **Death & Co, New York (see page 213)** *Small, simple, while being masters of a craft.*

✖ **Dead Rabbit (see page 212)** *If for no other reason but the drive and determination to be the first bar on everyone's lips globally.*

✖ **Milk & Honey, New York (now sadly closed)** *Realizing exactly how to tailor a bar to its environment, executing it masterfully and inspiring a tonne of knock offs who just don't get it.*

✖ **Sibs On The Mountain, St Thomas, US Virgin Islands (00 1 (340) 774 8967)** *Because all bartenders need a late bar; this one might just have the best location.*

✖ **Peruke & Periwig, Dublin [yes, it's his own bar, but his reasoning is pretty sound]** *The first bar in a long time to impress me. I thought, "That looks hard but like so much fun." I started work there a couple weeks later!*

FEATURE*

A DAY DRINKING IN...
DUBLIN

As a cultural city full of charm and twinkle, Dublin can claim to be one of the most charming and twinkly, especially given the number of great things to drink – and places to drink them. Historically, the Temple Bar area has been the destination of the visiting hedonist; a place packed full of welcoming pubs, bars and music venues. Dublin's nightlife has always been vibrant, and today an added level of sophistication has developed, with several world class cocktail bars adding to the ranks of great places to drink.

Start off your day for brunch, with a Garden Bloody Mary

at **The Camden Exchange** (camdenexchange.ie) – either the herbaceous vodka version with a homemade basil and ginger infusion, or the big, bold bacon-and chilli-infused version with bourbon.

Next stop is the **Guinness Storehouse** ↓ (guinness-storehouse.com) on St James's

Gate, for a tour of how the black stuff is made, trying a number of the famous brewery's new craft-angled beers along the way.

With your appetite well and truly whetted, wander over to Fleet Street and experience the delights of **Bowe's Pub** (see page 66), to experience one of Dublin's most highly regarded pubs. Licensed in 1880, the place has all the charm you would expect, a fine selection of Irish whiskies, plus some of the most sumptuous toasted sandwiches to balance out any pangs of hunger you may be feeling after lunch.

From here, you have a choice of a spirited late afternoon. Head over to the **Old Jameson Distillery** on Bow Street in Smithfield Village (jamesonwhiskey.com), which has just undergone a major

renovation and is one of the most definitive players in the history of Irish whiskey. Here you can see how the fortunes of Ireland's whiskey-making community have changed over the last two centuries, while trying some outstanding blends and single pot still expressions.

If you're looking for a more modern take on Irish whiskey, then head over to The Liberties area of Dublin to the newly constructed **Teeling Whiskey Distillery** ↖ (teelingdistillery. com) on Newmarket. At one point in the 19th century there were nearly 40 different distilleries making spirit in the area and once again, the feeling is that the renaissance of Irish whiskey has found new champions, with the number of smaller, craft operations rising by the year.

As the evening sets in, secure a later booking at **Peruke & Periwig** ↑ ↗ (see page 67) for a sumptuous gourmet meal and some of Dublin's finest cocktails, before heading to **Against The Grain** (galwaybaybrewery.com), a craft beer pub on Camden

Street with over 40 different world craft beers and ciders, ranging from smooth, silky blonde beers from Belgium, to punchy, zesty and lively IPAs brewed both locally in Ireland and from the USA.

As Dublin is seemingly a city that never sleeps, head down Harcourt Street to the **Dean Hotel** (deandublin.ie), one of Ireland's best boutique hotels, with a restaurant and bar that

Dublin's nightlife has always been vibrant, and today an added level of sophistication has developed, with several world class cocktail bars adding to the ranks of great places to drink.

rival the very best in New York or London. The cocktail menu is progressive, bringing in craft spirits alongside infusions and different bitters recipes. The Benton's brings together bacon-infused Bulleit bourbon with maple syrup and chocolate bitters or you could go toward the Guinness-influenced Cuban Espresso, with Havana Club rum, Guinness, espresso coffee, Pedro Ximenez sherry, vanilla extract and spicy bitters.

For a quick nightcap – if you're still standing, that is – head over to **Peter's Pub** (peterspub. ie) before last orders for a last celebratory brew or the mighty L. Mulligan Grocer (see page 66), arguably the best whiskey bar in the city, to sink a couple of Redbreast 15-year-old single pot still whiskeys, while reminiscing on how your day in this fantastic city just got better and better.

FEATURE*

A DRINK ABOARD...
THE VENICE SIMPLON-ORIENT-EXPRESS

The world of drinking can take you to some interesting places; basement bars, speakeasies, roof terraces, hotel bars, even airline lounges...the list of places to quench your thirst is almost endless. In this book we focus on the unique, the interesting, the entertaining, but above all, those places that provide an excellent experience. And there is one bar in the world, perhaps the most exclusive bar we feature in this book, that is unrivalled in its sheer and utter experience.

The Venice Simplon-Orient-Express train is less of a mode of transport and more a moving work of art. The 17 carriages date from the early 1900s, and each has been meticulously restored to its former glory. Perhaps the train's most famous outing was as the opulent centrepiece for the 1934 Poirot novel by Agatha Christie. Today it runs several routes, most famously from Northern France, to the very edge of Europe, Istanbul.

Our first destination, though, is the newly renovated Bar Car, named 3674 after its service number, which lies at the heart of the train and provides a drinking experience akin to the greatest hotels in the world. Step inside and you're faced with an entire American-style cocktail bar shrunk to fit inside a 1920s railway carriage. Decked out in vibrant blues and golds, at one end there is a full bar with white-coated bar staff and bar stools, offering the best seats in the house. All this before you hear the gentle tinkling coming

Decked out in vibrant blues and golds, at one end there is a full bar with white-coated bar staff and bar stools, offering the best seats in the house.

from the baby grand piano, which floats by accompanied by the rhythm section, the shaking of cocktails.

Alongside its own caviar list (yes, really...), head barman Walter Nisi and his team have created a new cocktail menu that reflects the train's golden era. You'll find classics, such as the Mary Pickford (c.1926), the Old Fashioned (c.1928), the Singapore Sling (c.1915) and the Sazerac (c.1850), alongside his own creations, such as the Guilty 12, inspired by *Murder On The Orient Express*. His Train Stabilizer, which takes Cognac, port and barrel-aged bitters, seems, after two at least, to do exactly what it says it will do.

This bar is one of the most exclusive in the world: it is only open whenever the train is in operation, working out at around just 100 days a year. Of course, you must be on the train to be in the bar in the first place. So when it comes to exclusivity, there is nowhere quite like 3674 aboard the Venice Simplon-Orient-Express; utterly unique, utterly chic, and utterly timeless.

FEATURE*

A DAY DRINKING IN...
PARIS

Paris. One word, so many emotions. If there is one emotion that is so closely linked with this city, however, it is love.

With such a wonderful history of culinary craftsmanship, Paris loves food, and loves anyone who loves food. In fact, it is flavours in general that are celebrated in the French capital and, as you would expect, the French have taken their dedication to food, to wine, to spirits and applied it fair and square to cocktails.

Just as Paris has grown to become a place to enjoy art, culture and food, it is Paris that also now takes the honour as the European city to watch this year when it comes to drinks; the mantle being passed on by Athens last year (which has excelled itself recently, with cocktail bars such as The Clumsies and Baba Au Rum establishing themselves as two of the best in Europe), and Berlin the year before that.

Paris's cocktail bars take the same theme as London's, with a mix of classic hotel bars and more esoteric joints. But whereas in London there is an

Paris's cocktail bars take the same theme as London's, with a mix of classic hotel bars and more esoteric joints.

almost definitive split between the white-coated hotel bars of the West End and the hipster hangouts of East London, this city is much more egalitarian in its geography.

For example, it's a mere half an hour stroll between the forward-thinking **Little Red Door ↗** on Rue Charlot and the wonderfully classical **Hemingway Bar** at the Ritz Hotel on Place Vendôme. In London, it can take 45 minutes to travel by public transport between The Connaught in Mayfair and Happiness Forgets in Hoxton Square...while Paris is a city of compact complexity, deliberately diverse and proud of it. This compact nature, on the whole, is what makes Paris a city to be enjoyed. A city to be loved.

Add to this, the general shopping paradise for those looking to bag a bottle of something unusual, which can easily be found at the whisky drinkers paradise of the incredible **La Maison du Whisky ↓**. This is a shop so complete, so forward thinking, so well respected that it can boast a number of exclusive bottlings direct from distilleries across a range of genres, and you have yourself an *inSeine* (please excuse the river-based pun) place to hang out.

This melting pot of styles, shops and drinking holes is what a city should be. Paris doesn't do one thing well, it does lots of things well. It takes you, the drinker, on a journey, as if it was planned out in some great ethereal master plan of what makes the perfect city. Plus, a general approach to fulsome flavour, unusual presentation and ease of navigation means you won't want to leave. Well, not until you've explored every nook and cranny of this amazing city.

So, Paris once again opens itself up to be explored, to be consumed. But most of all, to be loved, enjoyed and experienced. You'll just *Louvre* it.

PARIS*

CANDELARIA ↓

The first bar and restaurant created and curated by the engaging team behind Quixotic Projects in Paris, Candelaria focuses on the wonders of Mexico and particularly agave spirits. Head down to the intentionally ramshackle bar for a spot of brunch at the weekend and enjoy the wonderful twist that Tequila gives the Bloody Mary (a Bloody Maria) and enjoy some delicious daytime taco treats. From 6pm, it gets serious and the cocktails are full-on Mexican-inspired masterpieces, using mezcal, sotol (a lesser-known Mexican spirit) and some outstanding Tequilas. If you are serious about the flavours of Mexico, then there is probably no better place to explore the liquid forms than here.

✖

52 Rue de Saintonge, 75003 Paris +33 1 42 74 41 28 quixotic-projects.com

✖

IN THREE WORDS:
Mexican Mixology Masterpieces.
THE DRINK TO TRY:
The Domino.
THEY SAY:
"I've never been disappointed by any visit."
— MARCIS DZELZAINIS, FRANCE
PRICE RATING: ✱ ✱ ✱

CAVEAU DE LA HUCHETTE

An underground jazz haven in the Latin Quarter, which has become something of an institution. Opened post World War II, after the ominous arches were used by secret societies in the centuries before, this subterranean gem has hosted legendary big bands to solo stars of the Jazz Age. These days, you'll find it doing just the same: be it raucous sax-fuelled dance sessions or subtle jazz trios. From a drinks perspective, it's all very simple: no fancy cocktails, just beers, wines and, if you're feeling flush, bottles of Champagne for your table. While it's fantastic that the Parisian cocktail scene is blossoming once more, you cannot underestimate the importance of places like this and how they have shaped the culture of a city for centuries.

✖

5 Rue de la Huchette, 75005 Paris +33 1 43 26 65 05 caveaudelahuchette.fr

✖

IN THREE WORDS:
Big Band Boozin'.
THEY SAY:
"Incredible live music and lots of cold beer...what more does one need?"
— ALEX WOLPERT, UK
PRICE RATING: ✱ ✱

LE GLASS ↑

This small dive bar has given the Pigalle area of Paris a real reason to be extremely cheerful. In fact, dive it most certainly ain't. Influenced largely by American themes (the hotdogs and boilermakers) the simplicity of these drinks masks what's to come, once you've nailed back your first Pickleback (IPA beer, bourbon and a shot of pickle juice). The cocktail menu is artfully constructed into a flavour map: ranging from Bohême – Audacieux – Serein – Corsé (we'll let you Google Translate these) but loosely speaking they range from light, elegant drinks, through to bold robust and complex beasts. A Bar de Triomphe!

This small dive bar has given the Pigalle area of Paris a real reason to be extremely cheerful.

✖
7 Rue Frochot, 75009 Paris
+33 9 80 72 98 83
quixotic-projects.com
✖

IN THREE WORDS:
Red Light Cocktails.

THE DRINK TO TRY:
If you can get past the name, Guitars And Dildos.

THEY SAY:
"For the nights of pure, unadulterated fun."
— REBEKKAH DOOLEY, UK

PRICE RATING: ✷✷

FOCUS*

STARTENDER
REMY SAVAGE

Remy Savage is the head bartender for Parisian uber-bar, Little Red Door (see page 78), a constant feature in numerous world's best bar lists and one of Paris's shining lights in the resurgence of the classic cocktail.

Tell us about the bar scene in Paris and France...
In France, we have an awesome scene. For years we were catching up with everyone but because it is such a small scene in France, we do it together; it is non-competitive, which is great. You are also getting personality from people more than from concepts, which come next.

How have you tried to change the landscape of Parisian cocktails?
We try to add philosophical aspects to drinking and the menu at Little Red Door has no words, only pictures. The one drink on the menu which I love is Drink No. 9: it is the only drink where the visual presentation is not done by a traditional artist, but by a musician.

Where do you drink when you're off duty?

I usually like to start the night at **Little Red Door**, which is a good sign, I think – you should want to drink in your bar, right?! Then depending on the mood of the evening, it is very easy to choose somewhere special, as Paris has so much to offer. I like to get a Margarita and a beer in **Candelaria** (see page 74), a Death in the Afternoon at **Bespoke** (bspk.fr), a Hurricane at our sister bar **Lulu White** (luluwhite.bar) and a classic Daiquiri at **Dirty Dick** (+33 1 48 78 74 58). I love going to Le Syndicat (see opposite) at the end of the night, and I usually finish with a dry Martini!

What's your favourite drink of all time?
At least over the last year I've not been able to get enough Death In The Afternoon's [a drink that brings together Absinthe and Champagne] and the simply delicious Suze and tonic.

What is your favourite city in the world to go drinking in?
It would have to be London.

REMY'S TOP FIVE GLOBAL BARS:

✖
**69 Colebrooke Row, London
(see page 18)** *Discovering 69 was
a small revelation for me. This
bar and its philosophy taught
me that there are very few rules
to follow and you can really
showcase your personality and
creativity in this industry. It's
still today one of my favourite
haunts, and is still serving some
of the world's most creative, yet
simple drinks.*

✖
**Bar BenFiddich, Tokyo
(see page 133)** ↑ *If you are in
the right mood, BenFiddich
might just be the perfect bar.
My experiences there have been
special and unique each time
and I find it hard to really put my
finger on why; it might simply be
that everything from the drinks,
the service, the orientation of the
lights, to the olive in my Martini
was just perfect, no more no less.*

✖
**Le Syndicat, Paris
(syndicatcocktailclub.com)**
*Le Syndicat is a very good
example of the current state of
our industry. The bar works with
French spirits and nothing else,
and even though this may seem
limiting, the strength of their
concept and the perfect delivery
make it great!*

✖
**Dante, New York (see page
209)** *I like Dante for a lot of
reasons: perfect playlist, nice
vibe and very good-looking bar,
but the thing that really stood
out for me was their Garibaldi
cocktail. It was exceptional in its
uniqueness, although it is simply
Campari and "fluffy" orange juice
– it is probably one of the most
delicious and clever drinks I
have experienced in a long time.*

✖
**Ruby, Copenhagen
(see page 106)** ↗ *I remember the
first time I stepped into Ruby;*

*within seconds I was in love.
The room is so perfectly designed
both in its details and as a whole,
that I knew I did not want to
leave. If my dream home bar
could look like anywhere in the
world, I hope it would be Ruby.*

PARIS & BORDEAUX*

LE MARY CELESTE ↓

A hat trick of bars for the Quixotic Projects folks proves that great things come in threes. Le Mary Celeste is a departure from both Le Glass (see page 75) and Candelaria (see page 74) but the thread of well-made fresh food and creative cocktails is clear to see. The emphasis here is the art of pairing: dishes aren't thrown together with a liquid accompaniment and everything, from the natural wines on offer to the cocktails, is curated to offer balance and

complement each course. Sit at the octagonal bar and take a voyage into the unknown.
✖
1 Rue Commines, 75003 Paris
+33 1 42 77 98 37
quixotic-projects.com
✖
IN THREE WORDS:
Voyage Of Discovery.
THE DRINK TO TRY:
The Rain Dog.
THEY SAY:
"They nail it, all the time."
— DAVIDE SEGAT, ITALY
PRICE RATING: ✳✳✳

LITTLE RED DOOR ↗

Artistic, avant-garde and undoubtedly stylish could very well apply to any number of places in Paris, but Little Red Door probably tops them all, throwing in sheer ingenuity and a little craziness for good measure. The bar, headed up by Remy Savage, has redefined the approach to the creation of the cocktail, looking beyond merely bringing flavours together, to applying art concepts – and architecture, too. The previous menu paired a number of different illustrations with each specific drink, and the current menu has applied various architectural theories in the design and aesthetic of both the vessel the drink is

consumed from and the way it is constructed. This may sound a little pretentious, but the results are staggering. Credit must go to the bar team here for helping to change not only the perspective of how we look at flavour but also the way we interact with our drinks and the environment around them. The reinvention of the Paris bar scene very much continues.
✖
60 Rue Charlot, 75003 Paris
+33 1 42 71 19 32 lrdparis.com
✖
IN THREE WORDS:
Architects Of Flavour.
WE SAY:
A game-changer in many ways, but also just a brilliant place to explore how making cocktails is a genuine art form in the right hands.
PRICE RATING: ✳✳✳

PRESCRIPTION ↑ ↓

St Germain's swish streets are better known for bookshops and art galleries, but here you'll find Prescription and it is just what the doctor ordered. Spanning two floors, the bar concentrates on well-made classics, but the bar team are more than happy to accommodate something off-menu that you may fancy trying. The low lighting and speakeasy vibe are nothing new, but there's a level of class on offer here and a distinctly Parisian streak to the vibe inside. Well played.

✖
23 Rue Mazarine, 75006 Paris
+33 9 50 35 72 87
prescriptioncocktailclub.com
✖
IN THREE WORDS:
Pick Me Up.
THE DRINK TO TRY:
Gotta be The Penicillin, hasn't it?
THEY SAY:
"A fresh, small bar, with a very nice ambience indeed."
— MARC ALVAREZ SAFONT, SPAIN
PRICE RATING: ✳✳✳

SYMBIOSE

A nifty little speakeasy-style operation that was opened in December 2015. Behind the concept are four friends – Lucas, Simon, Thomas and Felix – who clearly have a thing for the Old Fashioned, as it features heavily on the menu. Hidden behind an old grandfather clock in the joint's restaurant section lie the low vaulted ceilings of the bar, and once in, you'll be thrilled at what you find. Beautifully presented, innovative drinks, which mostly take their lead from the classic sweet/strong/citrus/spicy note of the Old Fashioned. C'est superbe!
✖
4 Quai des Chartrons, 33000 Bordeaux +33 5 56 23 67 15
✖
IN THREE WORDS:
Old-Fashioned Stories.
THE DRINK TO TRY:
An Armagnac Old Fashioned.
THEY SAY:
"An amazing cocktail bar, with a great range of Old Fashioneds."
— AMANDA GARNHAM, FRANCE
PRICE RATING: ✳✳

BARCELONA*

BAR BRUTAL ↓

While the concept of "natural wines" (those made without the interference of any chemicals during the vinification process) won't appeal to everyone, it's hard not to get swept away with the enthusiasm on display here. This very cool-looking bodega-style wine bar at the back of the Can Cisa wine shop has certainly demystified the category somewhat and offers a really excellent selection of wines at a very affordable price point. Here you feel like thoroughly exploring the recommendations of the staff, leaving any preconceptions you have about natural wine at the door. Go in with this attitude and you'll have one of the most palate-liberating experiences possible.

✖
Carrer de la Princesa 14, 08003 Barcelona +34 932 954 797 cancisa.cat
✖

IN THREE WORDS:
Brutal But Brilliant.

THEY SAY:
"Comfortable restaurant / natural wine bar in Barcelona... in an unpretentious way – a philosophy, not fad...!"
— **JEREMY GARA, CANADA**

PRICE RATING: ✳✳

BOADAS →

We've used the word timeless quite liberally across this book and in every case we've tried to justify it with regard to a drink, or a location to enjoy one. Boadas in Barcelona is understandably worthy of this description, given that it is regarded as the city's oldest cocktail bar, first established in 1933 and shares an extraordinary link to another classic bar, El Floridita in Havana (see page 274) – Miguel Boadas was the cousin of Narcís Sala Parera, the man credited with naming the now legendary Cuban drinking joint. Boadas was born in Havana and worked at El Floridita until 1922, when he moved to Spain and a decade later he established Boadas, decorating the bar in much the same way as his beloved El Floridita. The same can be said for Boadas and walking in is, indeed, like entering a time warp: the dark wooden decor is exactly the way it was back in the 1930s, with a few more paintings of the great man himself adorning the walls. Some places evolve naturally; places as legendary as Boadas simply gain a natural patina of perfection over time.

✖
Carrer dels Tallers 1, 08001 Barcelona +34 933 189 592 boadascocktails.com

nearly 20 bars around the world under his hugely experienced wing making some of the best drinks on the planet.

This incredible empire began over 30 years ago in Barcelona, and the original Dry Martini, founded by Don Pere Carbonell, established itself as a Martinería, by simply serving just Martinis. Once it was taken over by de Las Muelas, the classic look and feel has been impeccably maintained and today, alongside Dukes Hotel (see page 32) and The Connaught (see page 30) it is undoubtedly one of the most important places for any connoisseur to tick off their checklist of "Martini coupes to lift". The service, vintage gins and spectacular back bar are worth buying a plane ticket to Barcelona for alone.

✖

Carrer d'Aribau 162-166, 08036 Barcelona +34 932 058 070 drymartiniorg.com

✖

IN THREE WORDS:
Classic Among Classics.
THEY SAY:
"From ice to glass to spirit to garnish, this expresses individuality and intriguing personality!"
— **JOHNNY SCHULER, PERU**
"A beautiful bar with an old school feel and has the power to transport you to another era."
— **ALEX KAMMERLING, UK**
PRICE RATING: ✱✱✱✱✱

✖
IN THREE WORDS:
Art Deco Delights.
THEY SAY:
"If ever there was a cocktail bar that sings of the romance of cocktail culture it is here."
— **ALLEN KATZ, NEW YORK**
"At Boadas I discovered the cocktail world and that bars can be like churches."
— **JAVIER DE LAS MUELAS, SPAIN**
PRICE RATING: ✱✱✱

DRY MARTINI

One of the most celebrated and ubiquitous cocktails, the Dry Martini has graced the cinema screens and literature of the 20th century. You could say that it is truly legendary and, with that in mind, Javier de Las Muelas is a bartending legend in his own right. His own take on the Dry Martini has now become a globally recognized brand, with

BARCELONA & MADRID*

MUTIS ↓

Throughout the extensive interviews with our wonderful contributors one of the main questions we ask is where do you drink when off duty? To which the answer is, mostly, in the comfort of their own home,

entertaining friends and loved ones. But imagine your home was a bar – and a cracking one at that. Mutis is the secret element to Bar Mut (a tapas-style restaurant, which you'll find on a grand corner of the street) and takes over an entire floor of an apartment block off Avenida Diagonal. You'll need to ring ahead to get in, or ask the staff at Mutis very nicely, as the place is a private members' club, but it's worth the effort. Listening to live music, drinking classic cocktails in secret till the small hours, in

an old time cabaret-style setting is a thrilling experience.

✖

438 Avenida Diagonal, 08037 Barcelona +34 932 174 338

✖

IN THREE WORDS:
Home Sweet Home.

THEY SAY:
"You can look out the window and marvel at the fact that everyone else is going about their lives without even knowing this place exists."

— **MICHAEL VACHON, USA**

PRICE RATING: ✳✳✳✳

TANDEM COCKTAIL BAR ↑ ↗

A touch of the classics has descended on Tandem Cocktail Bar – and it really shows. No pretence here, just wonderfully constructed drinks, from a group of dedicated white-coated bartenders who are as friendly as they are highly skilled. It's hard to find fault in anything this bar does. The presentation of the drinks is fabulous, the atmosphere – a mixture of old-fashioned bar chic and a sprinkling of contemporary – and to top it off, a surprisingly comprehensive Japanese whisky list, which you wouldn't expect.

✖

Carrer d'Aribau 86, 08036
Barcelona +34 934 514 330
tandemcocktail.com

✖

IN THREE WORDS:
Peddling Great Drinks.
THEY SAY:
"A small and relaxing place that I feel totally at home in, with a nice, perfect balance of classic cocktails."
— MARC ALVAREZ SAFONT, SPAIN
PRICE RATING: ✷✷

LA VENENCIA

A wonderfully vintage sherry bar that looks and feels like it hasn't changed in years, which very much makes it a perfect addition. Just like El Guitarrón de San Pedro (see page 85), La Venencia is the sort of place we all dream of finding: uncluttered, no pretence, just simple, honest quality drinks at a price you can afford to make it your local. The shelves are lined with pretty much every sherry you could wish for: bone-dry manzanillas, rich, complex olorosos and sticky sweet Pedro Ximenez. For a sherry lover, this is as good as it gets. For those beginning their journey…this is as good as it gets!

✖

Calle Echegaray 7, 28014
Madrid +34 914 297 313

✖

IN THREE WORDS:
Blindingly Bodacious Bodega.
THEY SAY:
"It captured a charm that is almost unbeatable, comparable (although utterly different) to the most quaint of British pubs!"
— JAMES BOWKER, UK
PRICE RATING: ✷

FOCUS*

STARTENDER
JAVIER DE LAS MUELAS

Perhaps the undisputed godfather of the Dry Martini, Javier de las Muelas has now built his inimitable take on this classic drink into a global phenomenon, with an empire of nearly 30 world-class bars spanning everywhere from his home town of Barcelona all the way to Bali. We caught up with the *man with the golden stir* to talk about his roots into bartending and…his Martini recipe.

How did you get into making cocktails as a career?

My first moment of fascination for the culture of service was when I was only six or seven years old and I used to spend hours "helping" in the cellar in front of my house. The owner was my best friend's father and he sold wine and ice for fridges, as at that time there were few houses with electrical ones.

The conversations, the coming and going of customers, the relationships between them, got me fascinated. Years later, my friends took me to Boadas, [see page 80]. There I had my first contact with the world of cocktails and I was burned by the flame of the culture of service! I realized that bars are like churches – bartenders are priests, the back bar is the altar, customers are parishioners and cocktails are the offering.

I opened my first bar in 1979, The Gimlet in Barcelona. I remember that time with great affection. A very young team, with limited means but full of enthusiasm and with an endless desire for doing things well and in a different way. It was a great success. A few years after, I found Dry Martini.

As I entered its fantastic bar with the magnificent *mise en place*, dedicated only to the Dry Martini, I realized that if bars are churches, then Dry Martini was clearly the Vatican!

Where do you drink when you're off duty?

I am a qualitative drinker, just in special moments. I would taste but I don't normally make a daily break for drinks. I used to share a cocktail moment when travelling for pleasure, with my wife and friends. For me, that moment of relaxation in a nice bar is the perfect experience.

Your favourite drink of all time?

A Dry Martini. Drinking one means drinking history, music, literature, cinema, and art…

Speaking of which…want to taste arguably the finest Dry Martini in the world? Well, now you can make Javier's recipe at home:

✖

DRY MARTINI

2–3 dashes of dry vermouth
1 glass of Bombay Sapphire gin
a green olive, to garnish
a twist of lemon, to finish
*   (optional)*

Pour the vermouth and gin into a mixing glass, together with plenty of ice. Stir for 15 seconds. Pour into a martini glass and garnish with a green olive and add a twist of lemon, if liked.

CÓRDOBA & JEREZ*

LA BICICLETA ↓

When you have the mesmerizing architecture of Córdoba, it's hard for anything else to really grab your attention, but nestled away on the back streets, surrounded by numerous tapas bars, is La Bicicleta, a fine example of a bar that understands the concept of less is more. There are no frills here, but great G&Ts, beers and the odd cocktail, along with a no-nonsense wine selection. Pull up a chair, order a plate of jamon Iberico and manchego, and complement your day of sightseeing with a masterclass in keeping it real.

> **...a fine example of a bar that totally understands the concept of less is more.**

✖

Calle Cardenal González 1, 14003 Córdoba
+34 666 544 690

✖

IN THREE WORDS:
Free-Wheelin' Sippin'.
THEY SAY:
"An exercise in simplicity and just getting things right... memorable and exceptional."
— MARCIS DZELZAINIS, FRANCE
PRICE RATING: ✶

EL GUITARRÓN DE SAN PEDRO

Jerez is one of those places that seem to quietly pass people by, passed over in favour of the nightlife of Barcelona, or the hustle and bustle of Madrid. But given its cultural roots into one of the world's great drinks – we're of course talking about sherry here – it really should be at the top of every oenophile's travelling plans. While you're there, wend your way through the sprawling back streets and find yourself a seat at El Guitarrón de San Pedro. The selection of sherries is, as one would expect, outstanding and you can sip your way through a chilled fino or manzanilla to start, tuck in to some tapas, then explore the wider world of amontillado, oloroso and finally a Pedro Ximenez. You've heard the saying that everything tastes a little bit better when enjoyed where it's actually from? With Jerez – and sherry – there's never a truer word spoken...*es delicioso.*

✖

Calle Bizcocheros 16, 11402 Jerez de la Frontera, Cádiz
+34 649 656 918

✖

IN THREE WORDS:
Cream Of Jerez.
THEY SAY:
"Back-street tabanco *serving a huge range of sherries...and spontaneous flamenco sessions."*
— DAVE BROOM, UK
PRICE RATING: ✶

BERLIN*

ABSINTHDEPOT ⬇

The Green Fairy is alive and well and living in Berlin. Over the last few years, a number of absinthe-focused bars have popped up across the German capital, but none is more fun than the Absinthdepot. Located around the corner from the brilliant Casa Camper Hotel on Weinmeisterstraße, this place is more than just a bar to drink in – it is an homage to all things

absinthe. Operating as a shop during the day, open just after lunch for all your absinthe needs, it transforms into a bar at night serving some fantastic cocktails and showcasing their list of over 100 absinthes; they also offer tasting sessions. Just be careful with some of their creations, such as the wonderfully named Psycho Surfer (an absinthe and Cognac creation) and the equally gauntlet-throwing-down Hell On Fire, which mixes whisky, rum and, of course, absinthe!

✖

*Weinmeisterstraße 4, 10178
Berlin +49 30 2816789
absinth-berlin.de*

✖

IN THREE WORDS:
German Green Fairy.

WE SAY:
If you're going to indulge in the Green Fairy, do it with and around people of this ability!

PRICE RATING: ✶✶

BUCK AND BRECK

A bar that has redefined Berlin's cocktail culture, Buck and Breck takes its name from a classic Champagne and Cognac cocktail, which, in turn, recalls the nickname for a former US president, James Buchanan, and his vice president, John Breckinridge. This is a classic bar located close to the incredibly

cool Mitte area of Berlin, where style, design and community ooze from the buildings. It has a very small seating area, so make sure you've got a back-up plan ready if you can't get in, but once inside, the hospitality keeps the room warm.

The cocktails here are classics; you won't find foams, spheres or jellies but a simple list of some of the best known and most loved cocktails in the world. The only really inventive side of this little speakeasy is the window display, which rotates artwork, and means you'll have as much fun finding the bar as you will once sipping lush libations inside.

You are welcome to go off-menu (which is small but packed full of classics) and the bar staff are happy to oblige. They're a knowledgeable lot, reflecting the attitude that Berlin has recently adopted of doing things simply, but doing them well. Very well.

✖

*Brunnenstraße 177, 10119,
Berlin +49 176 32315507
buckandbreck.com*

✖

IN THREE WORDS:
Hidden German Gem.

THE DRINK TO TRY:
The Clover Club is fantastic.

WE SAY:
Seek it out not just for the drinks, but for the hospitality.

PRICE RATING: ✶✶✶✶

✖
IN THREE WORDS:
Nothing Jaded Here.
WE SAY:
Retro in feel, but possessing some very classy touches. A late-night hangout well worth seeking out.
PRICE RATING: ✳ ✳

IMMERTREU

Some bars chase the zeitgeist and others tradition. Immertreu chases neither, forging its own path, which encompasses a no-nonsense attitude, simplicity and genuine skill. Soft candlelight, old-fashioned cocktail glasses and vintage bottles give the place a timeless feel, but not in a retro way. Want Wifi? Forget it. Same goes for Happy Hour. In short, Immertreu is a place to find and settle in when the rest of the world is losing its head.

✖
Christburger Straße 6, 10405 Berlin +49 157 85921221 bar-immertreu.de

✖
IN THREE WORDS:
Titans of Teutonic Taste.
THE DRINK TO TRY:
The Rapscallion.
THEY SAY:
"The owner and bartender is in some respects a genius and a bit crazy too."
— **BERNHARD SCHÄFER, GERMANY**
PRICE RATING: ✳ ✳ ✳

CLÄRCHENS BALLHAUS ↑

Let's make one thing very clear here: you're not going to Clärchens Ballhaus for the innovative, forward-thinking, modernist cocktails. There aren't any. You go for a quintessentially Germanic night out, at a place that has seemingly been frozen in time. Located in the Mitte district, Clärchens Ballhaus is just that: a ballroom that is still in the same style as when it opened in 1913. Book yourself a table and order some food, and lashings of beer and wine while the room slowly fills up with groups of all ages. Once in full swing, the night becomes part-school disco, part-revivalist swing joint, part-1980s club, giving the overall effect of being in a Wes Anderson movie. It is truly an assault on the senses. And this is just the downstairs. Upstairs is the simply breathtaking Mirror Salon, with cracked 1920s mirrors on the walls. This really is a time-travelling venue that should be on the to-do list of every visitor to Berlin.

✖
Auguststraße 24, 10117 Berlin, +49 30 2829295 ballhaus.de

✖
IN THREE WORDS:
Time Travelling Temptations.
THE DRINK TO TRY:
Grab yourself a beer, or a flagon of local wine.
WE SAY:
The grand old lady of Berlin nightlife dances once again.
PRICE RATING: ✳

GREEN DOOR

One of the enduring fixtures on the Berlin cocktail aficionados' list, Green Door typifies the city's serious, yet laid-back approach to making great drinks. The bar is an intimate affair, with a long seated area and adjoining booths. The drinks are meticulously prepared and range from strong gin-based classics to sweeter, fruit-infused takes on the Sour. The best thing about Green Door is its undeniable lack of pretence – feel free to question the staff about the drinks and you won't be met with a blank response or feel like you should know more than you do.

✖
Winterfeldtstraße 50, 10781 Berlin +49 30 2152515 greendoor.de

BERLIN*

KANTINE KOHLMANN ↓

Walking into either entrance of Kantine Kohlmann (one for the bar, one for the restaurant) you'll immediately notice that this place is one cool hangout. Mid-century retro in style on the inside, graffiti-covered walls on the outside, the concrete and wood panelling on the walls makes you feel like you're in a Vogue photo shoot in 1969 and the poles (erm, yes...) and coloured lights add an oddly

San Franciscan disco element to the vibe. This is one of those rare places that manage to do retro well. The two main rooms (food in one, booze in the other) are connected by a corridor.
✖
Skalitzer Straße 64, 10997 Berlin +49 30 85611133 kantine-kohlmann.de
✖
IN THREE WORDS:
1960s Movie Set.
THEY SAY:
"This place rocks!"
— **KRISZTIÁN CSIGÓ, HUNGARY**
PRICE RATING: ✱✱✱

RUM TRADER

Like Schumann's (see page 91), no trip to Germany should really end before a visit to this cult nightspot, which is now into its fifth decade of business. One of its claims to fame is that it supposedly features in the Bond classic *Octopussy*, and given the author Ian Fleming's predilection for a fine cocktail, who are we to argue? The bar's theme is in the name: rum is the spirit of choice, with a smattering of gin, and the place is extremely cosy indeed, seating around 15 people at a push. If you are lucky enough to grab one, you're in for a treat.

The cocktails are mostly prepared on the whim of the

bartender (unless you specify what you want – and you'd better be sure here) and you need to prepare yourself for a little sarcasm along the way. Some folk of a more fragile mindset may be upset by the bartender's quips, but don't let that cloud your judgement – this is real drinking in a genuine, old school Berlin classic. If it was good enough for Fleming, it should certainly be good enough for you.
✖
Fasanenstraße 40, 10719 Berlin +49 30 8811428
✖
IN THREE WORDS:
Right Rum Time.
THEY SAY:
"This tiny (rum- and gin-oriented) speakeasy, in business since 1976, shows how hospitality endures through the ups and downs of fashion."
— **PHILIP DUFF, USA**
PRICE RATING: ✱✱✱

FEATURE*

A DRINK WITH...
HELMUT ADAM

Helmut Adam is a man undoubtedly with his finger on the pulse of the German bar scene. As one of the founders of the visionary magazine *Mixology* in the early 2000s, he also jointly established Bar Convent Berlin (barconvent.com) in 2007, a mecca for international bartenders to learn about, taste and experience new liquids and techniques in the drinks industry. He gave us his perfect night out in Berlin.

"I would kick off a night out in Berlin at **Beuster Bar** (beusterbar.com) for dinner. It is one of these newish bar restaurant places; traditionally in Germany we haven't had many restaurant bars; either restaurants or service bars. Recently a few places have opened that have the same quality of food as drinks, and this is one of them. It is also a neighbourhood place where everything is fresh every day.

I would then continue and go to a beer place called **Straßenbräu** (strassenbraeu.de), which is recently opened and one of the newer brewpubs in Berlin. Their selection is wide and

Traditionally in Germany we haven't had many restaurant bars; either restaurants or service bars. Recently a few places have opened that have the same quality of food as drinks.

experimental, so I'd have beer there and a chat to the brewer.

After, I'd head toward Mitte and on the way head into **Booze Bar** (facebook.com/booze.bar.berlin), where I'd order a Mezcal Sour. If you don't get stuck there, and you can do one more stop, I'd go to **Buck and Breck** (see page 86). Around the corner from B&B is a burger joint called **Rosenburger** and that'd be the night over!"

89

FEATURE*

A DRINK WITH...
STEPHAN BERG

One of the godfathers of the German cocktail bitters scene, Stephan Berg started a revolution in bringing new-found flavours to mixed drinks in 2006 when he founded The Bitter Truth Company with his business partner, Alexander Hauck, in Munich. In 2016 the duo celebrated their 10th anniversary.

Can you give us an idea of the Munich bar scene at the moment? Where's hot and what are the current trends?
After years of few changes Munich has seen a great number of places either new or old which really work hard and have wonderful beverage programmes. Some favourites for me are: **Schumann's** (the always famous place! See opposite), **Goldene Bar** (goldenebar.de), **Bar Tabacco** (bartabacco.com), **Circle Bar at the Heart House** (thecircle.bar), **Jaded Monkey** (jadedmonkey. de) and **Patolli** (patollis.de), just to name a few. Trends still veer toward the very classic-style drinks, but local ingredients play into the modern bar scene.

After years of generally few changes Munich has seen a great number of places either new or old which really work hard and have wonderful beverage programmes.

STEPHAN'S TOP FIVE BARS:

✖
American Bar at the Savoy, London (see page 22)
An all-time favourite of mine. A great team, great hospitality and more than 100 years history.
✖
Dante, New York (see page 209) *A cosy aperitif bar, where Naren Young installed an Italian-inspired cocktail programme.*
✖
Williams & Graham, Denver (williamsandgraham.com) *A speakeasy-style bar run by Sean Kenyon. Somehow hidden behind doors, stunning drinks, warm atmosphere and service.*
✖
Lobster Bar, Hong Kong (see page 151) *Located at the Shangri-La Hotel, this bar really lifted the standards of drinking in China and beyond.*
✖
Schumann's, Munich (see opposite) *A melting pot of locals, artists, fashionistas, all held together by Charles Schumann. Warm hospitality, fantastic drinks and even better food.*

MUNICH*

BAR GABÁNYI

A subterranean gem, right in the heart of the Munich, but easy to miss. When you're in, however, you'll want to stay and explore the glorious selection of 36 house specialities. The highlight of these is the unique and slightly insane Tikipedia, which brings together smoky single malt whisky, rhum agricole, lime juice, apple juice, grapefruit juice, absinthe, falernum, port and bitters (phew!). Come on the right night and you'll share the bar with a new jazz artist too. What's not to like?

✖

Beethovenplatz 2, 80336 Munich +49 89 51701805 bar-gabanyi.de

✖

IN THREE WORDS:
Subterranean Flavour Punchbowl.

THE DRINK TO TRY:
Tikipedia.

THEY SAY:
"No chi chi – unusual in Munich. Just solid, strong drinks."
— BERNHARD SCHÄFER, GERMANY

PRICE RATING: ✱✱✱✱

SCHUMANN'S ⬇

A demi-god in the bartending world, Charles Schumann was very probably one of the first people in Germany to instigate a revolution in cocktails – one where today, he still sits at the very top of the tree, admiring the surrounding vista of a new generation of great, highly innovative bars, winning awards and turning heads. Loosely speaking, Schumann's has an American bar vibe: classic drinks, coupled with great food – the Schumann roast beef and potatoes, washed down with a Martini or Manhattan is probably on our bucket list. The place is uncluttered and the back bar is spectacular to look at – nowhere will you find the number of bottles of Campari that they seem to delightfully show off. The drinks themselves are a reflection of the man himself: stylish, uncluttered

and confident, each with a genuine personality of its very own. Head upstairs and things get very serious indeed at the Les Fleurs De Mal bar, which offers a more intimate "bespoke" drinking experience, all taking place around one large wooden table that seats about 20 guests. For over 25 years, Schumann's has reigned supreme. Having witnessed the man himself in full flow, one suspects this is still very much only the beginning.

✖

Odeonsplatz 6 – 7, 80539 Munich +49 89 229060 schumanns.de

✖

IN THREE WORDS:
Munich Mixology Masters.

THEY SAY:
"A melting pot of locals, wannabees, artists, fashionistas… always warm hospitality."
— STEPHAN BERG, GERMANY
"I love it !"
— JOERG MEYER, GERMANY

PRICE RATING: ✱✱✱✱

NUREMBERG, ERFURT, HAMBURG & FRANKFURT*

GELBES HAUS

For over 25 years, *The Yellow House* has been lovingly attended to by its owner, Oliver Kirschner, and in that time he has sealed his reputation as one of Germany's most accomplished bartenders. The bar brings together an exceptional collection of over 120 craft gins, alongside wonderfully curated single malts and house creations that veer toward the classics, but bring in their distinct personalities – all directed by Kirschner and his team. Alongside the menu, Gelbes Haus runs regular cocktail courses and hosts specific whisky nights.

✖

Troststraße 10, 90429 Nuremberg +49 911 262274 gelbes-haus.de

✖

IN THREE WORDS:
The Haus Masters.
THE DRINK TO TRY:
The Woman On A Calm Evening.
THEY SAY:
"Still my Home-from-Home."
— BERNHARD SCHÄFER, GERMANY
PRICE RATING: ✱✱✱

MODERN MASTERS ↓

As the word "classic" goes, Modern Masters is something of a contradiction. In fact, taking one look at the front of the bar and café, it is anything but modern, with its beautifully preserved historical German architecture. On the inside things are a little different however. The bar's motto, dreamed up by chief "Master" Torsten Spuhn, is "a Journey through bar culture, which promises much enjoyment, diversity, lifestyle and entertainment". This strategy is delivered across some 200 drinks and over 400 spirits, which may seem a lot, but the effect is perfect

– peerless creations broken down into three distinct areas: "traditional and refined classics", "recent classics and evergreens" and "rising trends and next generation", playfully referred to as the "liquid kitchen-style". One thing's for sure...you're going to need a comprehensive holiday break in Erfurt to fully appreciate this place.

✖

Michaelisstraße 48, 99084 Erfurt +49 361 5507255 modern-masters.de

✖

IN THREE WORDS:
Comprehensive But Captivating.
THE DRINK TO TRY:
Suffering Bastard.
THEY SAY:
"You think you are stranded on Crusoe island and then you meet Friday."
— BERNHARD SCHÄFER, GERMANY
PRICE RATING: ✱✱✱

LE LION

We're sure that if you polled 100 bartenders from around the world, one of the common desires would be to leave a lasting legacy – in a drink that, over time, effectively became a classic. This much can be said of Joerg Meyer, owner and bartender of Hamburg's Le Lion, whose Gin Basil Smash

(see our interview on page 94) is certainly well on the way to achieving immortality. Le Lion is a reflection of Meyer's immaculate attention to detail and is very much one of the key bars responsible for the resurgence of the German cocktail scene. Inside, the decor harks back to the Parisian opulence of the 1920s and the drinks are complex tasting versions of the classics, which take time to prepare, but the adventure on the palate more than makes up for the wait. As for the aforementioned Gin Basil Smash, you'll find refreshment, coupled with an aromatic explosion. Destiny awaits.

✖

Rathausstraße 3, 20095 Hamburg +49 40 334753780 lelion.net

✖

IN THREE WORDS:
A Roaring Success.
THE DRINK TO TRY:
The Gin Basil Smash.
WE SAY:
Almost certainly Hamburg's best drinking experience – and quite possibly one of Germany's too. Plan your trip to Hamburg without a visit at your peril.
PRICE RATING: ✶✶✶✶

ROTE BAR ↗

A common recurring theme with many bars is also one of our major pet hates: seemingly impenetrable websites, but we'll make an exception for Rote. The fuzzy, hand-drawn graphics are actually linked out like a Choose Your Own Adventure map, and eventually lead you to the childlike scribbling resembling

a back bar. Here you'll find the menu: a comprehensive list broken down into "Cocktails", "Whiskies" and "Diverse". As classics go, you'll find everything from a French 75 to a very perky El Presidente. Another simple, effective but hugely skilful, no-nonsense vibe, with drinks that just...deliver.

✖

Mainkai 7, 60311 Frankfurt +49 69 293533 rotebar.com

✖

IN THREE WORDS:
Unsung Deutsche Heroics.
THEY SAY:
"No fancy shit. Just big flavoured drinks!"
— **BERNHARD SCHÄFER, GERMANY**
PRICE RATING: ✶✶

> ## Le Lion is a reflection of Meyer's immaculate attention to detail and is very much one of the key bars responsible for the resurgence of the German cocktail scene.

FOCUS*

STARTENDER
JOERG MEYER

Creating a truly original signature drink that will not only embrace simplicity, but demonstrate creative genius, travel continents and defy the shifting sands of time and trends in drinks is arguably the alchemy every bartender dreams of. For Joerg Meyer, the man behind Hamburg's outstanding Le Lion (see page 92), it was almost a happy accident. Meyer's Gin Basil Smash has become the stuff of legend and the drink was recently given a chance to take a world tour with its creator, when the man in question was asked to take on a number of international weekly residencies, including a stopover behind the bar at Gŏng (gong-shangri-la. com) on the 52nd level of the Shard building in London.

The elegance of the Gin Basil Smash is hard to define without actually trying one, but despite being simple to construct, the complexity of the flavour and aroma is incredible: the gin botanicals tend to bring out a spicy note in the basil, alongside a richer liquorice, almost menthol note too. For additional

> **Meyer's Gin Basil Smash has become the stuff of legend.**

elegance, Mr Meyer's version is served over cubed ice (rather than the traditional crushed ice) in a chilled rocks glass. "We have a sweeter type of basil in Germany, which gives a different approach to the drink, as well as purple basil, which gives you a very different-looking drink altogether – perhaps more liquorice notes," explains Meyer. "Some people really can't place the flavour at all!"

✕

MEYER'S GIN BASIL SMASH

*a handful of fresh basil
(try experimenting with
different types: larger
broader leaf styles give
less sweetness and more
peppery spice)
half a freshly cut lemon
(about 20ml juice)
20ml sugar syrup
60ml gin (Tanqueray 10)*

Muddle the basil and lemon
into a shaker. Add the sugar
syrup, some ice cubes and finally
the gin. Shake hard for at least
10 seconds, to release the colour
from the basil.

Fine strain into a chilled rocks
glass over ice cubes and garnish
with a single basil leaf.

JOERG'S TOP FIVE HANGOUTS FOR COCKTAILS:

✕

**Schumanns, Munich
(see page 91)** *Mr. Schumann
is a character – the last man
standing. So is his bar. You'll
either love it, or hate it. I love it !*

✕

**Dead Rabbit, New York
(see page 212)** *This is the perfect
bar, in every little detail possible.
Very laid back but absolutely
brilliant.*

✕

**Salon 39, Copenhagen
(salon39.dk)** *My favourite place
when visiting Copenhagen. The
best drinks and awesome food.
Here is the place to start the
night off!*

✕

**Dry Martini, Barcelona
(see page 81)** *My favourite
"Classic Bar". I love the style
of this place.*

✕

**Experimental Cocktail Club,
London (chinatownecc.com)** ↑
*I love the mix. Chinatown, great
drinks, good music, fancy people!*

VIENNA & ZURICH*

LOOS AMERICAN BAR

Similar to the American Bar at London's Savoy (see page 22), Loos American Bar is another classic place, which truly shows the influence of the early 1900s US golden age of cocktails. Inside, the place is breathtaking: Adolf Loos's Art Deco design panelling meets wonderfully opulent leather, with an immense wooden bar that looks like it has been transported forward to this century by a time-travelling truck. It's dark, sleek and very decadent – all this before you even order yourself a drink. Don't expect molecular nonsense here, or hipster craft waffle: big, classic drinks are the order of the day and the team behind the bar really know their stuff, whether it's a Perfect Manhattan (not too sweet or dry) or the best vermouth to use in a Negroni. Simple. Classic. Beautiful. Timeless.

✖
Kärntner Durchgang 7, 1010, Vienna +43 1 5123283 loosbar.at
✖

IN THREE WORDS:
Architects Of Cocktails.
THEY SAY:
"Super-skilled barmen, who see their cocktails as a form of art."
— **RAISE DE HASS, NETHERLANDS**
PRICE RATING: ✱✱✱✱

ROBERTO AMERICAN BAR ↓

Leaving the safety of success is quite often a huge driving force for individual enlightenment and in the case of Roberto Pavlovic, a former protégé of the famous Loos American Bar (see left), it was clearly the right thing to do. Roberto American Bar (the grammar pedants will be ticked off at the lack of apostrophe) is a lush, dark, expansive experience in drinking, dominated by a huge pearl embroidered centrepiece, which hangs above the bar. The drinks are rich, complex affairs: think dark, spicy rum Old Fashioned and other classics, such as the French 75, and the ambience in here more than matches their character. This is a bar to inspire anyone's vision for future excellence.

✖
Bauernmarkt 11–13, 1010 Vienna +43 1 5350647 robertosbar.com
✖

IN THREE WORDS:
Roberto's The Man.
WE SAY:
Stylish, if compact, the vibe here is very classy drinking indeed, and a visit to Vienna wouldn't be the same without a drink here.
PRICE RATING: ✱✱✱

KRONENHALLE ↑

Precise is a word that bartenders of a certain type like to use in their assessment of great drinks, and at Kronenhalle, one of the most elegant restaurant bars in Zurich, it is a word that certainly lives and breathes in every drink. The bar is a beautiful mixture of vintage wood and leather, dating back to the 1960s but modelled on the classical cocktail haunts of the 1920s and 1930s. From a cocktail perspective, everything is as you would hope: classic, with little hints of additional personality thrown in for good measure. The story goes that underneath the bar is kept a handwritten notebook with guests' favourite recipes, listed alphabetically and collated for many years. Alongside this wealth of history are the bar's mainstays and seasonal offerings: everything from a Mai Tai to a Dry Martini is a masterclass in skill and attention to detail.

✖
Rämistrasse 4, 8001 Zurich
+41 44 262 99 00 kronenhalle.ch
✖
IN THREE WORDS:
Precision Cocktail Masterpieces.

THE DRINK TO TRY:
Ladykiller.
THEY SAY:
"Very traditional, very Swiss, this is a polite and service-oriented place."
— HELMUT ADAM, BERLIN.
PRICE RATING: ✱✱✱✱

OLD CROW

Not to be confused with the Crobar in London (see page 31), this old crow is something of a worst kept secret among its legions of fans locally and now on a wider scale. You'll find him perching on a quiet side street,

The story goes that underneath the bar is kept a handwritten notebook with guests' favourite recipes, listed alphabetically and collated for many years.

and inside, a cosy, perfectly detailed bar area greets you. The back bar is fantastically stocked, with shelves groaning under the weight of bourbons, whiskies and gins, alongside regulation vermouths, Chartreuse and other delightful liqueurs. Then it dawns on you…some of these bottles are clearly vintage…very vintage indeed. Yes, this is why the Old Crow is somewhere that you want to shout about from the rooftops, but in doing so, you're likely to see the demise of some simply breathtaking old bottlings – Chartreuse from the 1870s, gins from the 1930s, old rums you didn't even know existed. You'll need at least half an hour over your first drink to simply digest the volume of greatness on offer here, and Markus Blattner and his team will be happy to plan your night-time travelling adventure. Brilliant stuff.

✖
Schwanengasse 4, 8001 Zurich
+41 43 233 53 35 oldcrow.ch
✖
IN THREE WORDS:
Squawks Of Delight.
WE SAY:
The attention to detail is incredible, the selection of spirits mind blowing and the location picturesque…what's not to like?
PRICE RATING: ✱✱✱

AMSTERDAM*

DOOR 74 →

Door 74 can make the lofty claim of being Amsterdam's first speakeasy-styled bar, and since it opened back in 2008 it has been thrilling customers with its timeless Prohibition-style chic. From the sliding panel in the nondescript front door where you are greeted, all the way through to where you are served incredibly well-crafted cocktails from a variety of frankly bizarre glassware (think drinking horns and glass skulls). Door 74 has clearly honed its craft to become one of the most important destinations in the city's cocktail culture.

✱

Reguliersdwarsstraat 74I, 1017 BN Amsterdam +31 6 34 04 51 22 door-74.com

✱

IN THREE WORDS:
Doors Of Perception.
WE SAY:
Stylish, quirky and without any whiff of pretension.
PRICE RATING: ✱✱✱✱

FEIJOA

A gem in the Amsterdam bar scene, Feijoa is the sort of place you could visit with no preconceptions and leave feeling empowered with the knowledge of a mixology god or goddess. The place is compact and behind the bar you'll find many fragile shelves of bottles only accessible by ladder, suggesting that the staff either are hoarders or have a broad understanding of ingredients. Once you've tried the cocktails, you'll definitely think the latter. Really well-balanced drinks and some unusual twists (acidic shrubs, juices and the odd appearance of the aforementioned Feijoa – a papaya-type fruit from New Zealand). All this is delivered with a genuine passion from a team who want you to leave with a greater understanding of cocktails than you had before you entered.

✱

Vijzelstraat 39, 1017 HE Amsterdam +31 20 427 82 15 feijoaamsterdam.com

✱

IN THREE WORDS:
Distinctly Fruity Fun.
WE SAY:
Located right near the Pathe Cinema), this is a great place to stop for post-film reflection.
PRICE RATING: ✱✱✱

THE TAILOR ↓

Housed in the uber-smart Grand Hotel Krasnapolsky in Amsterdam, The Tailor is one of those bars that deliver on their promises of bespoke. Tying in with the story behind the spiritual father of the hotel, A W Krasnapolsky – who was a tailor by trade, before opening a coffee shop – the bar has created a list of classically tasteful drinks, which each have a distinctly modern twist on them, courtesy of award-winning bartender Tess Posthumus (see interview on page 100). You'll find each drink ingeniously grouped into a different type of fabric:

Cashmere (Strong Concoctions) Silk (Floral Fruity and Bubbly) Cotton (Fresh and Easy) and Hemp (Herbal and Spiced) – each one a curated moment of joy, effortlessly tailored.

✖

Dam 9, 1012 JS Amsterdam +31 20 554 61 14 barthetailor.com

✖

IN THREE WORDS:
Sharp Dressed Drinks.

THEY SAY:
"One of the most famous hotel bars in Amsterdam. I have many memories here."
— RAISSA DE HAAS, THE NETHERLANDS

PRICE RATING: ✱✱✱✱✱

TALES AND SPIRITS

In a short space of time, Tales And Spirits has become an institution for any drinks industry professional visiting Amsterdam, and it's easy to see why. There's a real playfulness at work here, as well as huge creativity and an ability not to take oneself too seriously. The list comprises several house specials, a dozen or so signature drinks, and then the bar's can't-do-away-with-'em favourites, which are all inspired, descriptive and extremely well made. All this before we even touch upon the list of different iterations of the Old Fashioned – surely the most reinvented and versatile drink of the last decade, with the Charlie Brown (bourbon, roasted peanut liqueur and creole bitters) taking it off on a tasty tangent. With much more to come, the tale is surely only half written yet.

✖

Lijnbaanssteeg 5–7, 1012 TE Amsterdam +31 6 55 35 64 67 talesandspirits.com

✖

IN THREE WORDS:
Tellin' Tall Tales.

THE DRINK TO TRY:
Smoke And Mirrors.

THEY SAY:
"Be sure to check out the story written along all the walls."
— HALEY FOREST, USA

PRICE RATING: ✱✱✱

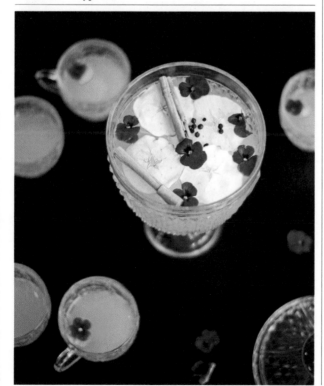

FOCUS*

STARTENDER
TESS POSTHUMUS

Tess is one of the Netherlands's most in-demand bartenders and drinks consultants, winning several national and international competitions and also being nominated as International Bartender of the Year 2016 at the prestigious Tales of the Cocktail expo in New Orleans. She regularly pops up behind some of the best bars in the world as a guest bartender and has recently visited Paris and London as a guest bartender, judged cocktail competitions in Milan and appeared in Thailand, America and Russia to give seminars and workshops.

Where do you drink when you're off duty?
A glass of wine at **Restaurant Breda** (breda-amsterdam. com) or **Auberge Jean & Marie** (aubergeamsterdam.nl) – those restaurants are owned by my best friends and they have very good taste in wine.

Your favourite drink of all time...?
There are so many beautiful drinks but if I need to choose just one it's the Corpse Reviver #2 –

a great gin-based drink, sour with a hint of absinthe.

What is your favourite city in the world to go drinking in?
London has so many great bars and cocktail history. Every year a lot of new places open so there is always something new to check out. Besides London, I also really love spending drinking time in New York, San Francisco, Berlin and Paris.

Take us through your perfect day out drinking in Amsterdam – where would you go and what would you drink?
The perfect day of drinking in Amsterdam will start off at **Teds** (teds-place.nl). This restaurant serves all day brunch and spirited high teas. Think Bloody Mary or Mimosa with eggs Benedict. Next up, make your way to Dam Square and behind

the square you'll find the Zeedijk area. Visit the **Wynand Fockink genever distillery** (wynand-fockink.nl) or another old and traditional bar for a "kopstootje" (a glass of genever with a small draft beer on the side). While in the area, pop by **The Tailor at the Krasnapolsky**, (see page 99), a hotel bar in a very classy Dutch hotel where I run the bar programme. Order one of the signature cocktails, which are paired with a little bite.

Okay, time to leave the tourist area and go for some good food. As I mentioned, restaurant Breda is owned by my best friends but besides being awesome, they really know how to cook. Delicious dishes and great wines. If by this time you're still up for a drink, walk toward Rembrandtplein and visit **Feijoa** (see page 98) for a quick drink before ending the night at Door 74 (see page 98).

As signature drinks go, Tess has a wonderfully playful one, with a definite bite to it! Here is the recipe for you to try at home:

✖
THE TESSMANIAN DEVIL

20ml Beefeater gin
20ml Strega (an Italian herbal liqueur)
20ml Lillet Blanc
20ml fresh lemon juice
a dash of Tabasco
a dash of Creole bitters
a pinch of chilli powder

Shake all the ingredients over ice and strain into a frozen Martini glass. Garnish with 2 chilli pepper horns on the rim. My little devil in a glass – enjoy!

TESS'S TOP FIVE BARS AROUND THE WORLD:

✖
Door 74, Amsterdam (see page 98)
It's been open since 2008 and I'm proud to say that I've been working there for seven years. The bar was the first speakeasy in the Benelux and has been on the "World's 50 Best Bars" list three years in a row. It's the place where I've learned the tricks of the trade and every time I step behind the bar it feels like coming home.

✖
Whitechapel, San Francisco (whitechapelsf.com) ↑
Keli Rivers is in charge here and she created a gin heaven. Besides a very extensive list of different gin brands and cocktails, they also stock some great genevers here.

✖
Artesian Bar, London (artesian-bar.co.uk)
This bar has won numerous prizes internationally, but that wasn't the reason why the place left a big impression on me. It was the great hospitality there that did the trick and made everybody in the room feel like a million dollars.

✖
Wynand Fockink, Amsterdam (wynand-fockink.nl)
It's not really a bar, it's a very old genever distillery with a small tasting room attached to it. Stepping in there feels like being transported back to 1700.

✖
Broken Shaker, Miami (freehandhotels.com)
In this bar at The Freehand Hotel, they showed me that tiki drinks don't have to be overly sweet and tacky; that it is a very fun but serious category of drinks. They serve some very tasty dishes as well.

ANTWERP & BRUSSELS*

DOGMA

The thriving thirst for deconstruction in cocktails shows no sign of abating and Antwerp's Dogma is undoubtedly among Europe's very best when it comes to either reinventing a classic drink, or coming up with a new twist on a drink you know and love. The bar is a mixture of gentlemen's club decor and New York loft-style shabby chic, with plenty of leather and exposed brick to give you a lived-in vibe. The drinks are anything but: tiki mugs, overflowing with garnishes, elaborate fogs and Negronis served from macchinetta coffee pots will give you the sense that these guys are really trying to have fun. At the heart of the bar's...erm...dogma lies an incontrovertible level of understanding about all that they do. Enjoy the ride.

✖

Wijngaardstraat 5, 2000 Antwerp +32 496 95 33 77 dogmacocktails.be

✖

IN THREE WORDS:
Conviction Of Cocktails.

WE SAY:
Fun, entertaining drinks delivered by a team who, deep down, are incredibly skilled and well studied.
PRICE RATING: ✳ ✳ ✳

DE HAUS

A relative newcomer to the Brussels drinks scene, De Haus wears its heart firmly on its bar apron, and in this case it is an aromatic juniper-flavoured heart. With well over 50 gins on the menu you know you're in the hands of a team who are hugely passionate about the wonders of all things botanical and the mastery of the serves here – especially the humble gin and tonic, which receives a glorious makeover in their hands. Better still, the bar offers workshops on how to perfect the art of a great G&T, and uses rose petals in its drinks with panache. Blooming marvellous.

✖

183 Chaussée d'Ixelles, 1050 Brussels +32 2 503 21 95 dehaus.be

✖

IN THREE WORDS:
Brussels Gin Giants.

WE SAY:
Arguably the finest gin bar in the city and the place to visit for a pepped-up G&T.
PRICE RATING: ✳ ✳

MOEDER LAMBIC

We couldn't curate a guide on the best places to drink without putting in a Belgian beer joint. As beer houses go, this one is pretty titanic: exposed brickwork, high ceilings and an immense display of beer. Yes, it caters for what you would expect: the big, broad-shouldered Belgian beasts that people travel far and wide for (if frothy, 8–9% Blondes are your sort of thing!), but there are enough different craft brews from around the globe to keep you occupied for a very long time indeed. Couple this with the platters of meats and cheeses and you'll be in hoppy heaven.

✖

Place Fontainas 8, 1000 Brussels, +32 2 503 60 68 moederlambic.com

✖

IN THREE WORDS:
Modus Operandi: Bier.
THEY SAY:
"The best beer geek place I've set foot in."
— **STAFFAN ALEXANDERSSON, NORWAY**
PRICE RATING: ✳ ✳ ✳

FEATURE*

A DRINK WITH...
ALAIN VERVOORT

Alain Vervoort knows a thing or two about bartending – and bartenders – he's been training them for the past six years and has been bartending for over 20. His Brussels-based academy, **Bar Connector** (facebook.com/ BarConnector), has provided a grounding for some of the brightest sparks in the industry, so we asked him to tell us the best places in Belgium where he feels you're going to get the drink and the service that you truly deserve.

✖

L'Apereau (lapereau.be)
If you visit L'Apereau you will be surprised, as Blankenberge is one of the most unexpected places for such a great cocktail bar, thanks to [owner] Jeroen Van Hecke's talent for educating young talented bartenders. A lot of top guys start their career under his expertise.

✖

The Dirty Rabbit (thedirtyrabbit.be)
One of the craziest cocktail bars in Antwerp and here, it's not all about the bartender...it's a mix. Here, you have the owner,

Kasper Stuart, something of a Hospitality Pope in Antwerp, always surprising people with new extravagant concepts. On the other hand you have the award-winning Dries Botty making interesting twists of classic cocktails.

✖

Le Corbeau (lecorbeau.be)
Ah, Le Corbeau...it's the story of my life. I've been a customer there since I was 16 years old, which means a long time ago! It's a typically old Brussels brasserie, [established in 1874], where you can eat some Belgian specialities, drink some very interesting beers – even in a Chevalier [a 1 litre glass] and, last but not least, on Friday and Saturday nights, dance on the table and – at the same time – enjoy one of the best Mojitos in town.

✖

Clover Bar II (+32 483 05 49 33)
I suppose this is the place I drink when I'm off duty in Brussels. Why? Because it's all about friendship; a quiet moment and, of course, the quality of the cocktails. You have to try the grilled chicken too...the best in town!

STOCKHOLM, GOTHENBURG & UMEÅ*

AKKURAT ⬂

With some bars, there's definitely the right "time" to visit them, and in the case of Stockholm's Akkurat, a cold, wintry day in January, with snow falling outside, made this visit just about perfect. Inside you'll find an array of winter warmers: an incredible selection of whiskies from around the world with a heavy weighting toward the peaty-smoky variety (see page 65 on the magic of Islay). The beer selection is equally impressive, given the number of Lambic-style offerings – genuine vintage beers which have been collected over the last 20 years and cellar aged. Couple that with hearty plates of home-cooked food and the occasional live band and you'll decide not to brave the elements again – preferring to simply curl up and hibernate here until spring has arrived. Wake us up in March, will you?

✖
Hornsgatan 18, 118 20 Stockholm
+46 8 644 00 15 akkurat.se
✖

IN THREE WORDS:
Welcome Whisky Wall.
THEY SAY:
"An unassuming casual bar with the deepest selection of whisky I've ever seen."
— **JEREMY GARA, CANADA**
WE SAY:
Stockholm's home-from-home when it comes to the best whiskies and beers. Essential visiting.
PRICE RATING: ✱✱

CORNER CLUB

You can find this gem right at the heart of Gamla Stan, around the corner from one of Stockholm's other fast-becoming-legendary bars, Pharmarium (see page 109). From a drinks perspective, Corner Club executes some exquisitely fresh, seasonal drinks, offered up by a team who are more than knowledgeable. It is the sort of place where you immediately feel welcome, the bartenders all delivering a passionate sermon about each drink. Should you want to try them at home, there's no secrecy in the recipes – most are posted weekly on the bar's YouTube channel, alongside some really useful tips for making the most of your cocktails. While this is undeniably transparent, there's still nothing like trying one from the guys themselves. Well worth a visit.

✘

Lilla Nygatan 16, 111 28
Stockholm +46 8 20 85 83
cornerclub.se

✘

IN THREE WORDS:
Join The Club.

THEY SAY:
"Leaving nothing to chance.
Great atmosphere, passionate
staff, and amazing cocktails."
— **JOHN HILLGREN, SWEDEN**

PRICE RATING: ✱✱

TWEED

Another gem in the popular
Gamla Stan area – and a cosy
one at that. Tweed is pretty
much modelled on a gentlemen's
drinking club, so you'll find the
abundance of leather armchairs,
rugs and knick-knacks you
would find behind one of the
mysterious, nondescript polished
doors on London's Pall Mall.
Here though, there are no secret
handshakes or knowing glances,
just lashings of fine whiskies,
gins and purportedly over
2,800 different labels of wine
to try. The bar is affiliated with
The Burgundy (theburgundy.
se), who clearly know a thing
or two about fine plonk and
have a terrific wine cellar bar in
their own right, with a similarly
impressive display of vintages
and around 2,000 different
labels. So settle in, order a single
malt and perhaps choose a cigar
for smoking later on the terrace.
Let's push on through till dawn.

✘

Lilla Nygatan 5, 111 28, Stockholm
+46 8 506 400 82 tweedbar.se

✘

IN THREE WORDS:
Tally Ho, Chaps.

WE SAY:
Comfortable, refined sipping in a
place that demands you relax.

PRICE RATING: ✱✱✱

STRANGER

This intriguing concept came
to our attention simply because,
like the owners, we consider
ourselves to be "curious booze
hounds". Heading down into
the basement space, which is
well hidden under Gothenburg's
South American-themed
restaurant Tranquilo, you'll sense
the vibe becoming distinctly
different. From the *Case File*-
style menu –broken down into
Negronis, Easy Sippers, Middle
Class Cocktails and Stiff Drinks
– a broad selection of classics
emerges from the pages with a
simplistic precision. There's no
mucking about here, just really
well-made drinks, using some
of the world's most exciting craft
spirits. Boozehounds, unite.
Things are getting stranger.

✘

Kungstorget 14, 411 10
Gothenburg +46 31 13 45 55
strangergbg.com

✘

IN THREE WORDS:
What Lies Beneath.

THEY SAY:
"Some of the best Manhattans
I've had in a long time."
— **ALEX WOLPERT, UK**

WE SAY:
A speakeasy with style, rather
than a "theme".

PRICE RATING: ✱✱✱

OPEN/CLOSED

The concept of the speakeasy
bar has clearly travelled far and
wide. Nestled in Umeå, northern
Sweden's largest town, owner
Emil Åreng has focused on the
natural environment of the
surrounding area and produced
a menu that is skilfully updated
on a biweekly basis, meaning
that visitors are seldom served
the same drink twice. It is an
endearing concept and one that
the bar clearly loves to have
fun with: everything from tiki
drinks (that particular menu was
simply entitled Tikileaks) to the
popular children's author Astrid
Lindgren (who wrote the Pippi
Longstocking books) is used as
influence on the drinks – yes,
you guessed it...the Pippi Colada
made an appearance. Despite
such cheekiness, the quality of
bartending is clear to see and
Emil is now a a highly decorated
bartender in his own right.

✘

Storgatan 44, 903 26 Umeå
+46 90 780 03 03
duaumea.se/openclosed

✘

IN THREE WORDS:
Revolving Door of Drinks.

THEY SAY:
"Innovative cocktails with a
biweekly shift of the cocktail list."
— **JON HILGREN, SWEDEN**

PRICE RATING: ✱✱

COPENHAGEN*

THE BARKING DOG

Modesty really is a wonderful virtue. When you visit The Barking Dog, they describe themselves as "a cocktail pub, where the music isn't too loud, and the service is above average". In all honesty, TBD is just about as perfect a find as it could be. The beers are superb, with an extensive array of pilsners, IPAs and saisons. The cocktails are beautifully laid out, with each one coming with a note on how they were conceived. In fact, as menus go, this one really does set a benchmark for simplicity and fun. Fancy a flight of mezcals? No problem. Same goes for vermouth and Tequilas, too. There's no pretence on display, just honest fun, delivered with a great deal of skill. Pun time…you'd be barking mad to miss this one, that's for sure. We'll get our coats….

✖

Sankt Hans Gade 19, 2200 Copenhagen +45 35 36 16 00 thebarkingdog.dk

✖

IN THREE WORDS:
All Bark no Bite.

THEY SAY:
"I'd go so far as to say it's one of the leading spots in Europe."
—**HANNAH LANFEAR, UK**
PRICE RATING: ✱✱

K-BAR ↓

Clearly, the art of bartending is about understanding how to bring flavours together in a sympathetic way, but alongside this, what about an ability to bring people together too? In the case of Kirsten Holm, owner of K-Bar (and of the K in the name, in case you were wondering), perhaps her talent for doing both of these things lies in her genes. Kirsten is the daughter of Jorgen Holm, a Danish ambassador, who spent over 40 years working in the US, Europe and the Far East. As he explains, "An open mind and sharp knowledge can mix the most opposite of

opinions. Taking elements away and adding new ones in another context creates a new result."

This is possibly the most eloquent approach not only to diplomacy, but also to the creation of cocktails. Kirsten has embraced this ethos, with the simple, relaxed list on offer, which comprises everything from a luscious rosehip- and hibiscus-infused Margarita to the short and strong In Absintia, with Old Tom gin, absinthe and smoky whisky. When the rest of the world is losing its head, find somewhere like this to regain perspective. Diplomacy rocks.

✖

Ved Stranden 20, 1061 Copenhagen
+45 33 91 92 22 k-bar.dk

✖

IN THREE WORDS:
Straight-Talking Drinks.
THEY SAY:
"Relaxed and inviting cocktail bar in the heart of Copenhagen."
— JON HILLGREN, SWEDEN
PRICE RATING: ✳✳✳

RUBY

Copenhagen is one of the coolest cities in the world. Take one look at the huge barometer on the corner of the building on the Rådhuspladsen and you could easily think that this acts as a cultural barometer too, especially when it comes to the bar world. Ruby takes its cues both from Japan and its contemporaries in Berlin and London. From the mismatched furniture, antique rugs and glassware, to the beautifully laid out back bar, everything screams perfection and precision. And that's just what you'll get. Order a

Martinez and you'll get a classic drink made with such panache, it suddenly won't make as much sense ordering one anywhere else. This is a serious haven for the cocktail enthusiast, but it doesn't take itself too seriously. As well as being a campus of skill, one thing's for sure, Ruby is no rough diamond – it's the genuine, highly polished article.

✖

Nybrogade 10, 1203 Copenhagen
+45 33 93 12 03 rby.dk

✖

IN THREE WORDS:
Highly Polished Precision.
THEY SAY:
"If my dream home bar could look like anywhere in the world, I hope it would be Ruby."
— REMY SAVAGE, PARIS
PRICE RATING: ✳✳✳

Ruby takes its cues both from Japan and from its contemporaries in Berlin and London. From the mismatched furniture, antique rugs and glassware, to the beautifully laid out back bar, everything screams perfection and precision.

STRØM

There's something quite modest about describing oneself as a "diamond in the rough", especially when it comes to a bar, but Strøm don't seem too unhappy with the description, especially given that they are asking their patrons to help shape it. Founded in 2012, Strøm is already setting the bar high on the mixed drinks front, in a city which already has its fair share of really well known cocktail joints. Cosy, classy and extremely laid back (which is something that seems to grow on trees in this city), the drinks are just wonderfully turned out: from a simple Jack & Coke to a Ramos Gin Fizz, you know it'll be one of the best you'll ever have. Hardly much rough to polish here, chaps.

✖

Niels Hemmingsens Gade 32, 1153 Copenhagen
+45 81 18 94 21 strombar.dk

✖

IN THREE WORDS:
Denmark's Drinks Diamond.
THEY SAY:
"Not many places can claim it, but these boys have it all nailed down."
— IAIN GRIFFITHS, AUSTRALIA
PRICE RATING: ✳✳✳✳

FOCUS*

STARTENDER
LAURA NISSINEN

Helsinki's Laura Nissinen describes her ideal day out drinking in the city, along with her all-time favourite bar picks.

Laura is the head bartender at A21 Decades in Helsinki (see page 110) – a career decision that almost didn't happen. "I wanted to become a chef when I started this career, but soon realized that customer service is my cup of tea. When I had a chance to take a bartending course at the restaurant school I decided to give it a go, and soon understood that this was the perfect platform for me to combine my love for flavours and customer service," she explains. In addition to working behind the bar, Laura has helped launch Birdtenders, a collective offering a platform for conversation and support to female bartenders.

Why is the Helsinki bar scene so important right now?
Helsinki is nestled between ocean and vast forests, so we have a unique setting and access to ingredients that big cities like New York, London or Paris cannot provide. Our

small community is bursting with energy and team spirit. We are also getting some help now from our government with new laws making our work a bit easier. Until now we haven't been allowed to use more than 4cl (1.4fl oz) of spirit in our cocktails, to advertise our drinks including strong spirits, to keep our bars open later that 2am and so on. With these changes we are ready to take our bar scene to the next level.

Your all-time favourite drink?
Usually I go for sour and fresh drinks, but when I want something extra special I choose the Hanky-Panky [containing gin, sweet vermouth and Fernet-Branca]. This cocktail is dear to me, because it was created by probably the best-known female bartender of all times, Ada Coleman, who is a huge source of inspiration for me.

LAURA'S PERFECT DAY OUT IN HELSINKI:

✖
Kellohalli (kellohalli.fi)
I would start my perfect day in Helsinki with a late lunch in the old Abattoir area at Kellohalli. On Fridays they have a "Street Food Friday" – a buffet with a large selection of fresh salads, tasty toppings, sauces and dips from a different cuisine each week. During the summer there is live music, and in the evenings a pizza oven is warmed up to serve the hungry crowd on the terrace.

✖
Latva (latva.fi)
Next, I would head to a cosy wine bar and pub, Latva. The name means "treetop", and it belongs to the same family as Restaurant Juuri – "root" in Finnish. Latva specializes in beers from Finnish microbreweries and also has a nice selection of wines served by the glass. You can pair your beverage with sapas, *a small snack similar to Spanish tapas, made from local ingredients.*

✖
Grotesk Bar (grotesk.fi)
This is one of my favourite places in town. During the summer they serve drinks on a cool inner yard terrace, and when the short Finnish summer is over the shakers are moved back inside to a space that once hosted one

of the oldest liquor stores in Finland, Alko. They have cool and whimsical drinks like Por Qué No, Parmesan? – which is made with bourbon, tepache [a Mexican fermented brew made from pineapple peel], lemon and Parmesan cheese.

✖
100Dogs (100dogs.fi)
This bar started off as a pop-up: their goal was to serve 100 hot dogs with bourbon each day. With a motto "Shitty drinks, average food and bad service", this place was inspired by Japanese dive bars. You certainly feel like you've stepped straight into Tokyo when you see the decor. Get rid of your coins with the old slot machines in the back room, pick a seat by the bar, enjoy some funky cocktails and eat a mouthwatering hot dog, before heading into the night.

✖
Navy Jerry's (navyjerrys.fi)
Navy Jerry's is a rum bar with an eclectic blend of Pacific kitsch and Naval officers' mess. The music is the best of the 1950s and 1960s, everything from Rockabilly to Motown, with DJs performing several times a week. This is the place where all bartenders end up after work for shots and Daiquiris.

✖
Primula (ravintolaprimula.fi)
When Sunday and the hangover hit you, it's time to head for a Sunday brunch. Primula is the bartender's favourite. Ease your headache with Bloody Mary "Caesar Style", Negroni or Michelada. For food there are options from Scandinavian-style smoked salmon with a poached egg to huevos rancheros.

LAURA'S ALL-TIME FAVOURITE BARS:

The American Bar at the Savoy, London (see page 22)
As a female bartender, the number one thing in London for me was to enjoy a Hanky-Panky in the American Bar, the home of the most famous female bartender, Ada Coleman. This place is full of history and style.

✖
The Gin House, Porto (facebook.com/theginhouse)
This small gin bar in the heart of the Port wine region in Portugal is a pure gem. Their selection of about 300 gins is very impressive, and each of them is served with a personalized garnish and big ice cubes chilled with liquid nitrogen.

✖
Pharmarium, Stockholm (pharmarium.se)
One of my favourite places in Stockholm. With its cosy atmosphere, candlelit tables and pharmacy theme, this is a place for long conversations and awesome cocktails. Their bar counter is curved so that you can have a seat next to the bartenders working, which makes it much more intimate.

✖
Employees Only, New York (see page 217)
This classic spot in New York is just the perfect combination of fun and great cocktails. Also, the food they serve is awesome! I was just learning to bartend when visiting this bar, and it made me understand the importance of hospitality.

✖
IceBar in SnowVillage, Ylläs, Finland (www.snowvillage.fi) ↑
In the forest near the Ylläs fell is a hotel made of ice and snow. I worked in the IceBar for one winter season and here I began to appreciate the small things we didn't have – running water, dishwasher, tonic water not freezing in your hand when poured into a glass. This is a perfect getaway from the buzz of city life: you can enjoy a cup of hot Glögi and even sleep in a bed made of ice!

HELSINKI & OSLO*

A21 DECADES

Contender for Scandinavia's best bar? Absolutely. A21 Decades sits perfectly in that niche between mainstream accessibility and genuine craftsmanship, ensuring that visitors leave with a broader understanding of the artistry of the cocktail and why they need to drink "better", rather than more. As bartender Laura Nissinen explains: "Our name comes from the address: Annankatu 21. The Decades bit refers to the theme of the menu: classic drinks from different decades with house twists made of seasonal ingredients." This is where A21 excels: you can explore Finnish flavours from the bar's Suomi menu, which includes birch leaves, sea buckthorn berries, rhubarb, bee pollen – all used in wonderfully innovative ways. A21 should really be renamed A1...it's that good.

✖
Annankatu 21, 00100 Helsinki
+358 400 21192 a21.fi
✖

IN THREE WORDS:
Totally A-OK.

THE DRINK TO TRY:
Sex In The Forest: a reinvention of the classic 1980s Sex On The Beach.
WE SAY:
A21 makes exploring the flavours of Finland a highly enjoyable, and educational, experience.
PRICE RATING: ✳ ✳ ✳

DR JEKYLL'S PUB

This is another outstanding Scandinavian whisk(e)y bar that sits right up there with Akkurat (see page 104), outlining the huge appreciation of this masterful spirit. The gothic feel of the place only adds to the mystery of the back bar, which is mostly focused on Scotch, but with a smattering of Irish and American whiskeys and world whiskies taking a perch too. Get your timing right and you may bump into a representative of a brand or two – Jekyll's is well known across the industry as a place where enthusiasts meet expert palates, so there is something for everyone to try.

✖
Klingenberggata 4, 0161 Oslo
+47 22 41 30 44 jekylls.no
✖

IN THREE WORDS:
Nowhere To Hyde.
WE SAY:
A bucket list visit for any whisky enthusiast.
PRICE RATING: ✳ ✳ ✳

HIMKOK

It's hard to know whether to call Himkok a bar that distils its own spirits or a distillery that runs a bar too. Either way, the results are groundbreaking and globally influential, putting Oslo firmly on the map as a drinking destination. With its stills producing vodka, gin and aquavit, a greenhouse for herbs, an outside garden area, walls lined with pickled and fermented goods, a glamorous cocktail bar downstairs and high-paced cocktails and beer on tap upstairs, Himkok is a drinking phenomenon. And under the watchful eye of Monica Berg (see opposite) it runs like clockwork.
✖
Storgata 27, 0184 Oslo
+47 22 42 22 02 himkok.no
✖

IN THREE WORDS:
Drinks of All Trades.
THEY SAY:
"The first time I went here my jaw hit the ground and never left."
— **GEORGIE BELL, UK**
PRICE RATING: ✳ ✳ ✳

FOCUS*

STARTENDER
MONICA BERG

Your favourite drink of all time…?
The Negroni.
What is your favourite city in the world to go drinking in?
Not to play home favourite, but probably London!

Monica Berg is one of the leading mixologists of Scandinavia. Former head bartender of Oslo's Aqua Vitae, she is highly praised for her innovative flavour combinations and has a minimalistic and elegant style. After moving to London in 2013, she joined Jason Atherton's Michelin-starred Mayfair restaurant, Pollen Street Social. Today, Monica works on various projects, splitting her time between London and Oslo. Her current project, Himkok, (see opposite) is a unique distillery bar in Oslo, which was shortlisted for the best new international cocktail bar at Tales Of The Cocktail 2016 and has become a new addition in the coveted World's 50 Best Bars.

Where do you drink when you're off duty?
To be honest, it depends, but I'm very lucky to have several of my favourite bars very close to me. **Peg + Patriot** (see page 44), **Sager + Wilde** (see page 47), **Dandelyan** (see page 31), **Bar Termini** (see page 49) and **Satan's Whiskers** (see page 47).

MONICA'S TOP FIVE BARS FROM AROUND THE WORLD:

✖
**Nomad Bar, New York
(see page 220)**
My absolute favourite bar in the world. I love the drinks and [Bar Director] Leo Robitschek has one of my favourite palates. It has next-level attention to detail and the best hospitality in the world.
✖
**Sager + Wilde, London
(see page 47)**
My favourite wine bar and hangout when I'm in London. I love how they select their wines and their approach to service. I'm not that strong on wine, but the team there are always very helpful and friendly about it.
✖
**Peg + Patriot, London
(see page 44)**
One of the most creative bars I know! This place has amazing drinks, amazing staff and is one of the few places truly fuelled by creativity in my opinion. If you haven't been – you need to go!

✖
**Operation Dagger, Singapore
(see page 156)**
From the moment I walked into this bar, I knew I would love it. The drinks, the team, the art – it's all incredible! The first cocktail I tried had bonito (dried, fermented and smoked skipjack tuna flakes) as an ingredient, and it was just so cleverly done. It tasted fantastic!
✖
**Le Syndicat, Paris
(syndicatcocktailclub.com)**
This bar's concept is great. I love the roughness of the entrance, contrasted by the warmth of the team. The best Flip I have ever tried in my life was their Flip Le Corse – I still dream about it!

BERGEN & VILNIUS*

NO STRESS

Housed in the premises which was once home to the popular clothing line, Stress (oh, the irony…), the bar is a wonderfully inviting display of colour and vitality. You leave your stresses at the door and go searching inside for a decent drink. You invariably find it quickly, from a menu which focuses on cocktails built around fresh ingredients and juices, as well as a healthy list of decent craft beers. The whole place is perfectly curated: everything invites you to de-stress and start living again. Save us a seat at the bar…we'll be back for a holiday soon.

✖

Hollendergaten 11, 5017 Bergen
+47 938 33 312 nostressbar.no

✖

IN THREE WORDS:
Just The Tonic.

THEY SAY:
"Whenever I walk through those doors I hear the theme from Cheers *playing in my head."*
—STAFFAN ALEXANDERSSON,
NORWAY

PRICE RATING: ✖✖

THE TASTING ROOM

One of the most beautiful cities in Europe, the ancient Hanseatic port of Bergen attracts huge numbers of tourists every year. But life in Bergen is expensive, so it can make a massive dent in the wallet, especially when drinking out. Laws prevent the sale of wines and spirits in supermarkets, bringing them under government supervision in its own stores, dotted around the country. This hasn't deterred some bar owners from offering a great selection of spirits to be experienced on a night out, and Bergen's The Tasting Room has one of the best selections in Norway, while its Swedish barman Staffan Alexandersson whips up some of the best cocktails seen in the Nordics.

✖

Engen 8, 5011 Bergen
+47 911 00 551 thetastingroom.no

✖

IN THREE WORDS:
Vi-King Of Whiskies.

WE SAY:
Well worth visiting if you haven't already spent all your money on beer.

PRICE RATING: ✖✖✖✖

KING & MOUSE

A little while ago, we received a request to visit Lithuania to host an event related to whisky. Given the fact that we love travelling, and whisky, we naturally said yes. Much like Akkurat in Stockholm (see page 104), King & Mouse is a welcome sight for the cold, tired traveller. This diminutive, but beautifully laid-out bar/shop holds around 300 different whiskies and you'll be hard pressed to find a team who know more about exactly what each one tastes like. Owner Sarunas Karalius (see opposite) opened one of the first dedicated whisky bars in the country (called 1608, in Kaunas) and King & Mouse is now his pride and joy. Expect everything from single cask malts through to great Irish and Japanese whiskies, and a handful of European malts and blends.

✖

Trakų g. 2, Vilnius 01118
+370 (657) 45 478 kingandmouse.lt

✖

IN THREE WORDS:
Kings of Whisky.

WE SAY:
A treasure trove of whisky – befitting the royal name!

PRICE RATING: ✖✖

FEATURE*

A DRINK WITH...
SARUNAS KARALIUS

We met Sarunas several years ago at a whisky tasting in Lithuania and it was quite clear that his passion for the spirit would lead to truly great things. Since that time, this once professional DJ has gone on to open King & Mouse ↗↓ (see opposite), with arguably the best selection of whisky you will find in the capital city of Vilnius.

Where do you drink when you're off duty?
Ha! It's a local pub called **Špunka** in Vilnius (spunka.lt) The place is absolutely tiny, just a little bit bigger than 20 square metres [215 square feet]. Despite its size it has a great choice of beers – mostly brewed by the local craft brewery **Dundulis** (dundulis.lt) and a brilliant atmosphere. What's funny is that alongside all the locals who visit, you can meet a wild pigeon called Astas, who flies in for his daily portion of barley!

Tell us about some of your favourite places to go drinking locally...
First up would be **Apoteka** (apotekabar.lt) in my home town Vilnius. Their whole premise is all about cocktails using local, seasonal ingredients. I can never get enough of one particular cocktail they make using wild blueberries, peated whisky and coffee – it's awesome.

From there I would go to **Alaus biblioteka** (beerlibrary.lt), which means "Beer library" and there's no denying it – it certainly is one! There are shelves of books on one side of the room and shelves with beer on the other, stocking around 300 beers and some 60 different styles. Incredible.

FEATURE*

A DAY DRINKING IN...
REYKJAVIK

If there is one place on this planet that really doesn't seem like it is on this planet, then Iceland would be that place. Bonkers to the extreme, Reykjavik is simply one of the most creative, encouraging and downright colourful places for cocktails in the whole world.

Start your adventure at **Loftid ↗**, (jacobsenloftid.is), arguably one of the most stylish and sophisticated joints in the city. There's a dress code, which really defines who drinks here, but the cocktails are inspired, many of them coming with little accompaniments (either to eat, to spray or simply to enhance the experience).

The craft beer scene is thriving in Reykjavik, with **Micro Bar** (+354 865 8389) offering a more down to earth approach to some equally inspired sipping. The list of imported beers is staggering, but then place these alongside the local brews – mostly those from the **Gæðingur microbrewery** (gaedingur-ol.is) – and you have a serious contender for a palate-enlightening experience.

Of course, coming to Iceland wouldn't be complete without trying to experience the northern lights and the aptly named **Northern Lights** bar at the **Ion Adventure Hotel** (ioniceland.is) is arguably one of the most comfortable, architecturally splendid places to catch a glimpse. If, like us, you find that your views are a little cloudy on the day you happen to arrive, fear not, the cocktail list will more than make up for any disappointment.

If there's just one bar that you can't afford to miss, though, in a city that hosts many great cocktail bars, it is **Slippbarinn**, (slippbarinn.is) – a sort of Icelandic version of London's Dandelyan (see page 31), and an undoubtedly hipster hotel bar. Housed in the IcelandAir Hotel in Reykjavik's marina, the cocktail menu features simple serves, such as the Negroni (who doesn't these days?), some non-alcoholic cocktails (including homemade lemonade) but it is on the creative side that things get really interesting. The Lazarus combines three types of bourbon with dry curaçao, cinnamon, lime, mint and pineapple, while the Fat Duck has duck-fat-washed Cognac, sugar, bitters and an absinthe wash. But to really make yourself feel like you're in one of the most incredible locations on the planet, try the Judas Hobo, which is mixed using a drill. No, really...a drill. There are also cocktails called Rentboys, Octopuilicious and Sourlock Holmes. We kid you not.

Whatever you do, get yourself on a plane over to Iceland as soon as possible. Yes, it has stunning, moon-like scenery. Yes, it has the blue lagoon. Yes, it (often) has the northern lights. But more than all of this, you'll have a truly bonkers cocktail experience.

POZNAŃ & PRAGUE*

WHISKY BAR 88

Not particularly known as a whisky connoisseur's paradise, Poznań has hit the ground running with this gem. Step inside the bar-cum-restaurant complex, part of the City Park Hotel, which is situated close to the retro-futuristic Poznan concert arena, and you'll be amazed at the rare whiskies on offer. Here, there's none of the geekish snobbery found at the top tier of whisky bars: Old vintage Ardbeg single malts sit in glass cabinets, but are a fraction of the price that they probably should be, plus the sheer weight of world whiskies is a true delight. No Polish whisky yet, but no doubt, they'll be the first to offer you a dram if it ever arrives.

✖

Wyspiańskiego 26A,
60-751 Poznań +48 888 321 888
whiskybar88.pl

✖

IN THREE WORDS:
Dram Fine Find.

THE DRINK TO TRY:
A Blood and Sand cocktail, made
with Lagavulin 16yo single malt.

WE SAY:
One of the least pretentious
whisky joints in the world.

PRICE RATING: ✳✳

HEMINGWAY BAR ↓

Old Papa was a huge influence on the drinking community. Alongside Havana's El Floridita (see page 274), Harry's Bar, Venice (page 123) and The Hemingway Bar at the Ritz in Paris (ritzparis.com), the big fella also made a considerable impression in Prague. This beautiful bar is festooned with classical detail: from the dark wood counters to the antique absinthe fountains, it's the sort of place that you can enter at one point in the day and then leave feeling like you've just been through a time tunnel to

the 1920s. The menu reveals a few cheeky twists, and all is not what it seems. Yes, you'll find the usual classic cocktails on offer, but also surprising, innovative serves: Hemingway's Gasoline comes served in a little petrol can and the Eau de Cocktail (which shouldn't deter men, despite being listed "for women") is delightfully fragrant and comes served in a perfume bottle. Hemingway is the sort of place you'll wish existed in every city because, as with the literature of its namesake, you'll come away feeling thoroughly enlightened.

✖

Karoliny Světlé 279/26,
110 00 Praha 1-Staré Město,
Prague +420 773 974 764
hemingwaybar.cz

✖

IN THREE WORDS:
Old Papa's Perfection.

THE DRINK TO TRY:
Hemingway's Gasoline.

THEY SAY:
"One of my most standout
memories."

— **KRISTEN VOISEY, CANADA**

PRICE RATING: ✳✳✳

ATHENS*

A FOR ATHENS

Athens is one of those cities where history is around every corner. But the key to understanding how our modern lives were shaped so effectively by Greek history is to look up, as from pretty much everywhere in the Greek capital, you can see the mighty Acropolis. Building regulations in the city have quite rightly dictated that nothing gets in the way of this incredible building, and its influence can be felt in every street. However, the ability to stop and take in this mighty building, while at the same time enjoying a wonderful libation, should be high priority on any visitor's to-do list when in Athens.

There are a few places where a great drink can be had with a wonderful view of the Acropolis as the sun sets over the city. You could choose to have a Metaxa 5 Star and soda on the roof at the St George's Hotel (sglycabettus.

gr/), which is about as far up into the forest-covered city suburbs as you'd want to be for brilliant views of the sunset and out to sea. Or you could find yourself at the historic Grande Bretagne Hotel (grandebretagne.gr) – which shares the same square in the middle of town as the Parliament building – where the roof terrace has a perfect spot for both photos and cocktails.

However, for a truly excellent experience head to the streets north of the Acropolis and settle in for a wet gin Martini at the rooftop bar of A For Athens,

There are some bars around the world that really stand out from the others, that just seem to give that extra few per cent more than most.

where you'll simply have every photo opportunity your phone could possibly handle!
✖
Miaouli 2, Athens 105 54
+30 21 0324 4244
aforathens.com
✖
IN THREE WORDS:
Ethereal Acropolis Experience.
THEY SAY:
"A view and great drinks mixed by a team headed up by Thodoris Pirillos. These guys know what the word 'service' means."
—ANISTATIA MILLER, UK
PRICE RATING: ✱✱✱

BABA AU RUM ↗

"House of Spirits" is how this place describes itself, and we have a funny feeling that when it says "spirits", it means it in the convivial, attitudinal way. For, as much as this is a bar with a wonderful selection of distilled drinks, it is also, first and foremost, a rum bar. That said, there is plenty on offer and the cocktails here come in all shapes and sizes, from the wonderful Star Sour (a tribute to London's Happiness Forgets – see page 36), through to the mezcal-driven Smokin' Mexican. It isn't all rum-based libations, we promise. In terms of the venue, this place is light and open with a wonderfully long bar with

just enough of a tiki feel to it. Bartenders decked out in aprons will tend to your every need, mixing drinks under their very own spotlight. Our tip is to get a seat at the bar: the real chef's table in this instance.

Baba Au Rum is yet another shining example of how good the cocktail scene is in Athens, and if you're planning a trip, please make sure you leave time for the Athens of the present while exploring the Athens of the past.

✖
Klitiou 6, Athens 105 60
+30 21 1710 9140
babaaurum.com
✖

IN THREE WORDS:
Rum Runners Extraordinaire.
THEY SAY:
"I love quality and quantity in Rum."
—**ARIS CHATZIANTONIOU, ATHENS**
WE SAY:
We simply love this place.
PRICE RATING: ✱✱✱✱

THE CLUMSIES

There are some bars around the world that really stand out from the others, that just seem to give that extra few per cent more than most. It could be through extreme detail, excellence in creativity, fantastic hospitality, liquid innovation or simply explosive flavours in your glass. And when all of these come together, you have something extremely special. In fact, you have The Clumsies. The drinks that are devised by the team here are simply outstanding, worked on in a small experimental kitchen space above the bar, and next to their private drinking room (complete with pool table and a smattering of interesting spirit bottles). The cocktail list isn't long, but don't be afraid to ask for a classic. The stunning stone walls are clad with a parquet wood effect on some. Mid-century Ercol chairs provide stylish comfort, while

the lighting, music and general hubbub are all at exactly the right levels and most of the glassware is bespoke for each cocktail.
✖
Praxitelous 30, Athens 105 61
+30 21 0323 2682 theclumsies.gr
✖

IN THREE WORDS:
Cocktail Gods of Athens.
THE DRINK TO TRY:
Ask for a Martinez with their own house Old Tom Gin.
WE SAY:
Simply a "must-do" when in Athens.
PRICE RATING: ✱✱✱

FOCUS*

STARTENDER
VASILIS KYRITSIS

Vasilis Kyritsis is the Co-Founder and Co-Owner of the highly celebrated The Clumsies in Athens (see page 117). The Clumsies is currently the bar on everyone's lips within the drinks industry and has really helped to shape the growing scene of great cocktail bars in Athens. We asked Vasilis to take us on his favourite night out in the city…

How did you get started working behind a bar?
When I started working in bars, I was lucky enough to work at a few of the most iconic Greek bars, such us **Pere Ubu** (pereubu.gr), **Eclipse**, **Aperitif** and **The Gin Joint** (theginjoint.gr), where I worked until the end of September 2014. In 2012, I won Bartender of the Year in a Greece bar competition and I represented my country in the Global Finals in Rio de Janeiro, which was just amazing. In 2015 I set up The Clumsies in Athens, which has been an incredible journey. We have been shortlisted for many of the top bar awards around the world. I consider bartending as the most creative job in the world.

Why is Athens such an important city for drinking culture at the moment?
Because a lot of good bars and restaurants opened in the centre of Athens, all with the common goal of offering good-quality drinks from talented bartenders, so a lot of tourists who come are enjoying creative cocktails and a perfect atmosphere in bars. Everything is in walking distance so you don't have to get a taxi or metro to enjoy cocktails, either.
Tell us about your perfect night out in Athens?
There are so many things to do! I would start by watching the sun set from the roof of **A For Athens** (see page 116), before heading over to **The Gin Joint** to drink a

perfect Dry Martini. I'd follow this up with a trip to **Baba Au Rum** (see page 116) to drink perfect tiki cocktails. For something a little more complex, I might aim for bar **"42"** (+30 21 3005 2153), then finish at **7 Jokers** (+30 21 0321 9225) till late morning.
For those who can't make it to The Clumsies, do you have a drink they could make at home?
My signature drink is the Johnnie Cola, which I developed because people in Greece love a long drink, and I really wanted to do a twist on Scotch and coke.

✖

JOHNNIE COLA

*50ml Johnnie Walker
    Gold Reserve
10ml pomegranate molasses
1 tsp vanilla-infused icing sugar
3 dashes of Abbots bitters
Fentiman's cherry cola
caramelized popcorn,
    to decorate*

Shake the first four ingredients together in a shaker and pour into a Collins glass. Top up with the cherry cola and decorate with popcorn!

ATHENS*

LOTTE BAR

Greece has some incredible hidden gems scattered across its islands. There is the brilliant Rachi in Lefkada, where the stunning terrace platforms above even the paragliders who are taking off below and the cocktails are creative, providing the perfect sundowner. (Try the Dark Side, a rum-based affair with a rim of toffee and biscuit around the vessel – rachi.gr.) And there are the more traditional tavernas that are the very DNA of these islands. One of those, which is easy to walk past, is Lotte Bar. A tiny café/bistro that doesn't shout about itself, but sits quietly, unassumingly, on the corner of two streets near the Atheneum museum. Lotte is Parisian in style and if you're sitting inside you could be forgiven for thinking that you're in 1930s France, with net curtains, a vintage gramophone lampshade and handwritten school ledgers for menus. It's quirky, but not over the top; think Alice Through the Looking Glass meets Cath Kidston. Stepping into Lotte,

you become Alice; things shrink and grow, and time seems to stand still. How very apt for a city where you are surrounded by so much history.

✖

117 42, Tsami Karatasou 2, Athens 117 42 +30 21 1407 8639

✖

IN THREE WORDS:
Small But Beautiful.

WE SAY:
This is a real escape of a place. A community minded bar.

PRICE RATING: ✱✱

MOMIX ↗

Molecular mixology has certainly been a passing trend across London's wave of hip bars, but not so in Athens, where the flair for all things scientific reigns large, especially at MoMix (which stands for Molecular Mixology), the first of its kind in Athens. Owner Aris Chantziantoniou is a man with more than a few scientific tricks up his sleeve, moulding the place into one of the most forward-thinking bars in Europe. His creations are far more than simply cocktails, as he turns drinks into jelly, sweets, spun sugar, foam and gases. It's an absolute blast.

✖

Keleou 1–5, Kerameikos, Athens 104 35 +30 697 43 50 179
momixbar.com

✖

IN THREE WORDS:
Science Fiction Drinking.

THE DRINK TO TRY:
One of the bizarre pearls or jelly cocktails served on spoons.

WE SAY:
Outlandish, innovative and forward-looking. Think Heston Blumenthal doing cocktails.

PRICE RATING: ✱✱✱

FEATURE*

A DAY DRINKING IN...
ATHENS

Mirroring the astonishing Acropolis, which dominates the middle of the Greek capital and is a focal point for modern culture, Athens is becoming a beacon for the creative cocktail scene in southern Europe.

Drawing on strong liquid history that has seen sweet Greek wines celebrated as highly as their Northern European counterparts, the rise of ouzo as a digestif, and the development of the wonderful drink that is Metaxa, a global brand devised in 1888 and now consumed around the world, the creativity

... the creativity of the country has moved into the bar scene, giving birth to one of the most exciting and vibrant scenes in the world.

of the country has moved into the bar scene, giving birth to one of the most exciting and vibrant scenes in the world.

Two of Athens's key bars of the moment are **The Clumsies** (see page 117) and **Baba Au Rum** (see page 116), which are doing much to push the reputation of Athens on a global stage. Indeed, trying such inspiring drinks as the Above & Beyond Punch (at The Clumsies) and the Duchamp's Punch (at Baba Au Rum), you can totally see why.

Add to this the incredible creativity of **MoMix** ✔ (see page 119), the carefully curated collection of booze in an actual cage at **CV Distiller** (+30 21 0723 1767) and the rooftops at **A For Athens** (see page 116), the **St George Lycabettus Hotel** (sglycabettus.gr) or the **Hotel Grande Bretagne** (grandebretagne.gr), where a perfectly made Martini slips down as easily as the sun setting behind the Acropolis.

LEFKADA & MYKONOS*

MAVROS LAGOS

Hidden in the back streets of the small Greek island of Lefkada is Mavros Lagos, or the Black Rabbit. It calls itself a wine bar, but it's very much a rum bar, evoking the spirit of Cuba like no other place. Outdoor seating is scattered under mature trees, and a projector throws footage of Havana high onto a wall above the bar. The cocktails are simple but refreshing and the bar is dotted with paper Panama hats with Mavros Lagos scribbled on the side, which visitors are encouraged to take away with them. Live music can be found some evenings, which adds to the laid-back atmosphere.

✖

Pinelopis St 4, Lefkada 311 00
+30 698 696 0000 1800.gr

✖

IN THREE WORDS:
The Black Rabbit.
THE DRINK TO TRY:
The Hemingway Daiquiri.
WE SAY:
The closest experience to drinking in Havana we've had in a long time.
PRICE RATING: ✳ ✳

SCORPIOS ↑

The Greek islands are some of the best places to drink in the world: sun, sand and great drinks. Occasionally there are places that live long in the memory, and Scorpios, on the stunning island of Mykonos, is one of those

The Greek islands are some of the best places to drink in the world: sun, sand and great drinks.

places. Spread across what seems like a red rock, this bar buzzes with life, drawing out the days as if the summer will never end, the sunsets slinking into the sea as you swig on a Singapore Sling. Seemingly risen from the rustic surrounds, this bamboo bar has stunning views of the Paraga and Kavos lagoons, and out to the Aegean Sea. It is a place where "intimacy is woven into the environment" according to the bar's owners, while at night, as the moon rises, it heats up to become a vibrant venue, the likes of which can only be found in places such as this.

✖

Paraga, 84600 Mykonos
+30 2289 029250
scorpiosmykonos.com

✖

IN THREE WORDS:
Sunset To Sunrise.
THEY SAY:
"Great holiday bohemian atmosphere."
— **RAISSA DE HAAS, THE NETHERLANDS**
PRICE RATING: ✳ ✳

ROME, MILAN & VENICE*

CHORUS CAFE

When you think of a typical London café you tend to think morning mugs of tea and bacon sandwiches. If you're in Rome... well, think again. As cafés go, Chorus is pretty awful. In fact, the description is totally misleading: on offer here is an absolutely stunning, refined and stylish Italian fine-dining restaurant and cocktail bar. The drinks list caters for the gin/whisky and classics lovers (a small, but punchy Martini awaits), and the vibe is ideal for an evening sundowner once you've finished perusing St Peter's Basilica, having changed into something with a bit more pizzazz.

✖

Via della Conciliazione 4, 00193 Rome +39 06 68892774 choruscafe.it

✖

IN THREE WORDS:
Martini For Breakfast?
WE SAY:
A vibey Italian masterclass of style and sophisticated drinking and dining.
PRICE RATING: ✳✳✳✳✳

THE JERRY THOMAS PROJECT ↓

To many of our esteemed panel of contributors, Jerry Thomas is as close as you'll get to a bartending god. This famous US giant of the bartending world entertained well-heeled drinkers back in the mid-1800s with wild showmanship, flaming drinks and recipes featuring his own infusions and concoctions. Over the past decade there has been a renaissance of all things Thomas (recreated cocktail bitters and the art of the Blazer cocktail – an incendiary drink, bringing together high-strength whiskey, boiling water, sugar and citrus, "thrown" in a flaming arc for added danger and thrill) and Rome's TJTP has created the perfect homage to the great man. This small speakeasy needs a password to get in (check out the website) but once you're here, you're transported back to a time when Thomas and his prowess behind the bar earned him a bigger salary than the president of the United States. Classics are stirred, thrown and slung, using a variety of homemade infusions. It's a delicious splash of history in a coupe glass.

✖

Vicolo Cellini 30, Rome
+39 06 96845937
thejerrythomasproject.it

✖

IN THREE WORDS:
Jerry Jerry Good.
THE DRINK TO TRY:
Ask for a Blue Blazer and be prepared to be thrilled...and

a little scared. Don't ask for anything with vodka – you'll be asked to leave.

THEY SAY:
"A classic speakeasy bar in the heart of beautiful Rome. It is really worth the trip to find it in the hidden alley."
—KRISZTIÁN CSIGÓ, BUDAPEST
"The mixologists there are your best friends in 10 minutes, their drinks are just as lovely."
—KESHAV PRAKASH, MUMBAI
PRICE RATING: ✱✱

CERESIO 7 ↑

This place is about as chic as you can possibly get: 1950s Hollywood rooftop pool-party vibe, incredible views, beautiful Italian people sipping beautifully made cocktails and small plates of tapas-style food. The interior is smartly designed and the bar itself is the real centrepiece: a lengthy tranche of engineered wood, behind which lie some outstanding spirits. The theme of the drinks is definitely Italian aperitif-influenced, with a few local twists including homemade bitters: the Unlike A Negroni No.2, using mezcal, white chocolate and bergamot

is aromatic, smoky and punchy. Just don't knock back too many and then embarrass yourself trying to do the backstroke at 10pm at night.

✘
Via Ceresio 7, 20154 Milan
+39 02 31039221 ceresio7.com
✘
IN THREE WORDS:
Dive Straight In.
WE SAY:
If the weather's good, this is the place to be in Milan, with a drink in hand, watching the sunset.
PRICE RATING: ✱✱✱✱

HARRY'S BAR

Has anyone seen the 1970s horror film *Don't Look Now*? If you haven't, it's a terrifying portrait of Venice in the winter; the beautiful architecture casting long, murky shadows, while a serial killer in a red duffel coat slices their way through the night. Anyway, we first visited Venice in November, a time of year when it draws a terrifying parallel with the film. Brooding and foreboding, the nights out were strangely empty – until we visited Harry's Bar. Another legendary outlet on the

list, which was patronized by Hemingway (see El Floridita on page 274), Harry's hasn't changed a great amount since the big man popped off to sip on his heavenly Daiquiri for good. The place is a simple affair: dark wooden stools run the length of the bar and the white-coated hosts hark back to the golden era when the bar was buzzing with the likes of Old Papa and his consorts. The Martinis are served short, strong and ice cold, straight from the freezer, which will infuriate the purists, who may want to see some artistry in their construction, but they sure do hit the spot. Similarly, the Bellini (which Harry's has become famous for) feels a little lacking in flair, but that's the point – what you see is what you get...and you get an experience straight from the pages of a Hemingway novel – a fresh, tasty one at that.

✘
Calle Vallaresso 1323, 30124
San Marco, Venice
+39 041 5285777
harrysbarvenezia.com
✘
IN THREE WORDS:
Venerable Venetian Virtuosity.
THEY SAY:
"Is it overpriced? Yes. Does it still have the atmosphere that it did in its prime? No. However, it still has something indefinable about it."
—MARCIS DZELZAINIS, FRANCE
PRICE RATING: ✱✱✱✱✱

MOSCOW*

CHAINAYA TEA & COCKTAILS

Tea and cocktails go together like...well...tea and cocktails. As a base, teas have been used to lengthen punches and other tall drinks for centuries, but here they are sipped like nectar, either infused into a small selection of incredible cocktails or on their own. Chainaya is to be found in Moscow's Chinatown, but be warned, like Delicatessen (see right), it's really not easy to find and requires some exploration down the back street behind a Chinese restaurant. It's also like a proper speakeasy, so you'll need to book, as they don't accept walk-ups. But once you do locate it, you'll fall straight in love. The basement is decked out with a teahouse vibe and you'll find all manner of infusions and unusual ingredients on offer, including some extraordinarily rare teas that you won't find anywhere else – certainly not in Moscow. Take the bartender's word on what to try and sit back, knowing that you're in safe hands – and in one of Russia's finest bars.

✖
1-ya Tverskaya-Yamskaya
ulitsa 29, стр. 1, Moscow 125047
+7 (495) 967 30 52
✖

IN THREE WORDS:
Brewing The Best.
THEY SAY:
"The place where you feel yourself, where time will never tell."
— **ELIZAVETA EVDOKIMOVA, MOSCOW**
"The first neo-speakeasy bar in a Chinese style, with a rare tea collection."
— **DMITRY SOKOLOV, MOSCOW**
PRICE RATING: ✳✳✳

DELICATESSEN ↗

Tucked away from prying eyes, Delicatessen is the sort of bar that Moscow has long needed and here it is, at last. This speakeasy-style place (it's tricky to find) has been making waves across Russia and now the wider world with its take on bohemian chic, which both New York and Berlin have done so well recently. The place has a genuine gastro edge and this is reflected in the plates of smoked fish, pastrami and other incredible dishes on the food menu. It's the cocktails, though, which really delight, and the playfulness on display disguises a genuine ability to create perfectly balanced drinks, using a wild back bar full of odd

infusions, bitters and miniature casks to mature cocktails in. Russia's cocktail revolution starts here....

✖
Sadovaya-Karetnaya ul. 20,
стр. 2, Moscow
+7 (495) 699 39 52 newdeli.ru
✖

IN THREE WORDS:
Wonderful Russian Delicacies.
THEY SAY:
"A happy atmosphere and the cocktails are an imaginative twist on the classics."
— **PETER DORELLI, LONDON, VIA ITALY**
"Famous for its homemade infusions, sophisticated food and great people around."
— **ELIZAVETA EVDOKIMOVA, RUSSIA**
PRICE RATING: ✳✳✳

FOCUS*

STARTENDER
DMITRY SOKOLOV

Dmitry Sokolov, Bar owner and educator, is a legend – or Tsar – in his homeland of Russia. He was one of the first bartenders to open a "proper" cocktail bar in Moscow, conveniently named Mr Help (see page 127) back in 2004, shortly after becoming the youngest ever winner of the Bacardi Martini Grand Prix World Finals in 2003. Today he is the man behind four different bars in the city, each with its own unique personality.

What do you drink when you're off duty?
My favourite drink is definitely rum – you can use rum in all drinks: tiki, old-style classic, modern mixology, drinking it by shots and just to sip, if it's an amazing old rum and the style of rum is a copy of my character!

Your favourite drink of all time...?
A Vanilla Daiquiri.

What is your favourite city in the world to go drinking in?
London – lots of different high class bars and restaurants; it's a city with history and the centre of European culture.

What changes have you seen in the Russian cocktail scene?
It changes very much: five years ago it was just about five bars. Now there are 15 good bars in Moscow, and guests are starting to understand the classics. In terms of trends for Russia, we are seeing more use of local products. It is more interesting to use our local products (for instance seabuckthorn, kvas [a fermented drink using black or rye bread], aged honey, baked Russian apple, red basil, birch cordial, dried apricots and lots more) and to share our culture all over the world, which is really starting to happen.

Take us on a great bar crawl drinking in Moscow...
Ok! To start, **Delicatessen** (see opposite), where I would drink a Pedro Manhattan – rum infused with cherries – and then a White Lady. I would end up in my bar, **Mr Help**, where I would drink a Cranberry Beeswax Old Fashioned and an Iron Lady – rum infused with two kinds of Russian plums and cranberry.

DMITRY'S FAVOURITE HANGOUTS ACROSS RUSSIA:

✖
Delicatessen, Moscow (see opposite)
A small bar and restaurant with amazing food and cocktails, as well as a great atmosphere.

✖
Apotheke Bar, Saint-Petersburg (hatgroup.ru/apotheke-bar)
A small cocktail bar with a big collection of whisky and rum.

✖
Chainaya, Moscow (see opposite)
The first neo-speakeasy bar in a Chinese style, with a rare tea collection.

✖
Moonshine Bar, Vladivostock (+7 (423) 207 70 51)
The first cocktail bar in the East of Russia. Amazing Russian seafood and a big collection of spirits.

FOCUS*

STARTENDER
ELIZAVETA EVDOKIMOVA

After cutting her teeth on the bar scene at Moscow's highly lauded Delicatessen for five years (see page 124), Elizaveta Evdokimova has gone on to consult for two new restaurants in the city (**Garden** and **Twins**) and, in 2017, embarked on a life-changing move to Shanghai to work alongside Chinese bartending giant Shingo Gokan on a new project.

Take us on your ultimate night out in Moscow...
Well, there could be more than one scenario of a perfect day out but today, let's pretend that it is a lovely summer's day and we'll be walking about! You could start with a raspberry G&T or one of the homemade infusions in **Delicatessen** before dinner, then drink a Pedro Manhattan with your food and finish it with a famous chiki-pookie shot.

Afterward, you could check out the famous **Chainaya Tea & Cocktails** (see page 124). Here, you should definitely drink the bartender's choice and try the food (even if you are full). Finish your evening in this bar with a shot of rum (but don't forget to buy one for the bartender!)

Well, my friend, checking the time, it is almost 3am [*we like this bar crawl!*] so you could have a nice 20-minute walk to **Noor** (noorbar.com). They have a great DJ and the bar is quite busy so if you don't want to waste your time in the waiting line for a fancy cocktail, just order a G&T (or it might be better to order two). When you decide that you are ready for another, 10-minute walk, go to the **Time Out RooftopBar** (timeout-bar. ru), and as it is now almost 5am [*crikey!*] you could watch the sunrise and drink a glass of sparkling wine. It's worth trying to convince the bartender to allow you to *sabre* the bottle, if you dare! So after a few more glasses of something sparkly, you *could* go home..or, if you want more, there is always **Barfly** (see right).

ELIZAVETA'S OTHER RUSSIAN FAVS:

✖
El Copitas, St Petersburg
(+7 (812) 941 71 68)
Small mezcaleria from super cool bartenders with so many small details and a very clear conception. And of course the best bar team in Russia.

✖
Public bar, Moscow
(+7 (925) 597 10 43)
The most intelligent bar in Moscow with beautiful and elaborate cocktails. If you want to feel the spirit of modern Moscow, you definitely need to check this place out.

✖
Kabinet, St. Petersburg
(+7 (911) 921 19 44)
Outstanding speakeasy bar with Bohemian guests and good drinks. If you want to go there, be sure that you have a tuxedo in your luggage!

✖
Barfly Booze & Noodles, Moscow (+7 (495) 650 27 79)
A legendary dive bar which opens 24/7 – plus they have really nice noodles!

MOSCOW*

MR HELP & FRIENDS →

Being a genuine pioneer is a tricky thing these days, as you'll usually discover someone else doing something similar, given our "glocalization" thanks to the web. However, for Dmitry Sokolov (see page 125), opening a decent, forward-thinking cocktail bar in Moscow must have seemed like a huge challenge indeed. As the youngest winner of the Bacardi Martini Grand Prix World Finals cocktail competition back in 2003, all eyes were on this new and talented bartender and his first bar – Mr Help & Friends was opened in 2004 and is arguably the first contemporary take on a cocktail bar in Russia.

Today, the place is a busy haven for anyone wanting a good time and a decent drink. The classics are catered for and, in addition, Dmitry has enlisted some incredible signature drinks from other star turns in the bartending world, including crackers like the Bare Faced Liar from Dead Rabbit's Jack McGarry (see page 212) and the Hunter from

Japanese bartending royalty, Hidetsugu Ueno of Bar High Five (see page 133). As Dmitry's empire grows, so does the confidence and quality of Russia's blossoming bar scene.

✖

1-ya Tverskaya-Yamskaya ul., 27, cmp.1, Moscow
+7 (495) 627 67 36 mrhelpbar.ru

✖

IN THREE WORDS:
Helping Palates Expand.

THE DRINK TO TRY:
Cranberry Beeswax Old Fashioned.

WE SAY:
Mr Help has come to represent the changing standards and times of Russian's vibrant cocktail scene.

PRICE RATING: ✱ ✱

Mr Help & Friends was opened in 2004 and is arguably the first contemporary take on a cocktail bar in Russia.

ASIA*

Countries

INTRO*

Perhaps the most diverse continent in the world when it comes to drinks culture, Asia is a cocktail of styles, flavours and inspiration. Historically, Japan has lead the way in terms of the sheer number of timeless bars, and over the next few pages you'll read about some of the finest examples currently taking service and innovation in the use of ingredients to a completely new level.

Casting the net further, Kyoto is also forging its own identity as an unmissable destination on the cocktail scene. Alongside

the more traditional whisky bars, you'll find the same sort of reverence for gin, and inspiring bars, such as the tiny **Nokishita Edible Garden**, have explored gin's botanical bonanza to create an unforgettable experience. The city also has its own micro gin distillery and is a short drive away from Yamasaki, arguably the founding fathers of the Japanese whisky scene. Finally, for genuine theatrics, **L'Escamoteur** (see page 141) brings smoke, mirrors and great drinks to another level of trickery.

The newly emerging drinks scene in Singapore is also hotting up, with many insiders predicting that the city-state is to become an influential player in the years to come and the unique, awe-inspiring creations at bars, such as **Operation Dagger** (see

page 156) point to a very bright – and tasty – future indeed.

From here, the cocktail renaissance across China continues apace and Shanghai in particular is developing its own inimitable style. Let's not forget the outstanding contribution from Taiwan too, alongside the growing interest in mixed drinks, craft beer and straight spirits, which is spreading out across the vast expanse of India.

TOKYO*

Enjoying the bar culture in Tokyo is also a wonderfully intense experience. There are scores of bars to visit on every street corner, some only big enough to accommodate a handful of guests, in the most unlikely of locations, such as office blocks, apartment buildings – even in the basements of shops, with their very own Beatles tribute band (abbeyroad.ne.jp)! Special mention needs to go to the Golden Gai area of Shinjuku ↗↓ – a concentrated area of some of the most insane, and tiny, bars you will ever come across, which stay bustling from 5pm until around 6am. Some resemble a front room with just a handful of bottles. Others, like **Bar Albatross** (alba-s.com) – our pick of the area for non-Japanese speakers – pack so much detail, including glitzy chandeliers and Tequila cocktails, into a compact space, that it brings a new meaning to Small Is Beautiful. *Kampai* ("Cheers")!

Special mention needs to go to the Golden Gai area of Shinjuku – a concentrated area of some of the most insane, and tiny, bars you will ever come across.

BAR BENFIDDICH

Something is bubbling away... strange herbaceous aromas hang in the air; glass jars containing all manner of extracts, infusions, lotions and potions line the top shelf of the back bar. What is this sorcery!? What we have in fact is Hiroyasu Kayama, the legend-in-waiting-cum-herbalist/chemist at work in his laboratory, Bar Benfiddich. The bar was opened back in 2013 and since then it has garnered a reputation for, shall we say, all things unusual. Top of Kayama's list of playthings are long-lost herbal liqueurs from another era, and he also recreates some classic flavours for himself. It's no surprise then that these make up a large proportion of his drinks, so any visit should be tempered with a curiosity to try a completely unknown flavour. Sit at the bar and you'll probably get to see the pestle and mortar at work, too. If it has the same inspiring effect as it did for us, you'll be heading down to your local kitchenware shop when you return home to buy yourself a box load of infusing jars....

✖
1-13-7 Nishishinjuku, 9F Yamatoya Bldg, Shinjuku 160-0023 Tokyo +81 3 6279 4223
✖
IN THREE WORDS:
Infused With Character.
THE DRINK TO TRY:
Something using Kayama's homemade Campari or Chartreuse.
THEY SAY:
"Benfiddich might just be the perfect bar."
—REMY SAVAGE, PARIS
PRICE RATING: ✱✱✱

BAR HIGH FIVE ↑

When you ask nearly 100 bartenders, drinks industry professionals and other assorted experts for their ultimate drinking havens, you expect there to be perhaps a little overlap on one or two bars. In the case of Bar High Five, located in the Ginza district (also home to the sensational Star Bar – see page 138), there seems to be a unanimous consensus on just how wonderful the place is. Run by the impeccably dressed Hidetsugu Ueno, High Five is the sort of bar which redefines any perception of craftsmanship one may have about cocktails. In his hands, any drink looks, feels and tastes like a work of art; from the precariously carved ice diamonds that are effortlessly slipped into a highball glass, to the simplicity of creating an elegantly stirred Martini, the calm poise on offer is quite mesmerizing to experience.

As you might expect with this level of establishment, there is no specific theme to the drinks, or menu as such: if there's something you are particularly looking for, they will deliver a stunning version, regardless of its complexity. The house specials really are just that: from the Full Bloom, a whisky or gin-based drink with sakura liqueur, maraschino liqueur and roasted tea bitters; to the simple Japanese classic, the Bamboo Cocktail, bringing together fino sherry, dry vermouth and orange bitters, everything is balanced to the highest degree.

If you had to choose just one bar to visit in Tokyo, we would say...impossible. But we'd be dragged kicking and screaming to the airport if we hadn't had another chance to visit the heady heights of High Five.

✖
Efflore Ginza5 Bldg, BF, 5-4-15, Ginza Chuo-ward Tokyo 104-0061 +81 3 3571 5815 barhighfive.com
✖
IN THREE WORDS:
Summit Of Skill.
THE DRINK TO TRY:
Plump for one of the specials – every one is unique.
THEY SAY:
"Hidetsugu Ueno's Martini is always my first order when I get there and it has never let me down."
— STEVEN LIN, TAIPEI
PRICE RATING: ✱✱✱

TOKYO*

BAR ORCHARD

A departure from the fast-paced claustrophobia that inner city Tokyo can bring, this Ginza gem focuses its attentions on a natural element, coupled with a dose of theatrics to entertain. And entertain it does. A number of the drinks incorporate fresh seasonal fruit, and rigid formality has been replaced by laid-back perfection, despite being located on the third floor of a nondescript office building. Raw peat, collapsible Japanese lanterns and caramelized figs all play a role in the highly engaging, creative cocktails served without pretension in a casual living-room-like setting. Genuinely refreshing and innovative stuff.

✖
6-5-16 Ginza, Chuo 104-0061, Tokyo +81 3 3575 0333
✖

IN THREE WORDS:
Garden Of Delight.

THE DRINK TO TRY:
The award-winning Perfume No.10, Takuo Miyanohara's signature drink.

THEY SAY:
"This was the ultimate experience in what can only be called modern-day Japanese hospitality."
— LIZA WEISSTUCH, NEW YORK

PRICE RATING: ✳✳✳

BAR TENDER GINZA

The Theatre of the Bar is a concept which many a great-mixologist-in-waiting so often seems to trivialize (see page 42 for our interview with cocktail legend Peter Dorelli on this very subject) or neglect completely, focusing on brash ingredients and flavours to tame the palate and dazzle the eyes. This is not seemingly a concept shared by Kazuo Uyeda, Japanese bartending legend and founder of Bar Tender back in 1997. His finely tuned ethos is to master the subtleties, nuances and micro detail of everything cocktail: from holding the shaker to pouring spirit from a jigger and gently stirring one's ice. Uyeda-san is widely credited as developing the Hard Shake technique (he's even written a book on the subject, that no bartender should be without), which, for the right drink, perfectly aerates and dilutes the contents of the shaker. With all this in mind, you get the picture that a drink in Tender

is like visiting another plane of existence in the cocktail world. The interior isn't flash or contemporary and the drinks themselves lack the sheer "wow" that is present in the other luminaries of the Tokyo cocktail scene, but it's hard to deny that absolutely mastery is at work in the balance of flavour and technique on offer. To see a white-coated bartender wielding a shaker in close-up, with all the precision of a samurai, makes a trip to Tender an absolute essential.

✖
Ginza Noh Theatre Bldg, 5f, 6-5-15 Ginza, Chuo-ku, Tokyo 104-0061 +81 3 3571 8343
✖

IN THREE WORDS:
Try a Little Tenderness.

THE DRINK TO TRY:
One of Uyeda-San's signatures – particularly The City Coral.

THEY SAY:
"A fantastic bar. This is where classic drinks gain perfection and guest service is second to none."
— MARIAN BEKE, UK

PRICE RATING: ✳✳✳✳

FOCUS*

STARTENDER
ROGERIO IGARASHI VAZ

Rogerio Igarashi Vaz is one half of the duo behind Small Axe Inc: a company in possession of one of Tokyo's finest bars, **Trench** (see page 136) and quite possibly the best-dressed man you'll ever see behind the stick. His mastery of local flavour, his love of discovering lost classics and his encyclopedic knowledge of absinthe have helped to create a global reputation for his drinks and impeccable service.

Tell us a little about Bar Trench.
Trench is well known for absinthe, but it is more than that; it is more than just cocktails, too. We used to have 140 different absinthes but we've cut this down to make room for other spirits. As we are located in a tiny street with high ceilings – we have a unique venue for Japan. It's called Trench because it is a place to rest, before you move on to the next stage. Maybe this is what makes Trench so special.
Take us through one of your signature cocktails.
We have plenty of signature cocktails but I'd choose one called Almost Dirty, which is a super-dry cocktail based around bamboo with celery bitters and mini tomatoes. It brings together sherry and vermouth at its heart.
Tell us about your favourite night out in Tokyo.
My ideal night out in Tokyo would be to start in the Ginza district for a drink, because it is formal, classic and you can have a good conversation. I'd then move on to another area like Shibuya, where Bar Trench is based, as there are many restaurants and more casual bars. To finish, I'd head over to the bar I have in my top five, **Qwang**, as that district is full of great clubs, too.

✖
You can read more about Rogerio's bar projects at small-axe.net

ROGERIO'S TOP FIVE BARS TO VISIT:

✖
Bar Qwang, Tokyo (qwang.sakura.ne.jap)
I've been going to Bar Qwang for about 13 years. They do great Thai food and have a fantastic selection of rums. It would be the first bar on any list I would make.

✖
Happiness Forgets, London (see page 36) *This is a cosy place, where everyone always wants to help you, even when it is busy.*

✖
Dersou, Paris (dersouparis.com) *This food pairing place in Paris called Dersou is great. It was relaxing and the food pairings worked brilliantly.*

✖
The Savoy, London (see page 22) *The American Bar has such history and is just a fantastic place to go drinking.*

✖
Oriole, London (see page 43) *I love the live bands and the Latin feel to the place. A great atmosphere plus great cocktails, which is what it is all about!*

TOKYO*

BAR TRENCH

Rather like the Ginza district of Tokyo, famed for its highly progressive micro-bars (see Star Bar on page 138 and Orchard on page 134), Shibuya can lay claim to a few absolute gems of its own, and Trench (along with its sister bar, Tram) arguably sits, somewhat ironically, at the top of the pile. With tradition at its heart, Trench is a very serious bar, specializing in absinthe – but pretty much every other spirit too – where the presentation and precision of every drink are calculated to the final degree. Under the watchful eye of the terrifically coiffured Rogerio Igarashi Vaz (see page 135), the enigmatic La Fée Verte is served in perfect historical glassware, louched with chilled water, then dripped slowly from vintage fountains through a dazzling array of vintage absinthe spoons. There's a sense of theatre here, and the ritualistic element to this often misunderstood spirit is firmly embraced. Close your eyes, breathe in the herbaceous notes from your glass and take a refreshing sip…and for a split second, there's nowhere on earth that transports you back to the Belle Époque quite like Trench.

✖

1F, 1-5-8 Ebisu-nishi, Shibuya-ku, Tokyo +81 3 3780 5291
small-axe.net

✖

IN THREE WORDS:
Drip, Drip, Sip.

THE DRINK TO TRY:
One of the many historical recreations of absinthe.

THEY SAY:
"An absolutely amazing bar, where the traditional Japanese bartending and laid-back atmosphere are mingling with great music."
— **KRISZTIÁN CSIGÓ,**
BUDAPEST

PRICE RATING: ✱ ✱ ✱

CAMPBELLTOUN LOCH ↓

An extraordinary bar. Finding the Campbelltoun Loch isn't easy, but once you've located the wrought-iron steps down into this basement hangout, past the carved wooden entry sign, you know you've found whisky perfection. For a whisky connoisseur, just the empty bottles that sit stacked around the entrance are enough to evoke a few tears, alongside a tingle of excitement about what they haven't opened yet. The bar itself is a tiny rectangular room, with enough space for just ten guests, where you'll find a veritable feast of rare and ancient single malts from all over the world. Ask nicely and you may get to try

small measures of these priceless treasures for a fraction of the cost of a full glass. Miss this and your trip to Tokyo will be incomplete.

✘

Matsui Bldg B1, 1-6-8 Yurakucho Chiyoda-ku, Tokyo +81 3 3501 5305

✘

IN THREE WORDS:
Rarity In Abundance.
THE DRINK TO TRY:
One of the bar's signature own-bottled Islay malts.
THEY SAY:
"Simply the most chaotic corridor dedicated to rare single malt in the world."
— DAVE BROOM, UK
WE SAY:
The place to know your Laphroaigs from your Karuizawas.
PRICE RATING: ✱ ✱ ✱

HELMSDALE BRASSERIE & BAR

One would usually be correct to recoil in horror at the words "theme pub", with their gaudy and inaccurate attempts to recreate a little taste of home for the mildly xenophobic tourist. Fortunately, there are no such problems at the Helmsdale, which is essentially a Scottish pub in Shibuya...and what a pub it is. The attention to detail is superb, with a stunning array of vintage and rare Scottish single malts, draft cask-conditioned ales (with the occasional guest ale) and vaguely Scottish-influenced food, including fresh seafood, venison and bizarrely the Scotch egg (technically invented in London by Messrs Fortnum & Mason, but full marks for trying!). Come along with your tongue firmly

in your cheek, but be prepared to be amazed at the whiskies on offer. The open-air sister site in Karuizawa (complete with takeaway fish and chips!) is equally quirky.

✘

Minami-Aoyama Mori Bldg, 2F 7-13-12, Minato-ku, Aoyama, Tokyo +81 3 3486 4220 helmsdale-fc.com

✘

IN THREE WORDS:
Theme Done Well.
THE DRINK TO TRY:
Undoubtedly one of the many single malt whiskies on offer.
WE SAY:
Scotland's cuisine curated for the non-Scottish traveller. A reminder of just why the place is still so revered internationally.
PRICE RATING: ✱ ✱ ✱

If you're looking for the heart and soul of whisky culture in Japan, this is it. A classic.

MARUGIN ←

It seems quite lazy to start this review with "if you only pick one place to drink a Highball..." but there really is no other way. Marugin is *the* original highball bar (whisky and soda), where Japan's drinking phenomenon started. The vibe is *tachinomi* (standing) – busy, bustling and noisy. Chicken wire lines the walls, along with vintage adverts for the drink of choice, Suntory's Kakubin whisky. In the centre of the room lie the bar and kitchen – where glass mugs of foaming glory are dispensed from a brass tap. Try the yuzu, honey and ginger version, or the Mega Highball, a huge glass that will make your friends very size conscious. As you sip this liquid perfection, order skewers of chicken hearts, edamame, freshly sliced tomato with salt and roughly chopped cabbage with a dipping sauce.

✘

7–1 Ginza, Chuo-ku, Tokyo +81 3-3571-8989

✘

IN THREE WORDS:
Heavenly Highball Haven.
THE DRINK TO TRY:
A Suntory Highball: Kakubin whisky, soda and ice.
WE SAY:
The heart and soul of whisky culture in Japan. A classic.
PRICE RATING: ✱ ✱

137

TOKYO*

MORI BAR

Like his contemporaries at Bar Tender (see page 134) and Star Bar (see right), Takao Mori has taken the concept of career bartending very seriously indeed. When you consider the transient nature of a bar, it's little wonder that in the western world, bartending has been seen as anything but a steady career. But in Japan, the craftsmanship and reverence reserved for the elder statesmen of the bartending world is truly staggering. Mori-san has been making drinks for decades before the term "molecular mixology" was ever a phrase, and his simple, fluid movements behind the bar, creating alluring, perfect classics, are a sight to behold. Mori Bar is a conservative place – wear the wrong clothes and you won't be welcome, or turn up half-cut and you'll be frowned upon – but to be able to simply sit at the bar and watch a master at work, pouring you a Martini, puts the word bartending into real perspective. Sometimes a whisper can be far more effective at leaving a lasting impression than someone screaming at you.

✖

Niibori Guitar Bldg 10F, 6-5-12 Ginza, Chuo-ku, 104-0061 Tokyo +81 3 3573 0610

✖

IN THREE WORDS:
Mastery, Mr Mori.
THE DRINK TO TRY:
A Mori Martini.
THEY SAY:
"A little hard to find, but it is well worth looking for if you're in Ginza."
— ALEX DAVIES, KYOTO
PRICE RATING: ✱✱✱✱

STAR BAR

Within seconds of entering Star Bar, located in the vibrant Ginza district, you are transported back to the decadence of the 1930s and some of the most elegant drinks you are ever likely to be served. Seating around 20 people, Star Bar does "classic" like no other. In many ways, it is as if some of the great drinks of yesteryear were actually invented just for the sheer pleasure of watching them being made under the total mastery of the maestro himself – owner and legendary Japanese barman Kishi-san. Try Kishi's Manhattan (perfectly balanced on the precipice between rich, sweet and an indescribable, deft dryness) and you'll never look at the drink in the same way again. As with Campbelltoun Loch (see page 136), the whisky selection (some 300+ bottles) is also worth a few moments of gazing/weeping over. If you only have one night in Tokyo, beat a path to the Star Bar and get ready for Kishi's broad, beaming smile at the door – but we recommend phoning ahead for a table or a seat at the bar.

✖

Sankosha Bldg B1F, 1-5-13 Ginza, Chuo-ku, Tokyo +81 3 3535 8005 starbar.jp

✖

IN THREE WORDS:
Timeless Cocktail Perfection.
THE DRINK TO TRY:
The Manhattan, or Kishi's Ramos Gin Fizz.
THEY SAY:
"I could pick 100 bars in Tokyo alone, but this is the one I always return to."
— DAVE BROOM, UK
"Impeccable service and fanatically brilliant drinks. Awesome."
— RYAN CHETIYAWARDANA, AKA MR LYAN, UK
WE SAY:
The elegance of these classics doesn't come much closer to perfection.
PRICE RATING: ✱✱✱✱

STAY UP LATE

Tokyo is undoubtedly one of the most unique cities when it comes to bar culture, and Stay Up Late perhaps typifies the rich diversity the city has been celebrated for. This third-floor bar is difficult to find, and, as with many of the microbars in the Shimbashi district, it fills up very quickly, with just 10 seats at the bar. But the most remarkable feature is the wall of 6,000 CDs, which play a very important part in the theme of the bar. Before you are served a drink, you must select a favourite rock track from the exhaustive collection, which the owner, Yuji Okumura (aka the "Human Jukebox") will select with encyclopedic precision. The bar serves a range of Japanese craft beers and whiskies, with the classic Highball serve proving popular among its many regulars. As the name would suggest, you can go some way to working through your favourite rock classics with last orders way into the small hours.

✖

2F, 7-29-7 Nishi-Kamata, Ota-ku, Tokyo stayuplate.jp

✖

IN THREE WORDS:
Select, Drink, Rock-out.

THE DRINK TO TRY:
Okhotsk Blue Ryuho Draft from the Abashiri Brewing Company in Hokkaido.

WE SAY:
(Probably) the only place in the world where you can drink with Cheap Trick, A Flock Of Seagulls and Meatloaf and not feel remotely ashamed.

PRICE RATING: ✱ ✱

ZOETROPE ↑

An intriguing bar, which is named after the ancient spinning cylindrical device that gives an illusion of a moving image. However, there are no illusions here as you stare at the incredibly well-stocked back bar with a good few hundred rare Japanese single malts. Zoetrope is probably one of Tokyo's leading bars in this field, lovingly curated and cared for by the owner, Atsushi Horigami. Enjoy one of his many whisky recommendations while watching old films from the age of silent movies, which are projected onto the back wall. A very unique experience indeed and certainly top of the visitors' list for any Japanese whisky aficionado.

✖

Gaia Bldg #4 3F, 7-10-14 Nishi Shinjuku, Shinjuku-ku +81 3 3363 0162

✖

IN THREE WORDS:
Film Meets Booze.

THE DRINK TO TRY:
The Hanyu Card Series Japanese whiskies.

THEY SAY:
"The smallest (in room size) whisky bar I've ever been to. But a large selection of amazing whisky."
— JANE OVEREEM, TASMANIA

PRICE RATING: ✱ ✱ ✱ ✱

OSAKA*

Osaka is Japan's second largest city and also plays home to the largest business area in the country. But after the sun sets on the numerous pristine glass-panelled skyscrapers, Osaka has a wonderful nightlife, from traditional restaurants to a burgeoning community of bars, serving cocktails, beers, sake and Japanese whisky. Much like Tokyo, the best bars have managed to stay in business by establishing a niche and becoming recognized as leading authorities in their particular field of drink, including whisky, tequila, sake, shochu and everything in between.

BAR AUGUSTA

Heading into the Kansai region of Osaka will undoubtedly bring you face-to-face with many irresistible treats – from a spirits perspective, none more so than Bar Augusta. On offer is another exceptional range of original cocktails, with classics the order of the day, but with a close eye on the current trend toward perfectly mixed whisky Highballs – all tenderly served by immacuately attired staff. Rather like Star Bar in Tokyo (see page 138), Augusta brings a wonderful sense of the old-fashioned right into the 21st century.
✖
Arakawa Bldg 1F, 2–3 Turuno-cho, Kita-ku, Osaka +81 6 6376 3455 bar-augusta.com
✖
IN THREE WORDS:
Osaka's Sublime Service.
THE DRINK TO TRY:
A classic Japanese Highball.
WE SAY:
A demonstration of why Japan's bartending is not just a profession, it's a way of life.
PRICE RATING: ✹✹✹

ROGIN'S TAVERN

Rogin's is the sort of bar that typifies a wonderful obsession within Japanese bar culture to be the very best in their particular field. In this case, it is American whiskey, specifically bourbon. The nondescript sign on the outside does little to indicate anything other than that you are about to enter a bourbon bar, but once you're inside, a wealth of absolute treasures awaits you. Their extensive bourbon list even dates back to some highly sought after pre-Prohibition bottlings, as well as many small batch bourbons, vintage rye whiskeys and award-winning whiskeys from all over the USA.
✖
Moriguchi, Honmachi, Osaka +81 6 6997 3200
✖
IN THREE WORDS:
Kentucky Fried Sushi.
THE DRINK TO TRY:
A Sazerac rye whiskey on the rocks.
WE SAY:
The sheer "time capsule nature" of some of the old bourbons here is worth saving up for.
PRICE RATING: ✹✹✹✹

KYOTO*

CAAMM BAR

Standing for Creative Alcohol And Mood Music, this should really tell you everything you need to know about what lies within, but if you still have doubts, they'll immediately dissipate as soon as you poke your head through the 1970s-style beaded door curtain. One of Kyoto's real hidden gems, located on the second floor of what looks like an apartment building, it is owned by Yoshihiro Tabuchi, who has assembled what can only be described as a spirits library with thousands of bottles (mostly whisky) spanning all walls of the bar. With such an extensive spirit selection it's almost tempting to try and outfox the barman and ask for something really obscure, but we guarantee you'll probably come off the loser.

✖
Kiyamachi-Dori Sanjo Agaru Higashigawa, Nakagyo-Ku, 2F Yurika Bldg, Kyoto 604-0961 +81 75 212 2202
✖
IN THREE WORDS:
Library Of Spirits.

THE DRINK TO TRY:
One of the rare independently bottled whiskies.
THEY SAY:
"With such an extensive spirit selection, this is a great place to go solo, bring friends or to take a date."
— ALEX DAVIES, KYOTO
PRICE RATING: ✱✱✱

L'ESCAMOTEUR ⬇

Utterly bonkers. While some bars can come across a little wacky – and not in a good way – heading up the steps into L'Escamoteur brings on a tingle of excitement. It's part Alice in Wonderland, coupled with a dash of Victorian apothecary and a big dose of Abracadabra thrown in for good measure – everything you would expect from a place named "The Conjurer". The bar is nuts to look at: knick-knacks are strewn everywhere and there's plenty of

Victorian glassware, and vintage cocktail paraphernalia slung around by a top-hat-wearing team. The drinks themselves are magic – in every sense of the word. Owner Christophe Rossi was a professional magician before becoming a bartender, and he has applied the same out-of-this-world approach to his concoctions: smoke, magic flash paper, science lab equipment and a little conjuring are all used to great effect. This is bartending, sleight-of-hand style!

✖
Kyoto-shi Saiseki-dori Shijo sagaru 138 banchi 9, Saitocho, Shimogyo Ward, Kyoto 600-8012 +81 75 708 8511
✖
IN THREE WORDS:
Magicial Mystery Tour.
THE DRINK TO TRY:
The Shiso Sour or The Smoky Old Fashioned.
THEY SAY:
"Their menu is my favourite in Japan so far, with a mix of classics and signature drinks."
— ALEX DAVIES, KYOTO
PRICE RATING: ✱✱

KYOTO, SAPPORO & NAGASAKI*

THE MARBLE ROOM

A very retro-modernist approach to bar culture and design. The decor looks like a 1950s take on the future, with lots of large cushions to laze around on and bucket-style seats for the more austere drinkers. By day, they serve a range of coffees, teas and cakes, and in summer you can step outside onto a small balcony and gaze down on the Komo River below. At night the atmosphere changes into full-on cocktail mode as the best-dressed and affluent members of Kyoto's hip scene gather to try the latest creations.

✖

135 Nakagyo-Ku Pontocho Sanjo-sagaru, Pontocho Biru 4F
+ 81 75 213 0753

✖

IN THREE WORDS:
Casual Kyoto Escapism.
THE DRINK TO TRY:
An outstanding coffee or local IPA.
WE SAY:
Perfect for idling away an evening in zen-like thought, with a few great drinks.
PRICE RATING: ✱ ✱

ROCKING CHAIR ↑

The concept of the speakeasy has been well explored throughout this book and most of the very best ones are hiding in plain sight. However, Rocking Chair is such a pig to find if you haven't been there before that it might as well be classed as a speakeasy too. With its comfortable seating in the style of an old house, complete with several rocking chairs, it's very easy to feel right at home here and the drinks are out of this world. Again, much in the style of some of the best Tokyo bars, you simply tell them the spirit you like and they will find something you'll fall in love with (English is not really an option here, so keep it simple). There's even a selection of different ports, which might seem incongruous, but is the perfect fit at the same time.

✖

434-2 Tachibana-cho, Bukkoji-sagura, Gokomachi-dori, Shimogya-ku, Kyoto
+81 75 496 8679
bar-rockingchair.jp

✖

IN THREE WORDS:
Rockin' The Joint.
THE DRINK TO TRY:
An amazing concoction using Bowmore smoky whisky, Benedictine and Jagermeister!
THEY SAY:
"A seriously comfortable and classy place to stop in after dinner."
— ALEX DAVIES, KYOTO
PRICE RATING: ✱✱

BOW BAR

Whatever their location, the best bars in the world take the drinker on a journey of discovery: some into the flavours and culture that surround them, others to locations far away, giving a hint or a theme, often telling a story along the way. Bow Bar does something a little different. In fact, this little whisky bar based in Sapporo city transports the drinker effectively back in time, thanks to the insanely good selection of rare whiskies on offer. By rare, we don't simply mean long-since-depleted limited edition bottlings, but whiskies from another time altogether.

Here you'll find Scotch blends and single malts dating back

to the 1930s and 1940s – once *everyday* whiskies from long since closed and demolished distilleries. Each time you peer into the glass, you take in the aroma of a bygone era, highlighting just how far whisky has come since then.

✖

Floor 8, Hoshi Bldg, 7–5 Minami4, Nishi2, Chuo-ku, Sapporo +81 11 532 1212
thebowbar-sapporo.com

✖

IN THREE WORDS:
Time-Travelling Whisky.
THE DRINK TO TRY:
Try a vintage bottle of whisky, side by side with a more modern expression.

Each time you peer into the glass, you take in the aroma of a bygone era, highlighting just how far whisky has come since then.

THEY SAY:
"When having a drink here, it seems I become a historian, falling into a time tunnel. Amazing!"
— STEVEN LIN, TAIPEI
PRICE RATING: ✱✱✱✱

COCKTAIL BAR JOY

Not necessarily the first destination of the classic cocktail afficionado, but this bar is a must-see due to the superb amount of mixology on display and the 500 bottles of vodka and gin available. Every concoction from the Singapore Sling to the Japanese version of a Piña Colada is catered for with a typically Japanese sense of refinement and sophistication. With classic jazz cuts providing a wonderful drinking soundtrack, this bar is at the height of its powers and represents a modern take on a bygone era.

✖

With Bldg 7F 10-21 Hamanomachi Nagasaki, 850-0853 +81 958 26 5014

✖

IN THREE WORDS:
Gin, Tonic, Joy.
THE DRINK TO TRY:
A refreshing G&T, followed by a wonderfully made Singapore Sling.
WE SAY:
Be prepared to take a seat and idle the night away, perusing some very authentic classic cocktails.
PRICE RATING: ✱✱

SHANGHAI*

BAR CONSTELLATION

Constellation has grown steadily in popularity over the years, but it still has bags of appeal. With an impressive 500 single malts in stock it's certainly an eye-opener for anyone wanting to explore a drop of the dark, smoky stuff. The bar is also well endowed with other spirits and it has an extensive cocktail menu. As spaces go, it's very low-lit, and, shall we say, "cosy", but the drinks take pride of place and its small size means that it can get pretty busy at times. Go early if you want to ensure getting a seat.

✖

86 Xin le Lu, Xuhui District, Shanghai +86 21 5404 0970

✖

IN THREE WORDS:
Touch The Stars.

THE DRINK TO TRY:
Any of the dazzling, star-studded rare whiskies on offer.

THEY SAY:
"This is the place to head if you're a serious (or even a not so serious) whisky drinker."
— JOSH WANG, CHINA

PRICE RATING: ✺ ✺ ✺

HEYDAY JAZZ BAR ↑

Jazz and cocktails are, of course, inextricably great pairings, and the sultry, velvet-smooth tones of a smoky torch song complement pretty much any classic cocktail. What's surprising is that Shanghai is full of them (jazz bars, that is) and one of the best has to be Heyday. The decor is perfect: chic and in keeping with the style of the bands and the serves, both of which hark back to the golden age of jazz in the 1920s and 1930s. In fact, much like a perfectly formed Cmaj7 chord, every element here is in perfect harmony – from the small plates of light bites to the barrel-aged cocktails. Even if jazz "ain't yo thang", you'll still find something to sing about here.

✖

550 Tai'an Lu, near Xingguo Lu, Shanghai +86 21 6236 6075
heydayjazz.cn

✖

IN THREE WORDS:
Sultry, Soulful Sippin'.

THE DRINK TO TRY:
One of the barrel-aged cocktails.
THEY SAY:
"They excel in every aspect including the drink, food, music and environment."
— DEREK CHANG, CHINA
PRICE RATING: ✳✳✳✳

LAB WHISKY & COCKTAIL

This awesome split-level whisky bar has a reputation for being a serious contender in a whisky-fuelled, connoisseur-led Shanghai night out. Yes, it may appear a little intimidating for the uninitiated, but one thing that Lab does brilliantly is to help demystify the complexity of whisky (arguably created by other whisky connoisseurs) and allow the genuine flavours to flourish. Alongside the strong selection of single malts from Scotland and Japan are a number of whisky cocktails that playfully deliver on the style of the whisky. If you're a fan of smoky stylings, the Laphroaig Project plays on the distinctly medicinal notes well, but balances them with more herbaceous flavours.

✘
1093 Wuding Lu, near Jiaozhou Lu, Jingan District, Shanghai +86 21 6255 1195
✘
THREE WORDS:
Precision Whisky University.
THE DRINK TO TRY:
Start with the Old Fashioned.
THEY SAY:
"The first professional whisky bar in Shanghai and the model others pursue."
— STEVEN LIN, TAIPEI
PRICE RATING: ✳✳✳

OJI

If bars were Russian dolls Oji would be the tiny doll, right at the centre. This new offering from Japanese bartender Naoji Oji opened in 2016, and is a bar within a bar – which is a neat concept. Oji is well hidden inside another highly regarded bar (El Ocho) and when you do locate it – we won't spoil it for you – it's a find and a half. No menu, but don't let that put you off, the team here will whip you up something outstanding using whatever spirit you desire.

✘
3F, Bldg A, 99 Taixing Lu, near Wujiang Lu, Jingan District, Shanghai +86 131 6277 3450
✘
IN THREE WORDS:
Pick Up the Phone.
THE DRINK TO TRY:
Oji's Whisky Sour.
THEY SAY:
"A bar inside another bar. Oji has quickly become one of the most sought-after Japanese craft cocktail bars in Shanghai."
— DEREK CHANG, CHINA
PRICE RATING: ✳✳✳✳

If bars were Russian dolls Oji would be the tiny doll, right at the centre.

UNION TRADING COMPANY

Clearly when great minds think alike, even greater things occur, and Union Trading Company typifies this scenario perfectly. The bar, opened in 2014, is the brainchild of chef Austin Hu (the man behind American-styled restaurant Madison) and Yao Lu (see page 146), one of the luminaries and architects of Shanghai's explosion of fabulous cocktail bars (formerly the creative force behind popular joints Alchemist and The Public).

The duo have come together delivering double the creativity with a highly inventive cocktail list, which regularly changes, reflecting the spontaneity and vision of the staff. Expect big bold drinks, but also beautifully garnished masterpieces, all delivered with a mastery of knowledge in the spirits department.

✘
Bldg 2, 64 Fenyang Lu, near Fuxing Zhong Lu, Xuhui District, Shanghai +86 21 6418 3077
✘
IN THREE WORDS:
Union Of Perfection.
THE DRINK TO TRY:
At the time of writing, the Fuxing Spritz.
WE SAY:
An absolute bartending delight!
PRICE RATING: ✳✳

FOCUS*

STARTENDER
YAO LU

Texan born Yao Lu is the co-owner of Union Trading Company in Shanghai (see page 145). In the relatively short space of time since the bar opened (back in 2104), it has been awarded numerous "Best New Bar" accolades. In addition to his drive for innovative new flavours in cocktails, Yao is responsible for developing extensive bar-training programmes across China and in his native USA.

Where do you drink when you're off duty?
I usually drink at my own bar, to be honest. Most of our guests turn out to be close friends and it's almost like hosting a house party every time I'm hanging out. If I have to pick one outside of the Union, it's probably **Speak Low** (579 Fuxing Zhong Lu, Huangpu, Shanghai). They are just a couple of blocks down the street and our teams have a great relationship. Those guys not only excel in cocktails but also just happen to be some of the coolest cats in the industry!

Your favourite drink of all time...?
Depends on who I'm vibing with, if you know what I mean.
Where is your favourite city in the world to go drinking in?
As of this very moment, I have to say Shanghai. In the past five years I have seen an incredible development of cocktail culture and a general understanding of what each concept is trying to convey. When I just moved here, every cocktail bar was either Ginza-inspired (see the Tokyo bar profile on page 135) or flair only. Now the scene has blossomed into a creature all of its own, with incredibly talented bartenders and operators each providing something unique for the city. It totally deserves a chair in the modern cocktail city conversation.

YAO'S TOP FIVE DESTINATIONS FOR OUTSTANDING COCKTAILS:

✖

Anvil Bar & Refuge, Houston, Texas (anvilhouston.com) →

I guess you can say this was my alma mater bar – the first bar I worked at that taught me everything I know to become a bartender. Every single one of my co-workers was the best in the city and we all hustled as a team. Without the experience I had with Anvil, I would be nowhere close to where I am right now.

✖

Jigger & Pony, Singapore (see page 155) ↓

A superstar bar team, chill vibes and delicious cocktails.

✖

28 Hong Kong Street, Singapore (see page 154)

One of the first bars that opened my eyes to the attention to detail on service – the way they treat

guests is peerless, and that hip hop soundtrack they have just keeps my head nodding the whole night.

✖

The Pontiac, Hong Kong (13 Old Bailey Street, Central, Hong Kong)

Your neighbourhood dive...meets Coyote Ugly...meets some of the

best cocktails in Hong Kong. This bar represents everything I love – loud music, lively atmosphere, plus delicious cocktails!

✖

Code Name Mixology, Tokyo (r.goope.jp/spirits-sharing)

Let me put it this way, there are absolutely no reasons for any of their cocktails to exist – none of them are necessary and yet I am so glad they do! Everything is insanely delicious, mind blowing and weird. [Bar owner] Shuzo Nagumo is the Japanese Albert Einstein and only he can come up with a Breakfast Martini that literally tastes like tomato, eggs, bacon and black pepper, in that order.

147

HONG KONG*

BUTLER

Discretion, expertise beyond belief and the ability to blend into the background are arguably among the most important virtues for the best butlers. The butler in question here is in possession of all three – and many more. Not only is it well hidden, but it is very small indeed – perfect for an intimate meeting or ultra-quiet drink. This is where Butler really comes into its own: each creation is simply perfect – tailored to the drinker's particular tastes, whether you like your gin and tonic bolder and more robust, or your Manhattan slightly drier than most. This attention to detail is delivered by Masayuki Uchida, a Japanese bartender who sought wider opportunities in Hong Kong and struck gold. The team always delivers, with the modest humility that Japanese bartending is famous for.

✖

5/F, Mody House, 30 Mody Road, Tsim Sha Tsui, Hong Kong +852 2724 3828

✖

IN THREE WORDS:
What Ho, Jeeves!
THE DRINK TO TRY:
Tricky – no matter what, they'll make it exactly to your tastes. But be sure to try the mentaiko spicy cod roe as a snack.
THEY SAY:
"Japanese bar service in Hong Kong; no cocktail is impossible."
— EDDIE NARA, HONG KONG
PRICE RATING: ✱✱✱✱

CHIN CHIN

In terms of whisky bars, Kowloon certainly isn't resting on its laurels, and Chin Chin, situated in the Hyatt Regency Hotel, has over 120 different whiskies from around the world. The decor is an interesting mix of rustic Chinese kitchen vibe and very cosy lounge chairs, perfect for unwinding with an early evening whisky and soda, before moving on to a flight of outstanding single malts or classic cocktails. On a clear evening, the outdoor terrace offers an excellent backdrop of Tsim Sha Tsui at its finest: bright lights, hustle and bustle and the aroma of a city ready to be explored. There's also a live band every night.

✖

3F, Hyatt Regency Hong Kong, 18 Hanoi Road, Tsim Sha Tsui, Hong Kong +852 3721 7722

✖

IN THREE WORDS:
Savour The View.
THE DRINK TO TRY:
A blended Scotch and soda, on the rocks.
THEY SAY:
"One of the best live band performances in Hong Kong... and the whiskies."
— EDDIE NARA, HONG KONG
PRICE RATING: ✱✱✱✱

PING PONG 129 ↗

Located in Hong Kong's Sai Ying Pun district, this is one of a number of bars that are springing up in the area. Away from the well trodden path of Soho and the Central area, the spaces become larger, more malleable and ultimately more roomy – a rarity in this city. Ping Pong's venue is a classic example of this, an old ping pong supply store, which feels incredibly spacey. A "gintoneria" (try saying that after a few cocktails...), it has a distinct focus on gin and tonic, especially the Spanish way of serving in large fish-bowl glasses. Their creativity when it comes to serving is second only to their level of detail, both in the serve and on the list, many of which can only be found in Hong Kong at this bar. There is also a clever and unique selection of tonics, which show off how much a G&T is really a T&G!

✖
129 Second Street, L/G Nam Cheong House, Sai Ying Pun, Hong Kong +852 9835 5061 pingpong129.com
✖
IN THREE WORDS:
Tonic And Gin.
WE SAY:
The place to get some space in Hong Kong. Oh, and a great G&T while you're at it.
PRICE RATING: ✳✳✳✳

QUINARY

The last decade's trend toward innovative, molecular-level cuisine has been a consuming passion for many of the world's finest and most highly regarded chefs. Everyone from Ferran Adrià at the now legendarily brilliant El Bulli to Heston Blumenthal has pushed the boundaries of flavour to the realms of the unknown. In drinks, the same passion for expanding our palates to the back of beyond is also flourishing, and Quinary, in Hong Kong's Central district has,

since 2012, followed in the finely aromatic, smoke-filled footsteps of the aforementioned chefs.

Lead by chief "scientist" Antonio Lai, here you'll find boutique redistilled spirits and infusions, bringing in distinct flavours of the East, alongside elegant classics reimagined and reprised. The bar itself feels comfortable, but at its heart is a metallic-tinged lab mentality, meaning you'll get some of the most finely engineered drinks on the planet.
✖
56–58 Hollywood Road, Central, Hong Kong +852 2851 3223 quinary.hk
✖
IN THREE WORDS:
Science Fiction Flavours.
THE DRINK TO TRY:
The Cinema Set: a sort of perfect 1950s Old Fashioned.
THEY SAY:
"Probably the most innovative cocktail creations in town!"
— **EDDIE NARA, HONG KONG**
"Very hospitable and very efficient."
— **KARL TOO, MALAYSIA**
PRICE RATING: ✳✳✳

SCHNURRBART

You have to admire the chutzpah of Schnurrbart: slap bang in the middle of a busy thoroughfare in a buzzy Hong Kong district, yet seemingly sharing nothing in common with its surroundings. This authentic German brewpub and restaurant has existed for over 25 years and sees no sign of losing its distinct appeal. Despite being over 900 kilometres (over 5,000 miles) from the motherland, Schnurrbart retains a level of authenticity that you don't expect and it certainly hasn't fallen into the "theme-pub" area. With some fabulous Pilsners on offer (the Veltins is outstandingly refreshing) as well as the obligatory flights of revivifying schnapps, it's easy to create your own personal Oktoberfest – albeit with a very different backdrop to Munich.
✖
29 D'Aguilar Street, Central, Hong Kong +852 2523 4700
✖
IN THREE WORDS:
A Wunderbar Bar.
THE DRINK TO TRY:
A few pints of Veltins Pilsner.
THEY SAY:
"Schnurrbart stands out like a sore thumb being an authentic German pub in the heart of Lang Kwai Fong."
— **ALEX KAMMELING, UK**
PRICE RATING: ✳✳

FEATURE*

A DAY OUT DRINKING IN...
HONG KONG

Meet **Steven Notman**, whisky expert and our man on the ground.

Hong Kong is well and truly an international city. Where East meets West. Where drinks, trends and cultures are drawn from Taiwan, Korea and Japan, but equally taking influence from west coast USA – and, of course, London.

Hong Kong offers a versatile nightlife, catering both for people on a slender budget and for those seeking the ultimate decadence in food and drink.

A must-do Hong Kong experience is to take the star ferry to Kowloon and enjoy the stunning views of Hong Kong island. While on the "Kowloon side" visit John Drummond and James Leung at **Tiffany's New York Bar** at the Intercontinental Grand Stanford Hotel (hongkong.intercontinental. com). The large island bar boasts one of the most diverse selections of whiskies in Hong Kong, with 200 different whiskies along with signature cocktails and craft beers. A vibrant and cosy atmosphere and a must for whisky lovers visiting Hong Kong.

On your return journey back to Hong Kong island you will arrive into pier number seven. Take a five-minute walk down to pier number three and find yourself a seat at **The Beer Bay** (62 Peel Street, Central) for a perfect place to enjoy a simple sundowner. Frequented predominantly by people that live on the outlying islands, Beer Bay hosts a very large selection of craft beers, gins and wine, one of which is Gweilo pale ale – a superb draft offering. Take a seat on the steps and simply watch the world go by.

A 15-minute walk or a 5-minute taxi drive from Beer Bay is **ABC Kitchen** (abckitchen.com.hk) located within Queen Street cooked food market. The food court is no frills, which adds to the atmosphere, and the food certainly does the talking! There is an option to bring your own alcohol, so grab yourself a craft ale or two and try the roasted suckling pork or duck confit, which are both outstanding.

The Hong Kong cocktail scene has been developing a real sense of prestige for the past five years. It's worth putting time aside to visit **The Envoy** (theenvoy.hk), **Zuma Lounge's** ← Japanese delights at **The Landmark** (zumarestaurant.com) and the hidden whisky gems at **Stockton** (stockton.com.hk). But for sheer

perfection, visit **Quinary** ↓ (see page 149). The relentless hard work of bartenders Antonio Lai and Charlene Dawes has completely raised the benchmark for the art of mixology in Hong Kong. Quinary's philosophy focuses on engaging all five senses, and classic cocktails have a modern-day twist.

Just a five-minute walk from Quinary is **Paradis** (paradishk.com) located above the hustle and bustle of Wyndham street. It's a welcome change of pace and one of a few cocktail bars where you can truly relax. The ethos of Paradis is a blend of French exuberance and Caribbean culture, which is reflected in their menu. If you find yourself there during "Apwe Twavail" – the bar's take on Happy Hour – go for a Hipster Mary, a riff on the classic Bloody Mary cocktail and a true explosion of cultural flavour on the palate.

The rise in international hotel chains has potentially led to a

> **The Hong Kong cocktail scene has been developing a real sense of prestige.**

subtle "blandness" creeping into some of the more mainstream places, but in Hong Kong the artistry of the hotel bar is seen as a genuine institution, offering modern-day historic significance. Whether it's the **Captain's Bar** and the **Chinnery** at the Mandarin Oriental (mandarinoriental.com), **Dickens Bar** at the Excelsior (also part of the Mandarin group) or **Sugar** ↑ at the East Hotel (east-hongkong.com), each one is a fine example of a great standalone bar. However, when it comes to the quality of drinks, range, glassware, atmosphere and hospitality, the **Lobster Bar** at Shangri-La island (shangri-la.com) has it all, deserving the crown as perhaps the best bar in Hong Kong.

151

FOCUS*

STARTENDER
STEVEN LIN

Steven Lin is one of the doyens of the whisky resurgence currently sweeping across Taiwan. His bar, **L'Arrière-Cour** (see opposite), locally known as the Backyard Bar, is one of the true go-to destinations for anyone serious about the spirit. We asked him about why whisky has become such a popular spirit in his home town and about the tricky pairing of cigars and cocktails.

Where do you drink when you're off duty?
When dining out, I usually choose wines and Champagnes. Mostly I still have whisky when drinking alone, because it's not only a duty, but an important companion to me.
Your favourite drink of all time...?
Ha...whisky for sure!
Where is your favourite city in the world to go drinking in?
Taipei.
What do you look for in a bar, as a sign of true greatness?
If the atmosphere is like a calm harbour for souls.
Take us through making one of your signature drinks.

How did you come up with it and why does it work?
Since I'm a cigar lover, Cuban ones preferably, which are heavy and full-bodied, I normally choose an Islay peated whisky with Drambuie, adding in a few drops of bitters, then squeezing in a quarter of a fresh lemon, which I leave in the drink. It's the perfect match with my cigar.
Tell us why Taipei is such a great destination for quality drinks now?
The Taiwanese import many high-quality whiskies and wines and can sell them for very reasonable prices, because of the relatively low tax here. Because of this, Taiwan is like heaven for whisky and wine! Furthermore, don't forget the food here. Most Taiwanese people are spoiled with regard to tastes. I think they are the reasons why Taiwan is a paradise with quality drinks.
A final word of wisdom from behind the bar?
Observing is the start of taste.

Mostly I still have whisky when drinking alone, because it's not only a duty, but an important companion to me.

TAIPEI & TAIWAN*

ASTAR COFFEE HOUSE

Don't be deceived by looks here. Though you'd be forgiven for thinking this is a bustling café, it is, by definition, one of the truest speakeasies you can find in town. Behind the blackboard menus listing various Americanos and lattes you will see a hidden shelf of bottles, jiggers and shakers – a tell-tale sign of what comes later on. Cocktail-wise, there are no rules: no menu to speak of, so everything is ordered on a whim.
✖
No. 41, Alley 13, Lane 60, Section 3, Minquan East Road, Zhongsan District, Taipei +886 2 2503 5856
✖
IN THREE WORDS:
Deceptive...Devilishly Delightful.
THE DRINK TO TRY:
Park yourself early for a great cappuccino, but finish with a superb Martini.
THEY SAY:
"Even the owner will insist on Astar being called a café, but they sure do serve impressive cocktails."
— DEREK CHANG, CHINA
PRICE RATING: ✱

L'ARRIÈRE-COUR

As one of the oldest whisky bars in Taiwan, L'Arrière-Cour offers an astonishing selection of whiskies for such a tiny space. The emphasis is on Scotch single malts but plenty of Irish, Japanese and American whiskies get a look in. The staff clearly know their stuff too: well educated and well versed in the subtleties between everything on the back bar, they can guide everyone from novice to expert through what to start with and what to finish off the night with. The key here is to put your trust in them, as there is no menu, so let them entertain you.
✖
No.4, Lane 23rd, An-Ho Road Section 2, Da-An District, Taipei +886 2 2704 7818
✖
IN THREE WORDS:
Whisky, Whisky, Whisky.
THE DRINK TO TRY:
Erm...did we say they have a fine selection of whiskies?
WE SAY:
Your education starts here. Leave it up to the experts.
PRICE RATING: ✱✱✱

TCRC

"Miss this place at your peril," says our man in Taiwan – although it's actually not an easy place to find. The bar, which stands for "The Checkered Record Club" also doubles as a bit of an underground indie music haunt and is decked out with a distinctly vintage feel – from the differently coloured window panes and exposed brick, to the mismatched artwork and furniture, it feels carefully curated, rather than thrown together. The drinks are similarly curated affairs, based on the style of spirit that you like – the team here are very adept at reading your taste buds.
✖
117 Xinmei Street, West Central District, 700, Tainan City, Taiwan +886 6222 8716
✖
IN THREE WORDS:
Hip Happening Haunt.
THE DRINK TO TRY:
A cocktail or craft beer.
THEY SAY:
"I taste not only the passion, but also the persistence in their cocktails."
— STEVEN LIN, TAIPEI
PRICE RATING: ✱✱

SINGAPORE*

Singapore is a place of truly dazzling proportions. From the towering cityscapes to the bustling, highly colourful and deliciously aromatic streets, it encourages you to chuck in your culinary preconceptions, open your eyes and taste buds wide and explore until dawn.

The bar scene in Singapore has travelled light years from its associations with the ubiquitous Singapore Sling, despite still being the best place to take in a perfect example of this all-time classic. To put it simply, it is arguably the most vibrant place for cocktails in Southeast Asia and has developed a distinct, playful mastery all of its own, so much so that its collective bar community regularly features among the finest in international cocktail awards and Best Bar lists. Here is a scene that really wants to show off a unique mixture of innovation, professionalism and sheer wow factor – and it can turn it on in a heartbeat. A visit to **Operation Dagger** or **Native** (see page 156) will thrill your senses and take

you to places that you hadn't previously imagined the humble cocktail could. As great hotel bars go, **Manhattan** (see page 156) offers a truly sophisticated, yet genuinely progressive drinks list. Similarly, **28 HongKong Street** (see below) and **Jigger & Pony** (see opposite) prove that you can't keep a good idea down, and these stalwarts of the Singapore scene are still every bit as relevant today, pushing the boundaries in both high-end service and the pursuit of new flavours.

Singapore – you've truly surprised and delighted us.

28 HONGKONG STREET ↗

The penchant for speakeasy themed bars is a clearly defined trend in Singapore (see Operation Dagger) and one which was definitely bucked by 28 HongKong Street, when it first opened back in 2011. Rather like 69 Colebrooke Row in London (see page 18), taking a seemingly nondescript city location and turning on the liquid wow factor behind its closed doors has paid dividends and 28HKS has gained an international reputation for its mix of both innovative flair and crafted old-time classics. Add in some ridiculously moreish bar snacks and you have a recipe for a true destination bar.

✖
28 Hongkong Street, Singapore 059667 +65 6533 2001 28hks.com
✖
IN THREE WORDS:
Looks Can Deceive.
THE DRINK TO TRY:
The Whiskey Sour.
THEY SAY:
"The best bar bites in Singapore... My favourite is the Mac & Cheese balls!"
— **KARL TOO, MALAYSIA**
"One of the first bars that opened my eyes to the attention to detail on service."
— **YAO LU, CHINA**
PRICE RATING: ✱✱✱

ATLAS

Sometimes the best experiences come in small packages. In the case of Atlas, however, the opposite is entirely true. Arguably the most stunning-looking bar in the world, this vast Art Deco palace to all things gin (and Champagne) will leave you utterly speechless when you arrive. The high ceilings and gilded features instantly conjure up images of the beautiful ballrooms of Gatsby-era America. Behind the immaculate bar is a gin tower, rising up like a monolithic tribute to Mother's Ruin, where you'll find over 1,000 different gins from all around the world. Ask the bartender nicely and they'll take you upstairs for a little tour. The drinks are equally impressive: novel twists on the Martini and a vintage "Decades" section of the menu, where you can drink gins dating back to 1910 through to the 1990s.

With such an encyclopedic approach to this once humble spirit, Atlas will redefine how you drink gin for ever.

✖

Parkview Square, 600 North Bridge Road, Singapore 188778 +65 6396 4466 atlasbar.sg

✖

IN THREE WORDS:
World Of Gin.

THE DRINK TO TRY:
The house Martini made with a classic London dry gin, ambrato vermouth, orange bitters and Champagne vinegar.

WE SAY:
A stunning addition to the already titanic cocktail scene in Singapore.

PRICE RATING: ✖✖✖✖

D.BESPOKE

D.Bespoke is a rare place, designed for quiet, reflective drinking rather than a raucous evening. Inside this bar you'll find a truly unique and bespoke

service, where the cocktails have been created to match the sumptuous, high-class environment where bespoke glassware is matched perfectly to each drink, and the level of detail afforded to the entire experience matches this truly tailored experience. The dedicated team assembled by head barman and owner Daiki Kanetaka boasts fine mixologists from Japan and Denmark, bringing you service which is Ginza-Meets-Copenhagen, with a hint of English Gentlemen's Club blended in, soundtracked by easy listening jazz. As drinking experiences come, D.Bespoke isn't cheap. There's no menu to speak of, so ask the barman if there's anything you're unsure of before the journey begins.

✖

2 Bukit Pasoh Road, Singapore 089816 +65 8141 5741 dbespoke.sg

✖

IN THREE WORDS:
Ginza Meets Mayfair.

THE DRINK TO TRY:
It's bespoke, so let them know your thirst and they'll craft you a cocktail to meet your needs.

WE SAY:
The perfect balance of Japanese dedication and British old-school style.

PRICE RATING: ✖✖✖✖✖

JIGGER & PONY ↗

This is a classic cocktail bar to the last and Jigger & Pony provides a much needed rest in one of the most modern cities on the planet. Boasting a list of 24 cocktails spread across three different categories of classics, vintage

and signatures, this is a bar where the flavour is as important as the technique behind the stick, blending the best bartending practices from across Europe, Asia and America. The attention to detail, as well as a great selection of ingredients, means that whatever you order will be made to the highest possible specification. Alongside the cocktails, flights of spirits are offered for those looking to educate themselves on the bar's great selection before diving in for a cocktail or two.

✖

101 Amoy Street, Singapore 069921 +65 6223 9101 jiggerandpony.com

✖

IN THREE WORDS:
Simply Singapore Style.

THEY SAY:
"Superstar bar team, chill vibes and delicious cocktails."
— YAO LU, CHINA

PRICE RATING: ✖✖✖✖

SINGAPORE*

MANHATTAN

Possibly one of the grandest places you will ever come across to drink a cocktail. Manhattan oozes chic from every fold in its glorious soft furnishings, to the cosy leather chesterfield armchairs which will envelop you, becoming your only destination for the night. The bar conjures up a similar feel to that of the Savoy Beaufort bar (see page 22) in London, but with an all-American feel. As you arrive you're greeted by over 100 mini barrels, each with a different cocktail inside, gently resting away. The menu is artfully separated into the various eras of the history of the cocktail, with a distinctive twist: each represents a style of drink, meaning that you get a libatious – and very innovative – tour of one of the world's greatest cities with a genuine panache all of its own. Outstanding stuff.

✖

The Regent Hotel, 1 Cuscaden Road, Level 2, Singapore 249715 +65 6725 3377

✖

IN THREE WORDS:
Singapore Strait Talkin'.
THE DRINK TO TRY:
A delicious barrel-aged Negroni, or an Ultima Palavra (a heady mix of Brazilian Cachaça, Chartreuse tea and vermouth).
THEY SAY:
"An absolutely stunning place, with a whisky collection to match."
— **EDDIE NARA, HONG KONG**
PRICE RATING: ✖✖✖✖

NATIVE

Relative newcomers to the Singapore scene, the team behind Native have taken the concept of doing everything as locally as possible, and run a mile with it, to produce some stunning results. With a menu comprising just seven drinks, each one delivers a compelling story, using a curated selection of Asian spirits (think Indian whisky and Thai rum). The serves are as tasty as they are ingenious: ask for an Antz and you'll get a sweet, creamy delight using coconut yogurt, aged sugarcane and rum, topped with a freeze-dried basil leaf and... yes, some ants, which brilliantly add to the overall genius of the drink. Upstairs you'll find a small micro distillery, which the team use to create completely unique flavours and combinations.

Native seems effortless in its approach, which is a true reflection of the skill and creativity on offer. A genuinely inspiring drinking experience.
✖
52A Amoy Street, Singapore 069878 +65 8869 6520 tribenative.com
✖
IN THREE WORDS:
Playful, Local, Skilful.
THE DRINK TO TRY:
Antz – the only bite you'll get here is from the delicious Thai rum!
WE SAY:
Singapore's most trailblazing bar and a total must-try when heading down to Amoy Street.
PRICE RATING: ✖✖✖

OPERATION DAGGER ↗

There seems to be a common theme emerging among some of the most progressive drinks joints around the world, and by this we mean...anonymity. Operation Dagger is typical in hiding its very bright, highly innovative light under a bushel, so much so that finding it among the backstreets of Singapore's Chinatown is pretty tricky indeed. There are no frills at all on display here: a simple concrete grey basement bar, festooned with bare lightbulbs. The back bar has strangely coded bottles and jars – indecipherable

to the casual observer. The drinks themselves – listed on the menu as "Dangerous Drinking Water" – are truly inspirational indeed. Owner Luke Whearty has developed some beautifully simple-looking serves, which hide a highly complex blend of ingredients (obscure tinctures, bee pollen, vinegars and herbaceous smoke). In short, anyone else trying to replicate what's on offer here, but lacking the obvious skill on display, would be attempting a Mission Impossible.

✖

7 Ann Siang Hill, Singapore
069791 +65 6438 4057
operationdagger.com

✖

IN THREE WORDS:
A Cut Above.
THE DRINK TO TRY:
One of the Omakase pairing flights.
THEY SAY:
"The mixology equivalent of a three-star Michelin chef who bought a gastropub. Game changing."
— PHILIP DUFF, USA
"From the moment I walked into this bar, I knew I would love it."
— MONICA BERG, UK/NORWAY
PRICE RATING: ✳✳✳

SUGARHALL

"Fun dining, fine cocktails and lots of rums," reads the website for this refreshing bar, just a short hop from the Marina Bay area and next door to its sister bar, Jigger & Pony. With an ethos like this, what's not to like? Dig deeper still and you'll see that Sugarhall have really cornered the market on a specialist drinks area, in a city that is bulging with great bars. The rum selection is one of the most comprehensive we've come across, dividing over 100 rums into smart categories: "Spanish style – smooth and elegant after dinner sippers, traditionally from Cuba, Panama, Guatemala and Venezuela" and "English style – rich and full bodied, heavy molasses, traditionally from Jamaica, Trinidad and Barbados".

There's also a huge focus on the highly flavoursome and herbaceous Agricole style, which is a rum trend gathering apace internationally. If you have an evening to spare (and in a place like this, with so many rums, why wouldn't you?) check out one of their rum flights, or "fleets" as they playfully list them.

✖

102 Amoy Street, Singapore
069922 +65 9732 5607
sugarhall.sg

✖

IN THREE WORDS:
A Rambunctious Rumbellion.
THE DRINK TO TRY:
Dark 'n' Stormy.
THEY SAY:
"They have the best rum selection in Singapore."
— KARL TOO, MALAYSIA
PRICE RATING: ✳✳

SINGAPORE'S OTHER DRINKING DELIGHTS

With so many great bars to choose from you're never far from a remarkable drinking experience. Here's our list of the others you need to visit:

Start your cocktail odyssey off with a ridiculously spicy-but-tasty lunchtime Bloody Mary at **Ding Dong** (dingdong.com.sg).

Fancy a whisky? Head to the **Auld Alliance** (theauldalliance. sg) and be stunned by what is probably the best collection of single malts in the world. Still want more? Then head to **The Other Room** at the Marriott Hotel (singaporemarriott.com) where you'll find a stunning range of whiskies all extra-matured in unusual casks by head honcho Dario Knox.

Gin? **The Gibson's** (gibsonbar. sg) stunning twists on some classic gin-based drinks have to be experienced to be believed.

Where does it all end?! Has to be **Skinny's Lounge** (facebook. com/drinkskinnys) on the quayside: the perfect after-hours party bar for beers and shots - and possibly a spot of ill-advised late-night karaoke.

One for the road? Make **The World Is Flat** (theworldisflat. co) at Changi airport your final destination for a swift Aviation cocktail or decent draft beer before leaving Singapore with a head full of great memories.

KUALA LUMPUR*

COLEY

One of Kuala Lumpur's newest additions to the burgeoning world of the classy speakeasy. The name, and vibe, is built around the legend of Ada Coleman, head bartender at the Savoy for 23 years and one of only two female bartenders to work at the hotel. Coleman, or "Coley" as she was known, created the Hanky-Panky cocktail for the British actor Sir Charles Hawtrey who was looking for something a little bit punchy. In keeping with the fun and games, the drinks at Coley are playful, but supremely well-crafted, with a keen eye on garnishes and quality ice.

✖
8, Jalan Kemuja, Bangsar, 59000, Wilayah Persekutuan Kuala Lumpur +60 19-270 9179
✖
IN THREE WORDS:
Nothing Fishy Here.
THE DRINK TO TRY:
The Hanky-Panky.
THEY SAY:
"Makes me think of an every-sunday-brunch-time kind of bar."
— **KARL TOO, MALAYSIA**
PRICE RATING: ✱✱

HYDE AT 53M

The speakeasy trend has taken good root in KL and this is yet another example of how to do it well. Hidden behind a sliding back door, the place is similar to a jazz bar, with low lighting and a long bar top, behind which the magic happens. Unusually for a speakeasy-style bar, there is also an outdoor section where drinks can be enjoyed with a view. A huge cocktail list moves from classics to their own creations, all of which are beautifully presented, served in everything from a nest to on top of a fan and even one in a lightbulb!

✖
53, Jalan SS 21/1a, Damansara Utama, 47400 Petaling Jaya, Selangor, Kuala Lumpur +60 17-680 1357
✖
IN THREE WORDS:
Creativity In Cocktails.
WE SAY:
Venture here for a truly excellent experience and choose from a huge number of brilliantly presented cocktails.
PRICE RANGE: ✱✱✱✱

OMAKASE + APPRECIATE

Omakase + Appreciate is the unusual name for one of the best bars in a growing Kuala Lumpur cocktail scene. This speakeasy bar in an office basement (hidden behind a door that would look more suited to covering a boiler cupboard), the cocktail list is divided between those made by Shawn Chong and those from Karl Too. If you're wanting to go "off list" (or "Omakase" style), simply ask them to make you a drink to meet your palate, and they'll oblige. As a place to hang out, it is wise to remember that this is a small bar, and it is best to check their Facebook posts to see when, or if, they are open. At the time of writing, the pair had taken the whole week off to "recharge", which, given the popularity of this place, is utterly deserved.

✖
Ampang Bangunan Ming Annexe, 9 Jalan Ampang, Kuala Lumpur +60 32-022 2238
✖
IN THREE WORDS:
I've Found It!
THEY SAY:
"Superstar bar team, chill vibes and delicious cocktails."
— **YAO LU, CHINA**
PRICE RATING: ✱✱✱✱

BANGKOK*

TEENS OF THAILAND

A word of warning: if you're planning to Google this bar before heading there for a drink...make sure you include the word "Bar" in the search. We accept no responsibility for the consequences. Joking aside, when you get past the..."tricky" name, T.O.T. is a real gem of a place. With gin firmly the spirit of choice, the bar team have assembled an exceptional arsenal of juniper-powered goodness. The cocktails (everything from a simple G&T, to a French 75 ➚) are as elegantly presented as one would find in an upmarket hotel bar in Western Europe...for a fraction of the price. Worth taking a trip to Bangkok for, then?

✖

76 Soi Nana, Bangkok
+66 81 443 3784

✖

IN THREE WORDS:
Itsybitsyteenyweeny
Grabyourselfa Ginmartini.

THE DRINK TO TRY:
For sheer simplicity, it has to
be a G&T.

THEY SAY:
"As a gin-focused bar they have
an amazing cocktail list."
— **KARL TOO, MALAYSIA**

PRICE RATING: ✳

VESPER

A curious mix, this bar-cum-Italian restaurant was founded in 2014 by the husband-and-wife team of restaurateurs Choti Leenutaphong and Debby Tang. With the help of the chef from the brilliant La Bottega di Luca, their two passions are serious cocktails "served in an unpretentious setting" and, of course, Italian food with all the right touch points to make it truly authentic. The cocktails are just fantastic, with a heavy influence (as the name would suggest) on European classics and, as they call them "spirit forward drinks" – think Martini, Martinez and the Vesper itself. The venue has a slight American bar feel to it; with low ceilings and perfect lighting, you could easily be in a top-end hotel bar in Paris, London or New York. The cocktails have won this bar plaudits from across the globe and it is certainly the premium cocktail experience in Bangkok.

✖

10/15 Soi Convent Road,
Silom, Bang Rak, Bangkok
10500 +66 2 235 2777
vesperbar.co

✖

IN THREE WORDS:
Go For Classic.

THE DRINK TO TRY:
Well, come on...you have to order
a Vesper!

WE SAY:
Enjoy this place until closing.

PRICE RATING: ✳ ✳ ✳

JAKARTA*

LOEWY

This is a casual bistro hangout that provides a wonderfully relaxing atmosphere and a bar that has a buzz about it, serving some of the best drinks in the city. Forged on the idea of the traditional Parisian bistro by way of New York City, it holds a stylish and original vibe that is mid-century and modern with a muted colourway, wood and metal. The drinks firstly play off a selection of whiskies before moving into classic and twisted cocktails, and a few of their own signatures such as the Dragonfruit Pop (genever, dragonfruit purée, fresh lemon juice and Japanese soda) and a Hazelnut Martini (brandy, cacao liqueur, hazelnut liqueur and syrup, cream, shaved chocolate and cashew nut crunch).

✖

Oakwood Premier Cozmo, Jalan Lingkar Mega Kuningan E4.2 No 1, Jakarta 12950, +62 21 2554 2378 loewyjakarta.com

✖

Monty's has become one of the hippest hangouts in Jakarta, attracting an opulent crowd looking for good food and even better drinks.

IN THREE WORDS:
Jakarta's Best Cocktails.
WE SAY:
Head here as our top tip in the city.
PRICE RATING: ✦✦✦✦

MONTY'S

Monty's has become one of the hippest hangouts in Jakarta, attracting a well-off crowd looking for good food and even better drinks. Aside from the restaurant, which offers European-style food over two floors, there is a small lounge bar hidden away on the third floor, which focuses on whisky and some cocktails with a twist, such as pre-made libations that have been left to rest in oak casks that once contained red wine. The restaurant and bar often work together hosting pairing dinners, so look out for those.

✖

Jalan Raya Senopati No. 84, Selong, Kebayoran Baru, Jakarta 12110 +62 21 720 4848 montys.co.id

✖

IN THREE WORDS:
Chic City Hangout.
WE SAY:
A good place to find interesting drinks with a twist.
PRICE RATING: ✦✦✦✦✦

NEW DELHI*

EK BAR

Exploring the relationship between the stick and the kitchen, Ek Bar's real talent lies in finding a distinct parity betwixt the two. Here, you'll find some incredible food on offer – from the khameeri pizza to the tandoori paneer roll – everything is approached with a genuine understanding of balancing spice. The drinks follow this ethos and you'll find this eloquently reflected in the City Of Nizams: a gin-based cocktail, also bringing in the flavours of turmeric, served in an oversized glass, into which, a giant spice-infused ice cube is placed. The attention to detail is right up there with their European and Japanese counterparts, as is the playful creativity.

✘

D 17, First Floor, Defence Colony, New Delhi, Delhi 110024 +91 11 4168 8811

✘

IN THREE WORDS:
Spice Is Nice.

THE DRINK TO TRY:
The City Of Nizams.

THEY SAY:
"A concept that celebrates quirky 'Indianness' in everything, from its name to its motifs, food and drinks."

— KARINA AGGARWAL, INDIA

PRICE RATING: ✱ ✱

PIANO MAN JAZZ BAR →

The spirit of Jazz is alive and well in New Delhi, thanks in part to Arjun Sagar Gupta, the visionary behind Piano Man Jazz Bar. The place itself is a relatively small, intimate affair, with an outstanding fine-dining restaurant (amusingly called Dirty Apron) upstairs. Going hand-in-hand with the passionate cuisine are the cocktails: pretty much all classics, from the Prohibition era (the White Lady and Mary Pickford are the real highlights). Jazz appears to be something of a hipster pursuit in Mumbai at the moment and, fortunately, the golden age of parping trumpets and rumbling double basses is awash with fine drinks too.

✘

B 6–7/22, Safdarjung Enclave Market, opposite Deer Park, New Delhi, Delhi 110029 +91 11 4131 5181 thepianoman.in

✘

IN THREE WORDS:
Shake-it Again Sam.

THE DRINK TO TRY:
The hugely underrated Mary Pickford cocktail.

THEY SAY:
"There have been bars built around music before, but never one so astutely focused and dedicated to jazz."

— KARINA AGGARWAL, INDIA

PRICE RATING: ✱ ✱ ✱ ✱

FEATURE*

A DRINK WITH...
SANDEEP AURORA

If you could take a guess at which country in the world has the highest consumption of whisky, we're willing to bet at least one decent Manhattan that you wouldn't have picked India. In fact, by volume India's consumption of "whisky" is vast...but only really applies in name. You see, the large proportion of "Indian whisky" (with the exception of the few fine Indian single malt whiskies made in the traditional way) is not really whisky at all. With molasses as its base, it probably has more in common with rum than with what we traditionally think of as whisky. However, there is a growing number of outstanding places to drink not only Scotch but also Japanese whisky, alongside some of America's finest too. We asked Sandeep Aurora, one of India's best-known whisky experts, to point us in the direction of his favourite gems.

1911, NEW DELHI ↑

The horseshoe-shaped bar 1911 was placed as one of the best three bars in India to enjoy whisky, by the Icons of Whisky Awards a few years back. The bar pays tribute to the historic milestone that led to the emergence of New Delhi as a seat of power. Soft Montana leather chairs and period portraiture add to the range of whiskies, served in a truly Imperial style, on a tray with a set of urban glassware. Most of the customers are Europeans and their Indian guests. The staff are polite and the service is quite gracious.

✖

The Imperial, Janpath Lane, Connaught Place, New Delhi, Delhi 110001 +91 11 2334 1234 theimperialindia.com

✖

IN THREE WORDS:
Relax, Raj Style.
PRICE RATING: ✦✦✦✦

HARBOUR BAR, MUMBAI

A wonderful collection of great whiskies, this was Mumbai's first licensed bar and an icon since 1933. [Try the From The Harbour Since 1933 cocktail, a tribute to this fact]. The Harbour Bar is a favourite destination with whisky lovers as well as in-house guests. Comfortable seating, muted tones and a vibrant ambience, the bar is a must-try for all visitors to Mumbai. Whisky is best enjoyed at the Harbour Bar overlooking the Arabian Sea.

✖

The Taj Mahal Palace Hotel, B K Boman Behram Marg, Apollo Bandar, Colaba, Mumbai, Maharashtra 400001 +91 22 6665 3366 taj.tajhotels.com

✖

IN THREE WORDS:
Marble Whisky Marvel.
PRICE RATING: ✦✦✦✦

GURGAON & BANGALORE*

COCKTAILS & DREAMS SPEAKEASY

When you first visit a bar's website to find that the place has been built around the vibe of a hugely popular song (in this case, Country artist Toby Keith's "I Love This Bar"), you start to realize the significant impact a drinking joint can have upon a local community.

Established by Yangdup Lama, one of India's best-known bartenders and drinks experts, and Minakshi Singh, Speakeasy wears its heart on its sleeve. It is very much a speakeasy in style, harking back to the 1920s, so expect all the classics to be there, done with perfection by Lama and his team.

✖

Sector 15, Part 2, Near Galaxy Hotel, Gurgaon 122001
+91 87505 82297
cndspeakeasy.com

✖

IN THREE WORDS:
India's Hidden Depths.
THE DRINK TO TRY:
A lost Classic – the Monkey Gland.

WE SAY:
From classics to innovative new creations, this is one of India's finest.
PRICE RATING: ✳✳✳

THE PIANO BAR

Housing a high-end shopping area, and featuring a standalone Gucci outlet, the Oberoi is the place to stay when visiting Delhi. But no hotel-cum-shopping mall would be complete without a seriously high-end bar to relax in at the end of the day, with an aged single malt and a cigar. Step up, The Piano Bar. Located on the third level, with contemporary decor, enhanced lighting and elegant service, The Piano Bar is reminiscent of an exclusive club and boasts a wonderful range of whiskies (it has over 75 on the list). The adjoining Wine Room presents a connoisseur's wine list, with over 100 labels from the Old and the New Worlds.

✖

The Oberoi Gurgaon, Sector 19, Gurgaon, Haryana 122016
+91 124 245 1234 oberoihotels.com

✖

IN THREE WORDS:
Luxury In India.
WE SAY:
Luxury like this is hard to get right, but they've nailed here at the Oberoi.
PRICE RATING: ✳✳✳✳✳

TOAST & TONIC

Toast & Tonic is a restaurant and bar that takes its lead from the culinary scene in Manhattan, bringing a slice of the East Village to India. The bar at Toast & Tonic is designed to be relaxing, with the wood-chip back bar offering spirits and beers from around the world, a selection of wines plus a range of creative and interesting cocktails. Take their Old Fashioned, for example, which uses bacon-infused bourbon strained into a chilled rocks glass over an ice ball infused with coriander and orange. For India, this is utterly groundbreaking.

✖

14/1, Wood Street, Ashok Nagar, Bangalore +91 80 4111 6879
toastandtonic.com

✖

IN THREE WORDS:
East Village Style!
THEY SAY:
"Gin-cocktail haven!"
KARINA AGGARWAL, INDIA
PRICE RATING: ✳✳✳

FOCUS*

STARTENDER
YANGDUP LAMA

Originally hailing from Darjeeling, Yangdup Lama began his bartending career in 1995 with the Hyatt Regency, New Delhi, where he stayed until 1999, after which a life of mobile bartending beckoned. His first book, *Cocktails & Dreams*, was published in 2014 and he continues to educate India on the latest cocktail trends.

Where do you drink when you're off duty?
I usually like to pour a drink for myself, from my own little home bar, which is my own space to come and unwind. Usually, I enjoy company, and like to invite someone over for a drink, and share a tale or two.

Your favourite drink of all time...marooned on a desert island style...?
Ah! Well, a Mint Julep, or a Mai Tai; these are usually my favourites – but definitely a Mai Tai when the rum is right!

Where is your favourite city in the world to go drinking in?
Well...I'd have to say, Kathmandu. It is a city where one can find a drink, anytime, anywhere – from a vegetable shop to the nearest meat store to, of course, a fine bar. I enjoy it as a city to drink out in, as there are no strings attached. There's zero pretence, and no frills. And when I am there, I enjoy something even as basic as a typical Nepalese whisky, with the many friends I have there. Kathmandu, despite all odds, is my happy place, full of warmth.

Take us through one of your signature cocktails from The Speakeasy.
I think The Fog Horn would be the place to start. This was one of the signature [classic] speakeasy drinks, but I added my bit of a twist to it. I always felt that the gingerbread flavour was quite underplayed. Mostly, it's used in coffee shops as a core ingredient in flavouring coffees, cakes and pastries, but I knew it would enhance the flavour of a mixed drink. Also, the lack of availability of good ginger beer in India was a reason to find a steady supplement.

Do you think there's a range of cocktails that pair specifically well with Indian cuisine?
I would have to say that the best cocktails to pair with Indian cuisine would be the classic Gin & Tonic and any of the fizzy cocktails, which aren't very overpowering in flavour. The Bloody Mary, for instance, is a bit too much to blend with Indian flavours. Even a Classic Martini works, as it stays silent!

✖

THE FOG HORN

2 measures gin or vodka
½ measure fresh ginger juice
½ measure fresh lime juice
½ measure gingerbread syrup
ginger ale, to top up
mint sprigs, to garnish

Build the drink by adding each ingredient to a tall glass full of ice, then stir. Top with ginger ale and fresh mint sprigs to finish.

YANGDUP'S TOP BARS FROM AROUND THE WORLD:

✖

Absinthe Brasserie & Bar, San Francisco (absinthe.com) →
I love this place for its classic and simplistic approach to drinks and service. Their cocktails are simple and sincere and the food they serve complements the drinks. The most important factor regarding the service is how prompt it is.

✖

Rum Doodle, Kathmandu (+977 1-2191248)
Thamel is this quaint little street in Kathmandu, full of hustle, commotion, and mountaineers. You'll find Rum Doodle Bar there and it has so much character and warmth. They don't serve the best drinks, but the overall vibe of the place is cosy and everyone around is happy and cheerful. It's not as much about the cocktails here as it is about having a drink with strangers who are either back from, or headed out for, a mountaineering expedition and keen on sharing a story or two.

✖

Polo Lounge, Hyatt Regency, New Delhi (delhi.regency.hyatt.com)
This is where I learned how to pour a drink and started out as an amateur bartender. Even today when I visit the Polo Lounge, there's nostalgia, endless stories and beautiful memories of a bygone era. They make amazing Caprioskas and some great cocktails. The bar has remained one of the finest hotel bars in the country for the longest time.

Even today when I visit the Polo Lounge, there's nostalgia, endless stories and beautiful memories of a bygone era.

✖

28 HongKong Street, Singapore (see page 154)
For the obvious reason that they serve some of the finest cocktails in the whole of Asia!

MUMBAI*

AER AT THE FOUR SEASONS

This is a rooftop bar like no other. It's as if designers from the future have dropped in on Mumbai's Four Seasons and installed their dream rooftop bar. With a panoramic city and sea views, it covers the entire roof of this premier Mumbai hotel. Situated on the 34th floor, the sounds from the bustling streets of Worli below add an audio backdrop to remind you that you're in such an exciting and busy city. Open all year round, it is the ideal place to take in a sunset and they even have a canopy and windscreen during the monsoon season, to keep the cocktails flowing. The bar also hosts nights each month showcasing the best of Indian and international DJs and artists, making it a place to be seen in Mumbai.

✖

The Four Seasons Hotel Mumbai, 34th Floor, 1/136, Dr. E. Moses Road, 400 018 Worli, Mumbai +91 22 2481 8444

✖

IN THREE WORDS:
Rooftop Of India.
WE SAY:
Our first stop of the night!
PRICE RATING: ✱✱✱✱✱

THE BOMBAY CANTEEN

This place is a curious mix of a Parisian café and a bar with an Indian heart. Located in a recreated old Mumbai bungalow, it is a real mix of the old and new. The bar has become one of the Mumbai hangouts for those looking for a great cocktail. The menu features a unique selection of reimagined classic cocktails (broken down into "fancy drinks" and "good old drinks") with firm Indian roots, even down to using marigold leaf as a garnish. Try the Ganga Yamuna Margarita, made with mosambi juice (sweet lemon) and you'll discover their mantra that "each dish and drink has a story to tell".

✖

Unit-1, Process House, Kamala Mills, S.B. Road, Lower Parel, Mumbai 400013 +91 22 4966 6666 thebombaycanteen.com

✖

IN THREE WORDS:
Indian Inspired Libations.
THEY SAY:
"Great food and great drink."
—KESHAV PRAKASH, INDIA
PRICE RATING: ✱✱✱

WOODSIDE INN

One of the most popular places in Bombay for discovering craft beers, the Woodside is a curiously cosy joint, with a lot of soul. Arguably better known for its food (burgers, sliders and awesome breakfasts) you can choose from an array of both local and imported beers, plus a small cocktail list (the Mojito is a treat, stirred down with a piece of actual sugarcane).

✖

Plot No. 126, Todi Building, Ground–First Floor, Mathuradas Mill Compound, Senapati Bapat Marg, Lower Parel, Mumbai, Maharashtra 400013 +91 22 2497 5018

✖

IN THREE WORDS:
Wood Craft Wonders.
THE DRINK TO TRY:
If it's on tap, something from the Independence Brewing Co.
THEY SAY:
"Bombay's favourite 'neighbourhood' bar."
—KARINA AGGARWAL, INDIA
PRICE RATING: ✱✱

FEATURE*

A DRINK WITH...
KESHAV PRAKASH

Keshav Prakash is the founder and chief curator of **The Vault** (vaultfinespirits.com), a collective of some of the finest spirits from around the world. Keshav's journey into the world of fabulous drinks began after a long career in film making, during which he travelled extensively discovering the world's fine spirits and cocktail bars. He remains a story-teller, and took his experience back to his native India where the drinking landscape is unlike anywhere else in the world.

Tell us a bit about The Vault
The Vault evolved out of my own need for access to quality spirits in India, while small producers were on the lookout for a boutique importer; a guardian for their brands in this complex nation. [Much like America, India has different taxation and licensing laws in each state.] In my travels to several countries – Scotland, Mexico, Guyana, etc. – I met amazing people, visited many distilleries and bars, and I wanted to come back and share my stories. The Vault is really a

The Vault evolved out of my own need for access to quality spirits in India, while small producers were on the lookout for a boutique importer; a guardian for their brands in this complex nation.

platform being built to promote the culture of fine spirits.
What's your ideal evening out in Mumbai?
All my plans are based on who I'm meeting and the traffic to be navigated. I would start with a sundowner at **AER ↑**, the rooftop bar at Four Seasons, hit the back lanes to **The Bombay Canteen** to grab a bite and hang at their bar while the traffic toward Colaba eases out, and then make my way to the **Woodside Inn** for craft beers (see opposite for the bars).

UDAIPUR & JAIPUR*

OBEROI UDAIVILAS

Ah, Udaipur. The backdrop to one of the greatest Bond movies there is, *Octopussy*. Who can forget Roger Moore in a safari suit running through the streets to dodge yet another bullet and save the world from some awful evil? Well, in Udaipur they sure won't let you forget it, with some bars showing the movie nightly on their terrace while you knock back yet another bottle of Kingfisher.

But there is more to Udaipur than the tentacles of an evil international empire and 007. It is a simply stunning place, built on the banks of a giant lake (which can occasionally dry out under the searing heat of the sun) with the stunning hotel, the Taj Lake Palace, sitting in the middle of it and only accessible by boat.

As fun as the Lake Palace is to visit, you can only go there if you are a resident, and the view of it from afar is much better than the view from it, so it is best to settle in for a drink at nearby Oberoi Udaivilas, which looks out over the lake, and has incredible views of the sunset. The drinks list is great, with everything from top-end single malts to a classic Martini to help you watch the sun dissolve into the lake. Once night-time hits, you can don your black tie and play at being Bond.

✖

Haridasji Ki Magri, Mulla Talai, Udaipur, Rajasthan 313001 +91 294 243 3300 oberoihotels.com

✖

IN THREE WORDS:
Double Oh Seven.

THE DRINK TO TRY:
A Vesper – shaken, not stirred.

WE SAY:
Bring out your inner spy in this incredible hotel. If you can stay, get a room with access to the infinity pool and enjoy a cocktail from there.

PRICE RATING: ✖✖✖✖✖

POLO BAR

Imagine the scene – it's been a long day in Jaipur; the air is warm, despite the fact that the sun is low in the sky; and a thirst has been developed from hours in the baking heat, playing polo in the fields. There is, of course, only one option now the ponies have been taken away for the day, and that is a cold, wet Martini to refresh, revive and reinvigorate. And there is only one place this could be served: at The Polo Bar in the Rambagh Palace. This historic bar has, over the generations, seen many Martinis shaken (yes, shaken) and served to guests, from Jackie O to you. Centred in the main room of the bar is a small water feature, the sound of flowing water setting a tranquil atmosphere, punctured only by the light sounds of staff coming and going from behind the bar. Large windows look out toward the neatly kept gardens, while polo memorabilia adorns the walls. This is a place to be served, in the truest sense. Sit back, and be king of the bar for the evening.

✖

Taj Rambagh Palace Hotel, Bhawani Singh Road, Jaipur 302004 +91 141 238 5700 taj.tajhotels.com

✖

IN THREE WORDS:
Simply Indian Luxury.

WE SAY:
The head bartender is one of the longest serving in India, so make sure you get drinking tips from him.

PRICE RATING: ✖✖✖✖✖

FEATURE*

OFF THE BEATEN TRACK...
BARS IN UNDER 140 CHARACTERS

Karina Aggarwal is a writer who covers wine, spirits and food in India and runs India's premier beverage-focused website, gigglewater411.com (she is also on twitter as @giggle_water). We've asked her for her best bar suggestions, off the beaten track in India, in the length of a tweet... fingers at the ready, Karina...?

Gokul in Colaba Mumbai (Ground Floor, Nawaz Building, Kulaba, 10, Tullock Road, Apollo Bunder, Mumbai, Maharashtra 400039). Almost a rite of passage when it comes to Bombay. Dingy but safe, an unlikely combination in India.

Doolally Taproom, Mumbai (doolally.in). Sparse interiors and

bare walls allow nothing by way of soundproofing! Despite loud chatter there's nowhere quite as friendly and familiar.

Janta Bar, Bandra (Building 219, Dharmasthal Manjunath Bhuvan, NM Joshi Marg, Lower Parel, Mumbai). *Janta* literally meaning "public", just who this bar caters to. All kinds of people drinking cheap whisky rub elbows with each other.

Grappa Bar ↙ at the Shangri-la, New Delhi (shangri-la.com) is one of the latest bars in town – elegant, chic and with bartenders that you can always count on for classics.

Perch Wine and Coffee Bar, New Delhi (71, Khan Market, Khan Market, Rabindra Nagar, New Delhi, Delhi 110003) is not so much a wine bar in the truest, international sense of the word, but the airy, easy vibe of the place makes for a great night.

Masala Bar in Mumbai (masalabar.co.in) is stylish, edgy and entirely candlelit (but not in a soppy romantic way), mixing ambiance with cocktails.

Masala Bar is stylish, edgy and entirely candlelit (but not in a soppy romantic way)...

169

Countries

AFRICA & MIDDLE EAST*

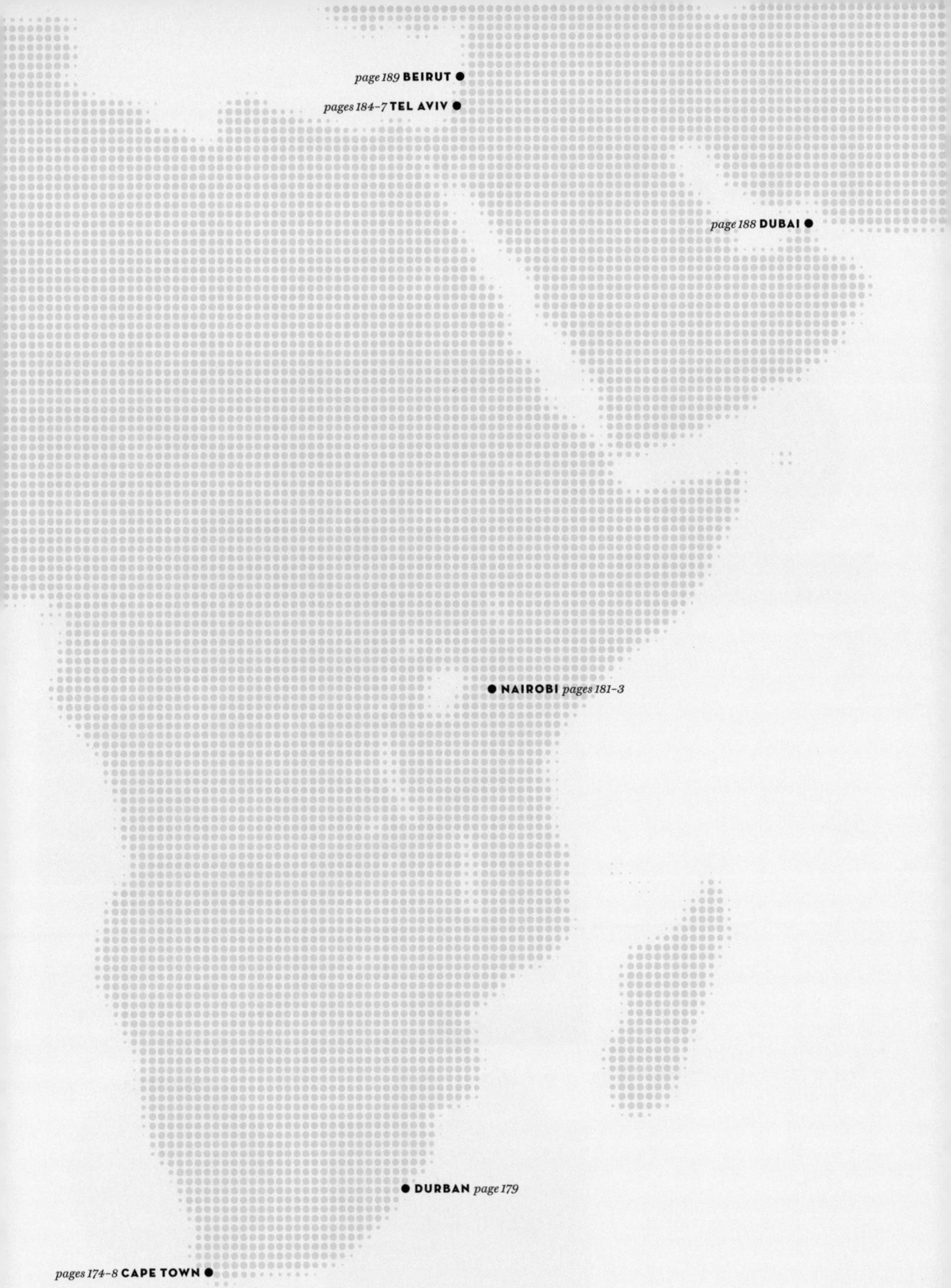

page 189 **BEIRUT** ●

pages 184–7 **TEL AVIV** ●

page 188 **DUBAI** ●

● **NAIROBI** pages 181–3

● **DURBAN** page 179

pages 174–8 **CAPE TOWN** ●

INTRO*

If you want an example of global diversity, you have to look at Africa. In this book, we cover bars from the far north in Morocco and the foothills of the Atlas mountains, through to the south coast and Cape Town – on the same continent but so very different in landscape, terroir and culture.

In the north of Africa, European influence flirts with historic local values, searing heat and desert terrain. While in the south, the lush landscape gives birth to wonderful wines and fantastic spirits, which make their way into the local cocktail scenes and drinking establishments.

Across the Middle East, there's rise in high-end drinking culture, with bars such as **Zuma ↗** in Dubai (see page 188) leading a flavour revolution in this part of the world. Look, too, for the excellent burgeoning scene in Israel, home to some of the leading bars that feature in this book.

In the north of Africa, European influence flirts with historic local values.

CAPE TOWN*

ASOKA

When you have Table Mountain as your backdrop, it's probably hard not to be a little envious, but Asoka can, quite rightly, be very proud of their very own vision of excellence. This restaurant and bar has become one of the most respected places in the city and right from the start of the evening you know your experience will be memorable. From the sumptuous platters of locally inspired seafood dishes and chargrilled vegetables to the drinks – fresh, bold, colourful and highly crafted affairs, bringing together fruit and spices, Asoka is an Instagrammer's dream come true. On top of that, how many other bars can boast of having a huge olive tree growing in it *and* a wonderful live band....

✖
68 Kloof Street, Gardens, Cape Town 8001 +27 21 422 0909 asoka.za.com
✖
IN THREE WORDS:
Highly Flavoursome Roots.
THE DRINK TO TRY:
The Porn Star Martini.

THEY SAY:
"The atmosphere is wonderful. Especially on their Tuesday Jazz nights. Jaw-droppingly efficient."
— **DEVIN CROSS, SOUTH AFRICA**
PRICE RATING: ✳✳✳

BASCULE BAR

One of the things that we are hopeful for with this book is that each entry will at least inspire a passing interest in a particular drink that you've never really been hugely keen on. In the case of the Bascule Bar, stretched splendidly across the basement of the plush Cape Grace Hotel on the Victoria & Albert Waterfront, we're talking whisky. It goes without saying that if, like us, you're slightly cock-a-hoop about the spirit, this is an excellent place to start. The menu today lists around 500 different whiskies from all over the world, including some absolute gems from South Africa, and it's probably fair to say that the bar helped to establish a real thirst – excuse the pun – among the growing community of South African whisky connoisseurs. Expect a quality, knowledgeable service, alongside the choice of many different flights and styles of whisky. Just be sure to steer clear from the rarities there – you'll have very little spending money left for the rest of your

trip, based on the legendary drams waiting to entice you.
✖
Cape Grace Hotel, West Quay Road, V&A Waterfront, Cape Town 8002 +27 21 410 7082 basculebar.com
✖
IN THREE WORDS:
Quintessential Quayside Quaffing.
THE DRINK TO TRY:
Start with a Bain's Cape Mountain single grain whisky.
WE SAY:
The menu reads like a Who's Who *of legendary drams.*
PRICE RATING: ✳✳✳✳

HANK'S ↗

Cape Town's Bree Street is fast developing into a perfect location for a fairly marathon drinking session. With the Orphanage (see page 176) helping to highlight the Cape's cocktail perfection, and Mother's Ruin (also page 176) flapping the flag for gin, now along comes Hank's, a whiskey joint with a vaguely Irish theme, possessing plenty of attitude and sassiness to suit the dark spirit of the moment. Since opening in early 2016, Hank's has become one of the city's most popular venues. The laid brick chambers are marvellously dark and tunnelled, hinting at a night that could end in mischief. In

fact, it's the kind of bar one can happily stay lost in until the wee hours of the morning. The jewel in the crown is the bar's excellent spirit collection (here you'll find some hard-to-get Japanese and Irish whiskeys) alongside the venue occasionally hosting live music and enlightening whiskey tastings from experts.

✖
110 Bree Street, Cape Town City Centre, Cape Town 8001 +27 82 535 5472 hanks.co.za
✖

IN THREE WORDS:
Hearty Hanky Panky.
THE DRINK TO TRY:
Must be Irish Whiskey.
THEY SAY:
"Hank's has a stunningly vibrant atmosphere."
DEVIN CROSS, SOUTH AFRICA
PRICE RATING: ✱✱✱

THE HOUSE OF MACHINES →

Among guidebook comments, "no visit would be complete without…" is perhaps the most lazy and overused phrase going, but here, its not an advisory

The House of Machines is a pretty legendary bar in Cape Town that ticks all the boxes…

note, it really does mean get your asses down here. The House Of Machines is a pretty legendary bar in Cape Town that ticks all of the boxes – fantastic drinks, great service, a beautiful crowd, live music, great beer on tap and delicious bar food. The venue itself is modelled on a haunted biker house – and as spirits go, don't expect to find your favourite ones on the shelves, as the bar only serves unique house spirits and well-designed pre-batched cocktails. For those of you with a "been there, got the T-shirt mentality," you can even do that, with some highly stylish threads to buy from The House shop. It's a thing, folks.
✖
84 Shortmarket Street, Cape Town City Centre, Cape Town 8000 +27 21 426 1400 thehouseofmachines.com
✖
IN THREE WORDS:
Marvellous Mechanical Masterpieces.
THE DRINK TO TRY:
An aged Manhattan or Negroni.
THEY SAY:
"Kick-ass bar with awesome live music every night, hot bartenders, delicious beer and the best Old Fashioned in the country."
— DEVIN CROSS, SOUTH AFRICA
PRICE RATING: ✱✱

FEATURE*

A DAY DRINKING IN...
CAPE TOWN

This outstandingly beautiful city has an equally impressive thriving cocktail scene, thinks bartender **Devin Cross**.

As the sun rises in Cape Town, so does the enthusiasm for exploring arguably one of the most exciting cities with a highly developed drinks culture. When you consider the wealth of great wines, beers and spirits that are crafted across South Africa, which have found international acclaim, it's little wonder that there are plenty of talented bartenders looking to explore such a hotbed of domestic flavour.

At the centre of of the scene is **Orphanage** (theorphanage. co.za) on Bree Street – arguably Cape Town's most famous cocktail bar. It's also the favourite haunt of every bartender in the city. Orphanage is largely credited as the cocktail bar that gave birth to the country's best bartenders and was for a very long time the benchmark for all other venues. The cosy interior, ever-changing cocktail menu and passionate team make this bar a Cape Town staple. As iconic venues go, this is one not to

miss – and neither is its Capone Reviver cocktail.

Cape Town has, in recent years become renowned for its gins. This popularity is arguably down to the proliferation of botanicals that grow in the Fynbos area of the western Cape, which distillers use to flavour their gin. At **Mother's Ruin** (+27 83 964 8300), a short hop down Bree Street, you'll find every one of these gins and many, many more. The bar boasts one of the biggest gin selections in the Southern Hemisphere. So grab a Negroni or even have a go at a Build-Your-Own G&T and settle in.

Another popular gin bar worth a visit is the aptly named **Secret Gin Bar** (theginbar.co.za).

> ...a Whisky Sour at The Leopard Bar at The 12 Apostles Hotel is a breathtaking experience and the views from the top floor, overlooking the Atlantic Ocean, are simply stunning.

one soon realizes that this venue was built for one thing – a unique experience. The menu, which features no brands or hints as to what spirit is used, is designed to make the guest reconsider any preconceived notions of what constitutes a cocktail.

As you enter the evening in the city, head to **Tjing Tjing** ← (tjingtjing.co.za), a rooftop bar in a 200-year-old building that offers a really interesting array of cocktails and vibe. With its great views, exquisite food and buzzing atmosphere you'll soon find you've stayed for far longer than you intended. Be warned though – this place is busy in summer, so get in early.

When it comes to your final few drinks of the day, you have a choice between two very different places indeed. For opulent hotel attention to detail, a Whisky Sour at **The Leopard Bar** at The 12 Apostles Hotel (12apostleshotel.com) is a breathtaking experience and the views from the top floor, overlooking the Atlantic Ocean, are simply stunning. But for a more tropical-themed vibe, head to Camps Bay and the **Caprice Cafe** ← (cafecaprice.co.za), located right on the beachfront, where you can sip sundowners and, if you stay long enough, maybe even a few sunrisers too.

This speakeasy-style joint is housed at the back of the Honest Chocolate Cafe on Wale Street and the small, intimate venue has somewhat of a cult following locally. Its history dates back to the last century when it was operated as a mortuary and – to add to the macabre element – the bar floor area once functioned as an embalming floor.

Another must-not-miss experience is **Outrage of Modesty** ← (anoutrage.com) on Shortmarket Street. This ultra-hip hidden bar is a seated venue only and while your first visit may feel a little daunting,

CAPE TOWN*

PUBLIK

Publik's approach to wine is forward thinking and democratic. The concept is simple – keep it natural and delicious. Dave Cope curates an ever-changing wine list that showcases the best of South African wine at a reasonable price. His relationship with vine growers and winemakers allows him to bring in new wines on an almost daily basis. If you're hungry, the bar's partnership with butcher Frankie Fenner and restaurant Ash represents the holy trinity of South Africa – great food, fantastic wine and magnificent biltong.

✖
81 Church Street, Cape Town 8001 publik.co.za
✖
IN THREE WORDS:
The Grape EsCape.
THE DRINK TO TRY:
The Black Rock Pinot Noir.
THEY SAY:
"It is definitely the best place to try our country's tastiest vino."
— **DEVIN CROSS, SOUTH AFRICA**
PRICE RATING: ✱✱✱

THE STACK ↑

Some stories are heartbreaking. Others are plain inspirational. In the case of The Stack, the story is both; the outcome, fortunately a happy one.

The first incarnation of The Stack, housed in the historic Victorian splendour of Cape Town's Leinster Hall, suffered a tragic inferno less than a week after it opened and had to be completely rebuilt. Needless to say, the phoenix has well and truly risen from the flames and owners Sarah Ord and Nigel Pace do a remarkable job at bringing contemporary, sophisticated fine dining and drinking to the area. The slick new bar has gained much chatter among the local cocktail cognoscenti and it's no surprise they're getting a lot of attention.

✖
Leinster Hall, 7 Weltevreden Street, Gardens, Cape Town 8001 +27 21 286 0187 thestack.co.za
✖
IN THREE WORDS:
Stacks Of Promise.
THE DRINK TO TRY:
The House Favourite – which is called The Stack.
THEY SAY:
"The cocktail list is one of the sexiest in town and the venue, now completely remodelled, is equally impressive."
— **DEVIN CROSS, SOUTH AFRICA**
PRICE RATING: ✱✱✱✱

DURBAN✶

LUCKY SHAKER ↓

Vibe and quality seem to be bywords for the style of drinks pioneered by Lucky Shaker. Nothing flashy, but always flawless and fun. The menu here is broken down into distinct categories – fruity, refreshing, dry and bold – with a tendency toward using fresh fruit or homemade syrups at the heart of the cocktails. There's also a distinct seasonality to each drink; head there for some winter sun with friends and find yourself surrounding a deliciously spicy punch that's the perfect antidote for the chilly nights. Likewise you'll find all manner of vibrant zestiness should you be heading over in the summer too.

✖
No 9B Mayfair On The Lake,
5 Park Lane, Parkside,
Umhlanga 4319, Durban
+27 78 450 6751 luckyshaker.com
✖

IN THREE WORDS:
Lucky Find Indeed.
THE DRINK TO TRY:
Seek out one of the punches if you're drinking with a party of people.
THEY SAY:
"Probably the best cocktail bar in the country."
— **DEVIN CROSS, SOUTH AFRICA**
PRICE RATING: ✱✱

THE CHAIRMAN

Given the rising interest in the rarity and connoisseurship of single malt whisky across South Africa, it was only a matter of time until this appreciation grew out to other areas of Africa, and Durban is one such place to truly recognize its reverence. The Chairman offers one of the most comprehensive collections of whisky in the city, alongside a fine understanding of both Cognac and rum. Couple this with its ample cigar selection, well-crafted cocktails and the best live jazz acts and you have a place worthy of true international acclaim. The decor is delightfully distressed and hipster. Expect to find the cognoscenti heading here to soak up the atmosphere.

✖
146 Mahatma Gandhi Road,
Point, Durban +27 79 753 6313
thechairmanlive.com
✖

IN THREE WORDS:
The Whisky Guv'nor.
THE DRINK TO TRY:
A Whisky Sour.
WE SAY:
If you're heading to the city, then a reservation at The Chairman should be on your list of evening pursuits.
PRICE RATING: ✱✱✱✱

MARRAKESH & NAIROBI*

EL FENN →

Emerging from the Sahara desert, Morocco is home to some of the most interesting hotels and hostels in Africa (try a cigar and a Martini in the Churchill Bar at La Mamounia), and none more so than Marrakesh's El Fenn. In the city in which Yves Saint Laurent designed and built his personal garden, this colourful riad was created by Vanessa Branson and sits just inside the city walls, providing the perfect, serene oasis, far from the madding crowds. Inside you'll find a cool space, with vibrant colours on the walls, pools of water calming the atmosphere, and sheer peace. The indoor bar downstairs is perfect for sitting and smoking a cigar, while upstairs on the 650sq m (7000 sq ft) roof terrace, the sounds of the city waft past gently. This suntrap is the perfect place for a pre-dinner Negroni (their restaurant is exceptional too) or Daiquiri as you watch the sun set over the city. More unique than the big chain hotels, and far more fancy than most other riads, you'll find a similar experience at Vanessa's brother Richard's place, Kasbah Tamadot, in the foothills of the Atlas mountains.

✖

Derb Moulay Abdullah Ben Hezzian, 2, Marrakesh 40000 +212 5244 41210 el-fenn.com

✖

IN THREE WORDS:
Moroccan Rooftop Bliss.

THE DRINK TO TRY:
A Negroni.

THEY SAY:
"Step into El Fenn and you leave the noise and madness behind."
— MARCIN MILLER, UK

PRICE RATING: ✱✱✱✱

ARTCAFFE

There's no doubt that Nairobi has a burgeoning interest in both cocktails and craft beer. Ranging from the splendour of the Kempinski Hotel's Balcony Bar (kempinski.com), serving a mixture of well-crafted classics, and the Juniper Social, with its quirky gin fizz served in mason jars, through to Brew Bistro (see right), which has taken its lead from the innovation and passion of craft breweries in Europe and the USA, there lies an interest for both tourists and locals to explore a new-found thirst for drinking culture on very different levels. Sitting in-between these is the Artcaffe, – or caffes, given that there are a number of these popular bistro/bar/coffeehouse/bakeries across the capital. Stop by the Westgate branch and you may be lucky enough to have a cocktail made by head bartender Joan Samia (see the StarTender interview on page 182), who is arguably becoming one of Nairobi's most famous bartenders. The list consists of simple classics – Daiquiris etc. – plus a fun line in Mojitos. The Spicy Thai brings together vodka, fresh pineapple, basil, chilli and lemon juice. Smart,

Smart, laid back and definitely tasteful, there's not a lot to dislike here.

laid back and definitely tasteful, there's not a lot to dislike here.

✖

Westgate Mall, Mwanzi Road, Westlands, 69671 – 00400, Nairobi +254 725 303030
artcaffe.co.ke

✖

IN THREE WORDS:
Cultured Café Cocktails.
THE DRINK TO TRY:
Joan's Nairobi Mule.
WE SAY:
A great all-rounder; head there and be pleasantly surprised.
PRICE RATING: ✖✖

THE BALCONY BAR

Within the plush walls of the Villa Rosa Kempinski Hotel lies this gem of Nairobi. The Balcony Bar is one of three which the hotel boasts and is the most refined, offering a wide selection of cocktails, alongside a focus on Champagne and Cognac. In fact, if refined pairings are your thing, then look no further than the Balcony's Triple Treat – an excellent selection of cigars, which the bartenders will help you pair with vintage Cognacs and dark chocolate truffles.

With a chilled-out soundtrack provided by various DJs and the occasional live band, the Balcony Bar is certainly one of the best places to start your evening with something fizzy and finish with the delicious complexities of an after-dinner brandy. Time to unwind in five-star luxury.

✖

Villa Rosa Kempinski Nairobi, Chiromo Road, 00800 Nairobi, +254 703 049 000
kempinski.com

✖

IN THREE WORDS:
Height Of Luxury.
WE SAY:
An excellent hotel bar, with bartending skills to match.
PRICE RATING: ✖✖✖✖✖

BREW BISTRO

An engaging operation, open since 2009, aiming to bring the best locally made craft beers to a wider audience. It's essentially a microbrewery, bar and restaurant, with a relaxed, modern-looking rooftop bar – the perfect location to enjoy a few pints of its wares. From the flights of German Pilsner-style brews to pale ales and heavier, Belgian influenced offerings, there's a definite sense of craft at work alongside some innovation with flavours. One of the seasonal offerings is inspired by Irish whiskey, with notes of vanilla and lighter fruits, and matured in bourbon barrels.

✖

Piedmont Plaza, Ngong Road, Nairobi +254 771 152350
thebigfivbreweries.com

✖

IN THREE WORDS:
Finely Crafted Character.
THE DRINK TO TRY:
The Nyatipa ale.
WE SAY:
Craft Beer is alive and well, living comfortably in Nairobi.
PRICE RATING: ✖✖

FOCUS*

STARTENDER
JOAN SAMIA

Joan Samia, head bartender at the Artcaffe (see page 180), is fast becoming one of Kenya's best-known bartenders, thanks to her victory in the 2016 World Class Kenya bartending competition. Since then, she went on to represent Kenya at the 2016 World Class finals.

Where do you drink when you're off duty?
When I'm off duty, I like to go to the **Brew Bistro Bar** (see page 181) and also catch up on what's happening in the Kenyan drinking scene and trends.

Your favourite drink of all time…?
The classic Margarita. Smooth and fierce!

Where would you most like to go drinking cocktails?
I would love to go drinking in New York, as for me it's the epitome of cocktail bars.

What's the most underrated cocktail in the world?
The Daiquiri to me is underrated. One of the best classic cocktails and yet always seen as a loser! But when made right, it's the best "anytime" drink.

Nairobeans are into cocktails…There is a hungry market and it's time to feed it! Kenyans like trends and the fact that they are ready to explore anything new means that it is time for the market to blow up.

What's hot in the Nairobi cocktail scene now?
Right now, Nairobians are into cocktails, which is the moment all bartenders and bar owners have been waiting for. There is a hungry market and it's time to feed it! Kenyans like trends and the fact that they are ready to explore anything new means that it is time for the market to blow up. The only challenge is to maintain the emerging cocktail culture.

✖
JOAN SAMIA'S NAIROBI MULE

2 coriander sprigs
15ml simple syrup
30ml lemon juice
60ml Ketel One vodka
60ml mango or pineapple
  purée
a mint sprig, to decorate

Muddle the coriander with the simple syrup, then add the lemon juice and vodka. Add crushed ice and stir. Add the fruit purée, then fill up with crushed ice. Garnish with a mint sprig and serve.

JOAN'S TOP FIVE FAVOURITE DRINKING HAVENS TO HANG OUT IN:

✖
Sweet liberty, Miami
(mysweetliberty.com)
What made the biggest impression is that it's the first bar I have been to that is run by ladies – and they really know how to make impressive cocktails.

✖
Broken Shaker, Miami
(thefreehand.com)
Altogether, their trio of concepts from the tiki bar, the fresh garden and the classic bar made a great impression on me!

✖
Dead Rabbit, New York
(see page 212)
Always praised for its great drinks and a multiple award-winning top bar of the year.

✖
The Aviary, Chicago
(see page 228) ↑
World-class cocktails and an award-winning bartender from the 2014 World Class finals.

✖
Door 74, Amsterdam
(see page 98)
I have two bartenders from there [who work with Samia] and they have such great characters. I would love to go and experience that.

TEL AVIV*

FRENCH 57

New Orleans comes to Tel Aviv! French 57 has taken the huge influence of cocktail mastery on display in New Orleans (see pages 230–3 for some truly authentic bars) and turned it into an Israeli art form all of its own. Founded by one of Israel's top mixologists (Oron Lerner – see our interview on page 186), this place features hand-crafted cocktails and creole food and drink. Expect plenty of Sazeracs, some brilliant Mardi Gras vibes and, if you ask nicely, the house Madame 57, made from a delicious balance of roasted mango-infused gin, pineapple, thyme, orange bitters and Champagne. Arguably *the* place for a contemporary twist on the classics in the city.

✖
Brenner Street 2, Tel Aviv-Yafo
+972 50 734 7452
french57.com

✖
IN THREE WORDS:
57 Shades of Excellence.
THE DRINK TO TRY:
The aforementioned Madame 57.

THEY SAY:
"Meticulously hand-made with the highest-quality ingredients, by barmen with a passion for excellence and tradition."
— **GAL GRANOV, ISRAEL**
PRICE RATING: ✱✱✱

IMPERIAL CRAFT ↓

The concept of the "bartenders' bar" has been discussed at points in this guide, and this phrase is undoubtedly the case when it comes to Imperial Craft, which nestles itself away in the city's Imperial hotel. The team behind this highly regarded cocktail joint includes six guys, each with a different skill set, who have come together to create arguably one of Tel Aviv's best drinking experiences. The menu changes regularly, but has established itself around eight flavour principles, which cover the whole gamut from Fruity, through to Deep and Aged, finishing with Spicy. The drinks themselves are very cleverly constructed, using infused spirits and an impressive range of spirits and ingredients.

✖
Ha-Yarkon Street 66, Tel Aviv-Yafo +972 73 264 9464
imperialtlv.com

✖
IN THREE WORDS:
Bar's Bustling Business.
THE DRINK TO TRY:
Although the menu changes, the team maintain they have knowledge of 150 different drinks.
WE SAY:
A bar-ometer for the growing cocktail scene that is steadily emerging in Tel Aviv. Ahead of their time, these guys are certainly spirited pioneers.
PRICE RATING: ✱✱✱

PORTER & SONS

A spacious and very smart gastro pub, with more than 50 types of beer on tap, and many more by the bottle. Here you'll find an incredible range of imported beers, from big, bold London porters (we suppose the clue is in the name!), as well as IPAs, Belgian Blondes and tripels and a fine selection of German lager too. The domestic craft brewing scene is very well catered for and Porter & Sons – along with the newly opened 55 Beers in Jerusalem (+972 9 887 0903) – are great places to try an array of local Israeli boutique beers.

✖
HaArba'a Street 14, Tel Aviv-Yafo +972 3 624 4355 porterandsons.rest.co.il
✖
IN THREE WORDS:
Family Flavour Fountain.
WE SAY:
Casual and relaxed dining and drinking, with a wealth of really excellent beers.
PRICE RATING: ✱✱

TASTING ROOM

The concept of tasting really pricey wines has well and truly undergone something of a transformation in the last few years and the Tasting Room wine bar is one such place, which aims to liberate drinkers from the elitism of fine wines. When you arrive at this uber-cool design-led bar/bottle room, you'll receive a smart card that you can top up with cash and then use under your own steam. The place features automatic machines, which dispense quantities as

tasting serves, half-glasses or full-glasses, choosing from a few dozen open bottles of varying price, so you can try many local Israeli and imported wines at your own pace, with simplicity. There are of course hundreds of wines by the bottle as well, should you find the one you: A: fall in love with and B: can afford!

✖
Eliezer Kaplan Street 36, Tel Aviv-Yafo +972 3 533 3213 tastingroom.co.il
✖
IN THREE WORDS:
Lots of Liberated Libations.
WE SAY:
A smart concept that has taken the wine world by storm.
PRICE RATING: ✱✱

WHISKEY MUSEUM AND BAR

One of Israel's latest outlets, which has dedicated itself to the huge local popularity of whisky. It's located in an amazing Templar tunnel underground in the Sarona district and features over 1,000 different whiskies by the dram: Scotch, Irish, American, Japanese and world whiskies. You'll also find many independent bottlings and rare editions, which aren't available anywhere else locally. Keep in mind that the place is kosher, so it's closed on Friday and Saturday – opening only on Saturday night and weekdays.

✖
David Elazar Street 27, Sarona, Tel Aviv-Yafo +972 3 955 1105 whiskeybm.co.il
✖
IN THREE WORDS:
Titanic Taste Temple.

THEY SAY:
"This is the best place to have a dram of whisky in Israel."
— GAL GRANOV, ISRAEL
PRICE RATING: ✱✱✱

BENNY'S CASK ALE PUB

This is a tiny pub off the beaten track located in a suburb of Tel Aviv, but it's well worth seeking out, if you're a serious cask beer fanatic – something that owner Benny clearly is. The place has only three taps and doesn't serve food but the ales are the real deal here and it's one of the only cask ale pubs in Israel. Expect to find local boutique brews, which are put into traditional beer casks and poured "old style" – giving you the malty, soft flavours you'd find in a traditional London boozer, rather than the traditionally carbonated fizzy brews. The beer on tap changes daily, so gives you more than a few good reasons to keep on returning!

✖
Saba Jerusalem Street 46, Kfar Saba +972 9 771 7627
✖
IN THREE WORDS:
Malt Advocates, Unite!
THEY SAY:
"A great place to experience really well poured craft beers at a decent price."
— GAL GRANOV, ISRAEL
PRICE RATING: ✱

FOCUS*

STARTENDER
ORON LERNER

O ron has been at the
forefront of Tel Aviv's
developing cocktail
culture for the last 10 years, being
part of the opening team for the
Imperial Craft and the man
behind **French 57** (see both on
page 184), combining the New
Orleans-influenced cocktails
and cuisine with Tel Aviv's local
produce and approach.

*When I'm off duty drinking
in Tel Aviv...*
First up, there's **Foster**
(Shlomo ha-Melekh Street
38, Tel Aviv +972 3 529 3510),
a neighbourhood bar run by
two of its bartenders. You'll
get recognized as soon as you
walk in, served great beer and
decent-priced liquor even late
at night. It's just a place that
makes you feel at home. If we're
hungry we'll probably head to
Minzar (Alenby Street 60, Tel
Aviv +972 3 517 3015) instead –
a dive bar that's open 24 hours
a day, serving great food and
high quality but cheaply priced
beer. Minzar is the kind of place
to go to be alone for a while, to
wind down – although you'll be

**Minzar is the kind
of place to go to be
alone for a while,
to wind down –
although you'll be
surrounded by
other bartenders
finishing their
shifts and looking
to wind down, too.**

surrounded by other bartenders
finishing their shifts and looking
to wind down, too!
*My favourite city to go
drinking...*
New Orleans. There's a huge
selection of bars and a lot of
surprises to find. You'll get
to dive bars serving amazing
cocktails (such as Frozen Irish
from **Erin Rose**, see page 231);
tiki bars offering Polynesian
vacations, such as **Latitude29**
(see page 230), **Cane and Table**
(caneandtablenola.com) and
Tiki Tolteca (tikitolteca.com);
classic old-style bars that sell
cigars for a truly southern feel
(such as **French 75** on page 232);
bars run by bartending mentors,
such as **Revel** (revelcafeandbar.
com); and modern bars with
cutting-edge innovation, such
as **Cure** (see opposite). And
everyone will be so nice and
welcoming you'll wish you could
just drink and eat nonstop.
*My Ultimate Tel Aviv
Bar Crawl...*
I'd say start with Happy Hour at
Imperial Craft (see page 184).
Book in advance and focus on
their early menu drinks like the
Painkiller #2 if they can still
make it. Then head off to **Thai
House** (thai-house.co.il), just
two blocks to the north, where
they make fresh fruit slushies
with some rum in it and great
spicy Thai food. From there,

I'd venture to **Cerveceria** (cerveceria.co.il) across the street for the largest selection of gins in the city and self-smuggled jamón from Spain. A brief 15-minute walk from there is **Beer Bazaar** (beerbazaar.co.il), offering a large selection of local beers in the middle of the closed souk – try their own brand, whatever is on tap. I'd cross from there to **Brut** (+972 3 510 2923), a local, very small and very adventurous restaurant serving great wines, and then their other bar, **Extra Brut**, which is right around the corner, serving the best pint of Guinness in the city. At the end – or at any time you feel you need to – I'd head to **French 57** (see page 184), for the perfect nightcap and dessert – Cheesecake Beignets.

One of my favourite recipes from the French 57 menu...
The Black Magic Julep, from our black menu – serving bitter and complex drinks to those who know to ask for them!

✖
BLACK MAGIC JULEP

10 fresh mint leaves
10ml simple syrup
25ml Fernet Branca
25ml Amaro Averna
25ml Four Roses Small Batch
  Bourbon
15ml Amaro Montenegro
15ml Amaro Nonino
2 dashes Angostura bitters

Smack the mint leaves, toss them into the glass, pour all the liquor in and leave to sit for about 5 minutes to absorb the flavours. Fill with crushed ice, garnish with a lot of fresh mint leaves and a dash of ground nutmeg and sip away.

ORON'S TOP FIVE GLOBAL BARS TO CHECK OUT:

✖
Rum Trader, Berlin (see page 88) ↑
This old-school-style bar works wonders. Their Rum Sour – and it's as simple as it reads – is by far the best I've ever had. The bartenders make great drinks effortlessly and the selection of cocktails and spirits is impressive.

✖
Seibert's, Cologne, Germany (seiberts-bar.com)
Seibert's has a visual language of its own – classic, elegant, well garnished, tasteful. It is the delicate touches that make the drinks look perfect.

✖
Cure, New Orleans (curenola.com)
It's really tough choosing a bar in New Orleans that stands apart from the rest, as all bars there are great! But Cure manages to combine the New Orleans atmosphere, hospitality and relaxed vibes with new and exciting drinks; especially their rare menu. Well worth the travel to Freret Street.

✖
Imperial Craft, Tel Aviv (see page 184)
The pioneer of the local cocktail scene, this bar is a symbol of how far motivation can get you. It is a superb bar, with a great selection of drinks and an amazing vibe that manages to be a hotel speakeasy-styled, well-designed bar, without overdoing it.

✖
One Flew South, Atlanta Airport, Georgia (oneflewsouthatl.com)
I make sure to have all my US connections go through this airport, just for this restaurant/ bar. Setting up shop in an airport – and doing it as well as they do – deserves a lot of praise. Being able to turn guests into regulars in an airport where thousands pass through daily is an indication of their hospitality.

DUBAI*

LITTLE BLACK DOOR

Hidden away unsurprisingly behind a black door in the lower reaches of the Conrad Hotel, this is a speakeasy-ish place where a simple knock of the large lion door knocker is enough to make your presence known. Even the website "KnockToEnter.com", gives you the instructions. Once inside you are greeted with chandeliers, exposed brickwork and comfy chairs, giving it the feel of somewhere between a Manhattan loft apartment, a European palace and a Victorian first-class train carriage.

When it comes to the drinks list, the cocktails are surprisingly complex and it might take you a while to read through them and get to grips with the explanations. A few of the cocktails reference Twitter handles and hashtags. All very interesting indeed.

✖

The Conrad, Sheikh Zayed Road, Dubai +971 55 623 1620 knocktoenter.com

✖

IN THREE WORDS:
Big Brass Knocker.

WE SAY:
One of the hottest hangouts in Dubai.
PRICE RATING: ✱✱✱✱

ZUMA →

This already uber-successful restaurant has highly lauded outposts in London and Hong Kong, breathing a super high-end life into beautifully cooked dim-sum cuisine. As restaurant/bars go, the place is absolutely vast, seating 300 covers, but you're not just here to sit and stare into your drink. The atmosphere is incredibly buzzy and the waiting staff have to be among the most professional, yet busy, in the business. The bar has a venerable treasure trove of different types of sake, which, let's face it, is a perfect accompaniment to izakaya-style cuisine. On the cocktail front, Zuma's mixture of fresh, vibrant Martini-style drinks brings another dimension to the proceedings, with the Rubabu (a rhubarb-infused sake, shaken with vodka and fresh passion fruit) a highlight. Under the direction of head bartender Jimmy Barrat, the bar has just developed a unique Solera system with rum brand Ron Zacapa, which uses four small American white oak casks, with different flavour components to

infuse and enhance the style of the rum once it hits your glass.

✖

Gate village 06, DIFC, PO box 506620, Dubai +971 4 425 5660 zumarestaurant.com

✖

IN THREE WORDS:
Asian-Influenced Perfection.
THE DRINK TO TRY:
The Rubabu
THEY SAY:
"Stunning cocktails personally supervised by master mixologists."
— KEN GRIER, UK
PRICE RATING: ✱✱✱✱✱

FEATURE*

BEIRUT'S HEDONISTIC HIGHLIGHTS

Beirut may not be the first place you would imagine to host arguably one of the world's most interesting and thriving drinks scenes, but spend a few days in this city, which is truly passionate about cuisine, and you'll understand why. From the old school cabaret leanings of **MusicHall** (themusichall. com) – an incredibly vibey bar/ music venue where young and old seamlessly mingle – to the sophisticated connoisseur heaven of **The Malt Gallery** (themaltgallery.com) – a ridiculously well stocked spirits shop and dram bar, which

Without doubt, though, *the* place to experience in the whole city is Central Station… and the magnificent hospitality, vibe and ingenuity of head honcho Jad Ballout.

plays host to masterclasses and bartender displays too – this is a city rich in conviviality.

If gin is your thing then a visit to **Propaganda Gin Bar** (caramelboutiquehotel.com) is essential; here you can enjoy over 40 types of international gins and a variety of exceptional cocktails. Head to the Mar Mikhaël area and your night then comes alive spectacularly. Want to experience the powerful flavours of Arak, the cloudy, aromatic local spirit? Then head to **Anise** (+961 70 977 926) for a taste of the Lion's Milk. Without doubt, though, *the* place to experience in the whole city is **Central Station** ← (+961 71 736 737) and the magnificent hospitality, vibe and ingenuity of head honcho Jad Ballout. This bustling bar is something of a miracle: a high-volume restaurant and bar, making unique cocktails with great skill, all served with the most precision-like service. It's little wonder that Central Station now ranks as a true leading light in the global cocktail scene.

AUSTRA-LASIA*

Countries

● CHRISTCHURCH *pages 202–3*

page 203 WANAKA ●

INTRO*

It is Australia first and foremost where the bar scene has developed most rapidly. Drawing on influences from London and New York it has grown some of the most unique and interesting drinking joints on the face of the planet. The Aussies know a thing or two about hospitality as well, so the order of the day in any of our recommended bars here is to sit back, enjoy and try to add to the atmosphere yourself. Don't be a guest, be a willing participant. And if you get a chance, try some of their own whisky and gin; both are exceptional, especially those that come from the wild isle of Tasmania.

Let's also celebrate the bar scene in New Zealand, where you'll find an equally eloquent bunch of hosts who will draw on the richness of local ingredients to really make you feel totally at home.

It is Australia first and foremost where the bar scene has developed most rapidly.

SYDNEY*

THE BARBER SHOP

If you look at the nu-vintage style of men's hairdressers sweeping the Western world, you'll notice that they look pretty similar to most of the cool, hipster bars that have been popping up from Edmonton to Edinburgh. So why not combine the two? Well, that's exactly what the folk at The Barber Shop in Sydney have done. As the sun slowly fades, this traditional barber shop comes alive as a "parlour entrance for ladies and gentlemen to venture past the partition door and discover a hidden treasure in the heart of the Sydney CBD," as they tell it. The clippers and razors are put away in favour of jiggers and Boston shakers, with gin the order of the day alongside boutique-bottled beers and artisanal spirits, and a selection of local and imported wines. The menu shows off classics from the UK and USA, including low-ABV options; some are even shaken up in a vintage "Crawley Imperial Shaker", a kind of steam punk-style mechanical cocktail-shaking device.

✖
89 York Street, Sydney, NSW 2000 +61 2 9299 9699 thisisthebarbershop.com
✖
IN THREE WORDS:
A Cut Above.
THE DRINK TO TRY:
A Fascinator from 1937.
WE SAY:
Stylish, hipster, but with a genuine substance too.
PRICE RATING: ✱ ✱ ✱

THE BAXTER INN ↗

One of the most highly recommended bars in this book, The Baxter Inn has won the hearts and minds of many of our contributors and it is easy to see why. Located right in the heart of Sydney, The Baxter Inn turns whisky on its head and introduces this once staid spirit into a fun-time, party atmosphere. With incredibly rare bottles of whisky open and ready to drink, there is a cornucopia of labels ready to be tried, but without any of the stuffiness that is often associated with whisky tasting. But this joint is not just about whisky – there are awesome cocktails too at this basement operation, and the beer selection will rival anywhere else in Australia. Set up by the guys behind The Shady Pines Saloon (see opposite), it is

another example of why visiting Sydney is a must for any serious booze-hound!
✖
152–156 Clarence Street, Sydney, NSW 2000 +61 2 9221 5580 thebaxterinn.com
✖
IN THREE WORDS:
Inn Good Time.
THE DRINK TO TRY:
Sometimes there's nothing greater in life than a Hauf 'n' Hauf: beer & whisky.
THEY SAY:
"Impressive back bar, high-quality cocktails, personalized service, all done in an exceptionally busy place. Seamless."
—**DAVIDE SEGAT, UK**
"Love the staff, decor, music and the amazing selection of whiskies."
—**JANE OVEREEM, TASMANIA**
PRICE RATING: ✱ ✱ ✱

HUBERT

What do you do if you're really, really good at bars? Open more bars! But when you feel like you've reached peak-bar, then what next? Go into food. And that is exactly what the chaps who set up The Shady Pines Saloon and The Baxter Inn (see left) have done. Having poached one of the best chefs in the country to run their kitchen, Hubert is a place to be seen. Walking through big wooden doors, you immediately feel welcomed into this palace of French-themed cuisine, the wood-panelling on the walls helping to create a cosy, homely but luxurious environment.

We aren't here to talk about the food (honestly, you're there to eat so get stuck in), but it deserves more than a passing mention, as this is, after all, a restaurant. But once you're settled in and your stomach is lined, hit the cocktail list, which is perfectly paired with the concept of "eating". In this subterranean hideaway, you're far more Franco than Aussie, so kick back, embrace the ambiance and enjoy some awesome food and booze.

✖

15 Bligh Street, Sydney, NSW 2000
+61 2 9232 0881
restauranthubert.com

✖

IN THREE WORDS:
Tricolour Goodness and Cocktails.
THE DRINK TO TRY:
The House Martini is an excellent pour-your-own pre-bottled affair.
WE SAY:
Be embraced by this sumptuous venue and enjoy all the flavours they have to offer.
PRICE RATING: ✶✶

LOVE, TILLY DEVINE

As you approach Love, Tilly Devine, you'll discover that this small bar, with its exposed, white-washed walls is a place that is very much focused around wine. It gives off an air of hipster coffee shop or a pop-up boutique, but inside you'll find welcoming workers and friendly faces,

ready to make your drinking experience one of the best in the city. In fact, they say themselves that "without being pretentious about it, we want this to be a bar where people come to drink well rather than to just get drunk", which is indeed a noble endeavour. With a wine list that currently sits at around 300 different labels from around the world, you might be hard pressed to find a place to sit down in this 40-seat bar, given the space afforded for all the bottles they have! But what about the name? Well, apparently it is a "direct reference to the former East Sydney heavyweight – brothel madame and militia boss extraordinaire – Tilly Devine". So there you go!

✖

91 Crown Lane, Sydney, NSW 2010 +61 2 9326 9297
lovetillydevine.com

✖

IN THREE WORDS:
Love Tilly's Wines.
THE DRINK TO TRY:
The port and tonic cocktail.
THEY SAY:
"This tiny little place looks achingly cool, but has no ego or pretension."
— JANE PARKINSON UK
PRICE RATING: ✶✶

SHADY PINES SALOON

There are many places that shine brightly in Sydney but if you're looking for something off the beaten track, a place where bartenders truly drink, then make your way to the The Shady Pines Saloon. The very name conjures up images of low lighting, bar stools, beer bottles and bourbon; and you'd be bang on the money with that assumption about this bar.

This is the sort of place to grab yourself a beer and a bar stool and chat to whoever may be sitting next to you. Home to many, if you're passing through just be sure to smile, as this place will make you happier than a hot water bottle in winter. Oh, and check out their website, which features a cowboy riding a giant rabbit. Yeah, we know! A giant rabbit!

✖

Shop 4, 256 Crown Street, Darlinghurst, NSW 2010
+61 405 624 944
shadypinessaloon.com

✖

IN THREE WORDS:
Ride That Bunny!
THEY SAY:
"This low-lit boilermaker-slinging haunt is where the bartenders hang out – and it plays country & western."
— DAVE BROOM, UK
PRICE RATING: ✶

FEATURE*

A DAY DRINKING IN...
SYDNEY

We spoke to **Sam Bygrave**, editor of *Australian Bartender* magazine (australianbartender.com.au) for his ideal day out exploring the best places to drink in this mighty city.

✖

Sydney is Australia's first city and it is chaotic and brash. It takes a lot of energy to live here; the streets can be hard to navigate (town planning seeming to have been done in the days when rum was the colony's currency), and it's loud.

Your first stop should be the **Hotel Palisade** ↗ in The Rocks and the **Henry Deane Bar** (hotelpalisade.com/henry-deane) on its rooftop, to take in the view with a cocktail in hand. Should the weather turn wet, you're best at **Bulletin Place** ↑ (bulletinplace.com) in Circular Quay – they've been named the country's best cocktail bar four years in a row and are the leading exponents of a distinctly Aussie approach to drinks: think summer in a glass, and you're getting there.

As the evening descends, the Clarence Street run is ideal.

Within a toss of a bar napkin there are three of the country's best bars: the Daiquiri at rum bar **Lobo Plantation** ↘ (thelobo.com.au) is a smart choice – or you'd do well to leave the choice in the hands of their bartenders. **The Baxter Inn** (see page 194) is unmissable for those who like whisky, craft beer or top-flight hospitality, which is why there's often a queue despite its location

Sydney is Australia's first city and it is chaotic and brash.

down a darkened alleyway. Luckily, Australia's premier gin bar, **The Barber Shop** (see page 194) is located opposite in the same disused alleyway – order a Genever Crusta here and pull up a perch outside to keep an eye on Baxter's queue.

From here it's time to pad your stomach: for those enamoured with burgers, the team from Mary's in Newtown (+61 2 4995 9550) are the city's best – their mash is a bounty of butter and potato that you must also try. Just around the corner is **Continental Deli & Bistro** (continentaldelicatessen.com.au), which specializes in canned goods of the highest quality (their canning programme, such as it is, includes a Mar-Tinny, which is perhaps as perfect a Martini as you'll find in Sydney, and an admirable Can-Hattan).

Next, visit Oxford Street, home to Sydney's gay community for decades, now undergoing a revitalization with an influx of new bartender-owned bars opening in the precinct. Start with a Spritz at the innovative **This Must Be The Place** (tmbtp.com.au); then duck over to

Bourke Street to **Dead Ringer** (deadringer.wtf) for a Sherry Cobbler; then a few doors down to Italian joint **Maybe Frank** (maybefrank.com) for a Negroni (and perhaps a pizza); before visiting **Shady Pines Saloon** (see page 195), the taxidermy-stuffed whisky dive that some six

years on from opening is still the original – and the best (get here on a Sunday and you'll see that the local hospitality crowd sure thinks so).

To finish the evening, head around the corner to **Big Poppa's** (bigpoppa.com.au). It's a combo of cheese, wine, cocktails and hip hop that stays open until 3am. Take their suggestion for wine, order the ragu, then ask the bartenders (they're some of Sydney's best) for one last drink. It will be a good one.

MELBOURNE*

BAR AMERICANO ↓

Some bars are small, others are tiny...and then there is Bar Americano. This is a proper "hole in the wall" style bar – one station, standing room for 10 people tops. Australia's first "standing room only" bar was opened in 2011 by Matthew Bax as an homage to the golden age of drinking, and they only serve classic cocktails – "No, the Espresso Martini is not a classic!" says Matt – and the menu changes on a regular basis. The no-photos policy is brilliant, too.

✖
20 Presgrave Place, Melbourne VIC 3000 +61 3 9939 1997 baramericano.com
✖

IN THREE WORDS:
Standing Room Only.
THE DRINK TO TRY:
The Americano.
THEY SAY:
"I had the best Americano of my life there. It's a drink you can go to when your taste buds are tired, a delicious all rounder."
— **HANNAH LANFEAR, UK**
PRICE RATING: ✱✱

BLACK PEARL ↓

There are some bars around the world who have given more back to the drinking scene in their country than they have taken out. Bramble (see page 58) in Edinburgh is a prime example of a place that has nurtured talent, and its very existence has allowed incredible bars and bartenders, such as Ryan Chetiyawardana and his Dandelyan bar (see page 31), to take flight.

In the southern hemisphere, a bar whose ripples are felt right across the bartending industry is Melbourne's Black Pearl. Its not just a hub of talent throwing out trained bartenders across the globe, but also a magnet for those looking for a top night out in this Australian city. The bar itself has a new look and feel to it, with clean lines and comfortable seats, and the menu is an entertaining browse made up of playing cards for each drink. This now legendary place just keeps turning out great

THE EVERLEIGH

When you have the lineage and heritage of the legendary Milk and Honey in New York to draw on, there is only going to be one outcome, and the Aussie cousin to the New Yorker is The Everleigh. This place has a wonderful, laid-back but classy feel and the cocktails are some of the best in the country. The wood panelling gives a distinctly speakeasy-cum-Mayfair-Club vibe, while the detail, from the glassware to the seating, all adds up to a beguiling mix of relaxing vintage with contemporary cocktails. Such is their eye for detail that they even have their own company to make high grade ice (The Navy Strength Ice Company), ensuring all their cocktails are chilled and diluted with the best frozen water around.

✖

150–156 Gertrude Street, Melbourne VIC 3065 +61 3 9416 2229 theeverleigh.com

✖

IN THREE WORDS:
Ice, Ice, Baby.

THE DRINK TO TRY:
If you're there in winter, ask for a Hot Toddy.

THEY SAY:
"Beautifully crafted classic cocktails. My Melbourne happy place."
— **JANE PARKINSON UK**

PRICE RATING: ✳✳✳

drinks, even as it celebrates nearly two decades in operation.

✖

304 Brunswick Street, Fitzroy, VIC 8065 +61 3 9417 0455 blackpearlbar.com.au

✖

IN THREE WORDS:
The Precious Pearl.

THE DRINK TO TRY:
Flick through the cartoon-like cards and go for the Early Bird. ↑

THEY SAY:
"Creativity and discovery! Very exciting interpretations and a wild and happy crowd!"
— **JOHNNY SCHULER, PERU**
"The Pearl has built a community around itself – owners, guests and staff – that extends a warm welcome to all who walk through the doors, in a way and to an extent that I have not seen anywhere else in the world."
— **PHILIP DUFF, USA**
"Absolutely wonderful ambiance. And Armagnac cocktails!"
— **AMANDA GARNHAM, FRANCE**

PRICE RATING: ✳✳✳

BOILERMAKER HOUSE

If you like whisky, you are in utter heaven here. There is an extreme selection of amazing bottles, which sit behind the bar like a line of soldiers defending the back wall...700 malt whiskies make up the main regiment and the 14 seats at the bar are utterly dominated by them. The bar hosts regular tutored tastings of whisky and beer, so they can pass on their extreme passion; these people are educators, not simply sales people. Then there are the beers: the seven beers on tap are supported by over 40 in bottles, and there is a meat and cheese bar...yes, a meat and cheese bar. If you don't like the sound of that, you should put this book away and go and read something else.

✖

209–211 Lonsdale Street, Melbourne VIC 3000 +61 424 270 082 boilermakerhouse.com.au

✖

IN THREE WORDS:
Meat And Cheese.

THE DRINK TO TRY:
A Boilermaker!

THEY SAY:
"This place is insane! Just google it and you'll see why! Whisky & Cheese, Whisky & Beer, Whisky & Cured Meats..."
— **JANE OVEREEM, TASMANIA**

PRICE RATING: ✳✳✳

FOCUS*

STARTENDER
TASH CONTE

Black Pearl (see page 198) is, in essence, a celebration of everything great about world-class bartending today. The combination of innovation, service and quality has placed the bar at the top of many drinks professionals "must-see" lists since it opened 15 years ago. Tash Conte is the visionary behind this undisputed cocktail gem.

What was the original ethos behind Black Pearl?

Black Pearl's ethos has been the same as it always has been for 15 years. It is about being a part of a family and about providing a space for people to be the best versions of themselves and what they love doing most, making drinks and being hospitable. People often ask what is the secret to longevity in this trade, and it's always the same answer for me. There is no secret! It is about consistency, ownership and allowing the team to excel in what they do.

Where do you drink when you're off duty?

Being a mum with a four-year-old and a husband who also works nights, you are never

really off duty! But when I do get the chance, there is a local bar/ restaurant called **Gerald's Bar** (+61 3 9349 4748) that I love. It's local and has an amazing array of wines that consistently change and the food just makes you feel at home.

Your favourite city to go drinking in…?

Apart from Melbourne, as it has a diverse range of places to lose time in, it would have to be Spain; in particular Barcelona, Madrid and Seville. All three cities are spilling with people in the streets, drinking and eating till all hours with not an unruly act in sight. We have a lot to learn from the Europeans in understanding that drinking is a part of life and not to treat it as an occasion to go mad!

TASH'S TOP FIVE DRINKING HAUNTS AROUND THE WORLD:

✖
Happiness Forgets, London (see page 36) *I love the fact that it is about the hospitality first and foremost before the drink. The energy behind the bar is contagious.*

✖
PDT, New York (see page 220) *It's the intimacy between the bartender, the drink and the space that I enjoy most at PDT; the cocktails are just delicious and elegant.*

✖
Café No Se, Antigua (see page 271) *This bar is unabashedly raw and is about the atmosphere, the company and enjoying the booze in its simplest form, straight up!*

✖
Bacchanal, New Orleans (see page 230) *Mounds of soul food teamed with Rosé and local musicians – enough said.*

✖
El Floridita, Havana (see page 274) *A bar steeped in American and Cuban history that makes Daiquiris from sunup to sunset.*

MELBOURNE*

HEARTBREAKER

Pubs: the beating heart and soul of any village, town or city, and in Melbourne Heartbreaker is a classic. You'll be guided in by the bright red neon sign that blinks through shutters like the lights on a landing strip. This is the sister bar to The Everleigh (see page 199) but boasts a narrowed-down list of just four cocktails (a Negroni, Martini, Old Fashioned and Manhattan) and a bottle shop as well to take away. With such a small list, the cocktails are pre-bottled at The Everleigh, which keeps the quality high and service fast. Of course, there is a selection of other drinks including beers and ciders, which can be consumed in a stylish bar where a pool table adds to the almost saloon-style of joint. All it's missing is a smoke haze and *Bat Out Of Hell* on a jukebox. Oh, no, wait...they have a fully loaded jukebox too!

✖
234a Russell Street (Lonsdale Corner), Melbourne, 3000
+61 3 9041 0856
heartbreakerbar.com.au

✖
IN THREE WORDS:
Public House Frolics.
WE SAY:
A proper pub experience, done better than almost anywhere.
PRICE RATING: ✳✳

THE TOFF IN TOWN ↓

This is a classic, down and dirty music venue/bar/restaurant that checks all the boxes for a night out. The Toff's main bar, or "carriage room", is utterly bonkers, and features a unique train carriage running down the

centre, made up of booths that can be reserved for dining and drinking where the doors can be closed to give extra privacy. For even more intimacy (make your own entertainment, we guess), you can even pull the blinds down and use the discreet buzzer for service, meaning you're just the flick of a knob away from intoxicating liquids. Created by chef Karen Batson, the food is Thai-influenced and the beers, wines and spirits list also features excellent cocktails that will almost put you on the Orient Express (see page 70).

✖
Second Floor Curtin House,
252 Swanston Street, Melbourne
3000 +61 3 9639 8770
thetoffintown.com
✖

IN THREE WORDS:
Choo, Choo, Choo!
THEY SAY:
"Great place to see music, nice cocktails, great food. Lots of different rooms for lots of different atmospheres."
JEREMY GARA, CANADA
PRICE RATING: ✳✳

TASMANIA, CHRISTCHURCH & WANAKA*

ROBBIE BROWN'S ↓

Close your eyes and imagine yourself in Kingston...the one in Tasmania, Australia. Now, if you want someone to open a bar, you want them to know about drink; so what better person to open a bar than someone who knows how to make the stuff. Enter, Jane Overeem. Jane, along with her father, Casey, is an experienced producer of whisky (Overeem single malt from Tasmania). Opened in November 2015, Robbie Brown's is a real family affair with a trio

of Sawfords (Mark, Jane and Brett) at the helm. Located on the stunning Kingston Beach, they serve oysters and burgers, all paired with locally made libations. What better way to spend an evening in Tasmania than on a beach with people who make booze and serve great food?

✖

32 Osborne Esplanade, Kingston Beach, Tasmania 7050 +61 3 6229 4891 robbiebrowns.com.au
✖

IN THREE WORDS:
Life's A Beach.

THE DRINK TO TRY:
Overeem Single Malt Whisky (the sherry edition) of course.

WE SAY:
The perfect place to experience Tassie hospitality firsthand.

PRICE RATING: ✱✱✱

DUX CENTRAL BREW BAR → ↘

This bar is a contemporary take on the modern industrial style. With exposed brick walls and black tiles, it is as if someone has taken a classic London pub and dragged it onto the set of *Mad Max*. Beer is the main focus here and the Brew Bar often boasts more than 200 of them, for all palates and purse-sizes; rumour has it that you can spend over $100 on one beer at Dux Central. Featuring their own Dux beers, local craft brews and plenty of other options, this is the perfect place for any ale angel to come and spread their wings. The staff here are well trained in explaining their incredible selection of beers, meaning that the chances of you ordering something you really don't like are pretty much zero.

Look out too for the Poplar Social Club next door – a sister bar and speakeasy with leather booths, Prohibition-inspired drinks and some new creations such as the Pavlova Sour using local NZ kiwi-infused vodka and enough fruit on top to be able to call this drink "one of your five a day".

✖

6 Poplar Street, Christchurch 8011 +64 3 943 7830 duxcentral.co.nz

✖

IN THREE WORDS:
Beer Is Best.

THE DRINK TO TRY:
One of the multitude of craft beers on offer, which the bar regularly rotates.

WE SAY:
Four venues in one (the Brew Bar, the Emerald Room, the Upper Dux and the Courtyard), this is a brilliant place to spend your whole evening.

PRICE RATING: ✱✱✱

A lake and mountains are the perfect garnish to any drink...

LALALAND LOUNGE BAR

As the bar itself says, "La La Land – *noun* – a fanciful state or dream world," so we have a good idea what to expect from this place...or do we?

Opened in 2011, this bar has one of the best views in the world. A lake and mountains are the perfect garnish to any drink, and it would be easy for the staff here to take their eye off the ball when it comes to delivering quality cocktails and rely on the location to pull visitors in. But they don't, giving as much time and dedication to serving brilliant cocktails and craft beers as you should to admiring the view. They also have a selection of local, award-winning spirits on offer, showcasing the genuine terroir of New Zealand.

✖
99 Ardmore Street, Wanaka 9305 +64 3 443 4911
lalalandwanaka.co.nz

✖

IN THREE WORDS:
Sit Back, Enjoy.

THE DRINK TO TRY:
A Te Anaka.

WE SAY:
The perfect relationship of cocktails, view and service.

PRICE RATING: ✱✱✱

Countries

NORTH AMERICA*

INTRO*

The birthplace of the cocktail, which grew in fame despite the onset of Prohibition, North America has had, and continues to have, a seismic effect on the world of hospitality and drinking. You only need to look at the sheer number of speakeasy-style bars in this book, from Singapore to Shoreditch, to see that. Couple this with the wonder that is Canadian whiskey, the ease with which it mixes, and you've got yourself a cracking pairing. Be it a tiki bar in the depths of the Vancouver winter, where the inside and outside worlds are in direct contrast with one another, through to hidden bars inside hot-dog shops and beyond.

With Europe and North America constantly pushing each other for greater innovation in the bar scene, it is often those that stick to the traditional rules of hospitality that win out, never forgetting that great drinks and great service come first.

North America is a continent united by great drinks, a true understanding of hospitality and the passion and drive to constantly innovate.

It is also no surprise to see such a concentration of bars in New York, a microcosm of every drinking experience under the sun from the trad-ale house of **McSorley's Ale House ↑** (see page 219) to the aforementioned father of the speakeasy, **PDT →** (see page 220).

North America is a continent united by great drinks, a true understanding of hospitality and the passion and drive to constantly innovate.

NEW YORK*

ATTABOY →

Milk & Honey in New York must go down as one of the most legendary drinking venues of the late 20th century. Its first home was on Eldridge Street, where Attaboy now sits. Run by two of Milk & Honey's former employees, Micky McIlroy and Sam Ross, this place is a real gem. In this unassuming venue the duo have managed to impart a neighbourhood feel to the place, and the bar industry's finest call it home. The place has no menu, so just let them know what you like and take whatever the bartenders want to make you; just as it should be.

✖

134 Eldridge Street, New York, NY 10002 +1 855 877 9900

✖

IN THREE WORDS:
Ghost Of Greatness.
THE DRINK TO TRY:
A Paper Plane, followed by a Penicillin.
THEY SAY:
"The first bar on my list whenever I go to New York."
—GEORGIE BELL, UK

"The guys come out with some fantastic drinks based on your preferences and have a wealth of knowledge to back it up."
—HAYLEY FOREST, USA
"There are always a million bars opening in New York, but I make sure to end my night here."
—KATIE EMMERSON, USA
PRICE RATING: ✱✱✱

BRANDY LIBRARY

TriBeCa in Manhattan is home to the Brandy Library, and it doesn't take an experienced bar-back to guess what their specialist subject is. But you'd be wrong, as this top gaff offers aged spirits of all kinds, not just brandy but Scotch, Irish and American whiskey; Cognacs and Armagnacs; Calvados; Rum...you name it, they've got it. They've even got their own private cask of Armagnac, which is very special indeed, and do preselected flights of spirits, which are brilliantly thought through and incredible considering the quality price. Oh, and look out for their Master Classes; you'll find it hard to get a better education anywhere else in the city.

It was opened in 2004 by Flavien Desoblin, who chose to call it the Brandy Library because "whiskey" had too many old school connotations. He has created an atmosphere where it is easy to stop, relax and, that rarest thing in New York, take your time. If you do this, you'll discover this mini-oasis in the midst of Manhattan madness.

✖

25 N. Moore Street, New York, NY 10013 +1 212 226 5545
brandylibrary.com

✖

IN THREE WORDS:
Aged Spirits Oasis.
THE DRINK TO TRY:
The house Armagnac.
THEY SAY:
"Every one of the bartenders is an encyclopedia."
— LIZA WEISSTUCH, USA
WE SAY:
The best place in Manhattan to chill out with a dram.
PRICE RATING: ✱✱✱

CULL AND PISTOL

New York is famous for bars that serve great drinks and oysters (see Maison Premiere on page 218, Dead Rabbit on page 212, and Employees Only on page 217) but Cull and Pistol, named after two different types of oyster, is the reverse: a great place to eat oysters while having a drink to boot. Hidden away in Chelsea Market, it has one of the best selections of oysters in the city and they don't laud this over their guests, but guide you through their selection with grace and goodwill. Once you have chosen your shellfish, simply tick the boxes on the paper slip and hand it over to one of the waiting staff while ordering a beer or one of their unique cocktails. Or both. Our tip is to sit at the bar and take in the ambiance, and if you can make it for the $1 oyster happy hour, then it leaves more budget for their cocktail list, which includes the excellent Oyster Shooter ↓ (Aloo vodka, house Bloody Mary mix, salted rim, oyster, black pepper), the perfect aperitif to your seafood platter.

✖

Chelsea Market, 75 9th Avenue, New York, NY 10011 +1 646 568 1223 lobsterplace.com

✖

IN THREE WORDS:
Chelsea Market's Pearl.

THE DRINK TO TRY:
The House Mary.

WE SAY:
The first place we head to in NYC, before blowing the cobwebs out with a walk along the High Line.

PRICE RATING: ✳✳✳

DANTE

Originally an authentic Italian joint called Caffe Dante, this opened way back in 1915 and quickly became a meeting place for Italian immigrants to have a coffee and chat about life back home. Many visitors passed through the doors, including Al Pacino and Bob Dylan, but in 2015, the Flotta family passed it on to an Australian family who have given it a new lease of life, while maintaining the famous hospitality in which this venue is soaked; the new owners call it "a love letter to the original".

Pictures of the original café stare down at you as you sip on a Sherry Cobbler, having chosen from their excellent food menu, flicking through some of Dylan's poetry. As the great artist once wrote, "a man is a success if he gets up in the morning and gets to bed at night, and in between he does what he wants to do." Dylan's choice was to drink here. And so should yours be.

Oh, and did we mention they have Negroni on tap?

✖

79–81 MacDougal Street, New York, NY 10012 +1 212 982 5275 dante-nyc.com

✖

IN THREE WORDS:
Like a Rollin' Stone.

THE DRINK TO TRY:
NEGRONI. ON. TAP.

THEY SAY:
"Nice and cosy aperitif bar in Manhattan."
— **STEPHAN BERG, GERMANY**
"Perfect playlist, nice vibe, and their Garibaldi cocktail is one of the most delicious and clever drinks I have experienced."
— **REMY SAVAGE, PARIS**

PRICE RATING: ✳✳✳

FEATURE*

A DRINK WITH...
ALLEN KATZ

Allen Katz is the co-founder of the New York Distilling Company in Brooklyn ➜ where he produces the award-winning Dorothy Parker American Gin, and the extraordinary Mister Katz's Rock & Rye, full of spiciness and sweet delight. He is also the director of mixology and spirits education for Southern Glazer's Wine & Spirits of New York.

Where do you drink when you're off duty?
It's hard to be off duty but if I were, I would go again and again and again to Clover Club in Brooklyn, one of the most complete cocktail bars I have experienced and fairly easy to get to from my home or my distillery.
Your favourite drink of all time…?
Rye Whiskey Manhattan, straight up with a lemon twist.
Where is your favourite city in the world to go drinking in?
I have lived in New York City for 25 years. It is my home and where I am most able to experience the thriving and evolving cocktail culture that is being shared in so many places around the world.

...spend the evening with a good friend and time passes – simply, joyously...

ALLEN'S TOP FIVE DRINKING HANGOUTS:

✖
McSorley's Ale House, New York (see page 219) *Thought to be the oldest bar in New York City, the beer is serviceable and there is nary a cocktail to be found. That's not the point. Go in the afternoon and spend the evening with a good friend and time passes – simply, joyously – in a perfect pub environment that exudes the classic character of the city.*

✖
Death & Co, New York (see page 213) *It remains a magnificent balance of delicious, approachable cocktails, great music and an energy that lasts from opening until the last drink is served.*

✖
Boadas, Barcelona (see page 80) *If ever there was a cocktail bar that sings of the romance of cocktail culture, it is here. The rhythm of the thrown cocktail, the vibrancy of Las Ramblas and the daydream of generations of happy drinkers.*

✖
Dukes Bar, London (see page 32) *This place is simplicity and sophistication at its best. Order an ice-cold gin Martini, straight up. There is no purer or more elementary pleasure.*

✖
French 75, New Orleans (see page 232) *Evocative of the 1940s, maybe earlier, life at the bar is an emotional escape, a time capsule that snaps back to present-day with some of the most delicious cocktails to be found in America's most unique city.*

NEW YORK*

DEAD RABBIT

Dead Rabbit. What can be said about this place that hasn't already been written? From the outside it might seem like a simple Irish bar on the southern tip of Manhattan Island, but behind this facade is something much deeper, much greater. On the outside it is Roddy Doyle. On the inside, James Joyce. Downstairs is a spit-and-sawdust tap room where you'll find "craft beer, bottled punch, and whiskeys of the world" and food is served daily, with a mixture of pies and stews, sandwiches and oysters. Upstairs, the magic starts to happen as you ascend to the Parlour where the cocktail list boast 72 different options, presented in an ever-changing (and highly collectable) menu, often featuring comic book style drawings and telling stories of local folk looking to do good through adversity.

Founders Sean Muldoon and Jack McGarry (see page 214) are the fantastically talented team behind Dead Rabbit, with experience of working behind some of the best bars in the world, and have used all their experience to turn Dead Rabbit into a multi-award-winning venture; building a highly respected brand that can be seen in the sheer number of plaudits and comments from other bartenders, below. Their latest bar, Black Tail (blacktailnyc. com), takes things to another level, with a Havana meets New York ideal that is sure to see them win even more awards.

✖

30 Water Street, New York, NY
10004 +1 646 422 7906
deadrabbitnyc.com

✖

IN THREE WORDS:
Alive And Kicking.

THE DRINK TO TRY:
Irish Coffee – the best in the world, with their unique mix.

THEY SAY:
"This is the perfect bar – in every little detail possible."
— JOERG MEYER, GERMANY
"Great beer, cocktails and their concept menus are world class."
— MARTIN MORALES, UK
"Always praised. Absolutely amazing drinks."
— JOAN SAMIA, KENYA

WE SAY:
The duo here keep getting better, so try a drink at Dead Rabbit and then head over to Black Tail for some more inspired drinking.

PRICE RATING: ✱✱✱

DEAR IRVING

Some bars are small rooms, with a single vibe that pulls you in (see Satan's Whiskers on page 47). Others are vast affairs that stretch across more than one level, with an assured attitude (see Nomad bar on page 220). But few try to offer rooms with different vibes, all under one roof. A curation of bar space, a tapestry of tastes, is hard to achieve without losing the original vision of the bar or simply confusing your customer. However, at Dear Irving in New York's Gramercy Park, the proprietors have managed to create a number of rooms that suit different tastes, while maintaining hospitality and warmth. Their four rooms take you from the reign of Louis XVI and Marie Antoinette via a Victorian manor house to the era of the Great Gatsby, all hidden behind an unassuming facade on Irving Place.

The cocktails are a thing of joy but first order the house-made ricotta flatbread to prepare you for the adventure ahead. The menu is split into their own house creations, classic and sipping spirits, beers and wines.

✖

55 Irving Place, New York, NY
10003 dearirving.com

✖

IN THREE WORDS:
Four-For-One.

THE DRINK TO TRY:
The Vice Versa.

THEY SAY:
"This is the most evocative and beautiful bar in New York in my humble opinion."
— HANNAH LANFEAR, UK

WE SAY:
Go four times, and sit in four different styles of room.

PRICE RATING: ✳✳✳✳

DEATH & CO →

Located in Manhattan's East Village, Death & Co first opened their doors on New Year's Eve 2006 and has since established itself as one of the top drinking destinations in New York City, having won multiple awards for their service, style and cocktail selection. The venue itself is a well-styled, Art Deco type of joint with copper, wood, and leather adding to the low light of this bar, giving it a truly night-time drinking joint vibe where Don Draper might not be out of place, lounging back with a well-made Martini. When it comes to the drinks, there is a good variety of styles, with a menu that is well laid out and easy to navigate and drinks listed as either stirred or shaken. This vintage approach is reflected in drinks such as the rum-based Artful Dodger, or the Tequila-based Aces & Eights. All in, this is a time capsule of a venue, which will take you right back to mid-20th century New York.

Such has been the goodwill for the drinks at Death & Co that they were one of the first "contemporary" bars to collate a modern guide to their cocktails, launching a book of the same name, which includes not only recipes, but also the theory and philosophy behind making great drinks, a guide to spirits as well as the physical tools of the trade.

✖

433 East 6th Street, New York, NY 10009 +1 212 388 0882
deathandcompany.com

✖

IN THREE WORDS:
Back To Black.

THE DRINK TO TRY:
The rum-based Touch of Evil.

WE SAY:
A legendary establishment and quite rightly so.

THEY SAY:
"A magnificent balance of delicious, approachable cocktails, great music and an energy that lasts from opening until the last drink is served."
— ALLEN KATZ, USA

PRICE RATING: ✳✳✳✳

FOCUS*

STARTENDER
JACK MCGARRY

Jack McGarry is one half of the team behind **Dead Rabbit** (see page 212) and **BlackTail** (blacktailnyc. com). In July 2013, McGarry won the Tales of the Cocktail International Bartender of the Year award. He is its youngest-ever recipient, and only the second in America, after the legendary Audrey Saunders of **Pegu Club** (see page 221). Immediately prior to being in New York, McGarry tended the bar at **Milk & Honey** in London (see page 40) and before that at **The Merchant Hotel** (see below), Belfast, which was declared the World's Best Cocktail Bar in 2010 at Tales of the Cocktail.

Here Jack takes us on a tour of some of his favourite drinking locations around the globe.

JACK'S TOP FIVE DRINKING HAUNTS AROUND THE WORLD:

✖
The Merchant Hotel, Belfast (themerchanthotel.com)
This was the bar that really made me fall head over heels in love

with world-class cocktail bars. It was run by my now business partner, Sean Muldoon. Sean has really set up to do something special with the programme there. I met him for a job opening and he showed me two pieces of ice – one that was cloudy and imperfect and the other that was perfectly shaped and crystal clear. He said "which type of ice do you want to be?" My answer mirrored my philosophy, which is similar to Sean's – I want to be the best version of myself; and to be the best, you have to work with the best. I wanted to be the crystal-clear piece of ice or,

at the very least, to strive for that daily pursuit of perfection.

So The Merchant Hotel was the bar that made the biggest impression on me as it greatly shaped the rest of my career.

✖
Duke Of York, Belfast (dukeofyorkbelfast.com)
Dead Rabbit was based on bringing world-class cocktail bars such as The Merchant Hotel and down to earth, but well run, Irish pubs such as The Duke Of York together under one roof.

The Duke Of York was the bar myself and Sean hung out in. We ran a programme in

Belfast called The Connoisseurs' Club and attracted some of the biggest names in the industry. Bartenders from all over Europe travelled to these sessions. We were isolated in Belfast and had to operate off the mantra that if the people won't come to us, we have to bring our bar to the people; so one way of doing that was these sessions.

It worked but the one thing that surprised us was that all these bartenders didn't hang out all that much in The Merchant Hotel. They opted for The Duke Of York. They loved the unpretentious Irishness and genuine hospitality at the bar. Of course, a great Irish whiskey selection and solid pint of Guinness didn't hurt either.

✖
Milk & Honey, London (see page 40) ↑
This bar shaped myself and Sean both for slightly different reasons. Milk & Honey was the bar that inspired Sean to do the initial programme he

developed at The Merchant Hotel: the ice programme, fresh juice, homemade syrups and classic drinks. The Merchant was known for its attention to detail and this was definitely inspired by Milk & Honey.

✖
The Hunting Lodge, Belfast
My first ever bar job! I started in this industry as a glass collector when I was 15. It was due to my mother and father getting fed up with me asking for money to do things. They said, "If you want something in life you've got to be prepared to work for it." It's the single best piece of advice I've ever received. My father put me in touch with a family member who ran bars in Belfast. His spot at that time was a neighbourhood boozer called The Hunting Lodge, at the bottom of my street. Upon meeting him he said two things to me: "I expect two things from my staff – that they are loyal and that you don't steal." It was in this bar that I fell in love with the industry.

✖
PJ Clarke's, New York (pjclarkes.com)
This one is more about seeing a particular bartender that altered my style for ever than about the actual place. It all clicked when I went to see Doug Quinn bartend at PJ Clarke's. He knew everyone's name, knew their drinks, had everyone in the room in the palm of his hand. It changed me for ever. I would never claim to have the memory Doug has with his guests but seeing him definitely made me a more centred, hospitality-driven bartender.

You can read more about Jack's multi-award-winning bar, Dead Rabbit, on page 212 or visit deadrabbitnyc.com.

NEW YORK*

THE EAR INN →

One of Manhattan's oldest drinking establishments, The Ear Inn is housed in a building that dates from 1770. This is a long time ago in the history of any city but, when it comes to New York, the date comes only 150 years into its existence. The place was built by James Brown, an African aide to George Washington, and since the 1800s the site has sold grog of many styles. At first it dealt in home brew, then it operated as a speakeasy, daring to serve booze during The Great Experiment. By the end of Prohibition, the bar had become world-famous with those passing in and out of the ports and piers of Manhattan, and as it had no name, it became known as "The Green Door".

In the late 1970s, current owners Martin Sheridan and Richard "Rip" Hayman, wanted a new name and sign quickly. To avoid the lengthy process of legally obtaining new signage, the pair just covered up the round parts of the pre-existing neon "B-A-R" sign, leaving it to read

"EAR". Clever stuff. Inside you'll find a bar that feels untouched since Manhattan was a proper trading port, part bar, part bric-a-brac stall. Swigging beer and eating hearty food is the order of the day here, and you might even bump into one of their friendly ghosts...or at least encounter a spirit of one kind or another!

✖
326 Spring Street, New York, NY 10013 +1 212 226 9060 earinn.com

✖
IN THREE WORDS:
Come Inn Ear.
THE DRINK TO TRY:
Swig some ale.
THEY SAY:
"Pours the best Guinness, possibly ever."
— **REBEKKAH DOOLEY, USA/UK**
WE SAY:
Place your bets as to who can see a ghost first.
PRICE RATING: ✶

EMPLOYEES ONLY ⬇

The brilliantly named Employees Only is a bar that truly knows it is a bar. The staff are amazingly trained, the doormen are some of the friendliest in New York and the cocktails just excellent. Mixed with a team in chef whites behind the bar, this classic spot in New York is the perfect combination of fun and great cocktails, and can get seriously hopping late at night with the music up and cocktails flowing.

Started by five visionaries in 2004, with another branch now open in Singapore, it has become a mainstay in the world of the New York drinker, but don't just think of this place as a cocktail bar; the food is also exceptional with oysters, bone marrow and lamb chops part of their menu. The cocktails are classic affairs – think Ginger Smashes, West Sides and Pisco Sours. This is a bar that will take you through to morning.

✖
510 Hudson Street, New York, NY 10014 +1 212 242 3021
employeesonlynyc.com
✖
IN THREE WORDS:
Keep 'Em Coming.

THE DRINK TO TRY:
The Quiet Storm is a great take on a Dark 'n' Stormy.
THEY SAY:
"Had high expectations and was not disappointed in the slightest."
— ANDY SHANNON, UK
"It made me understand the importance of hospitality."
— LAURA NISSANEN, FINLAND
WE SAY:
Just soak up the atmosphere as well as a great cocktail.
PRICE RATING: ✱✱✱✱

FISH MARKET

To call this a dive bar would be doing it a disservice, but a posh joint it ain't. It's located down in the Two Bridges area (and only a short hop from Dead Rabbit, see page 212), which has been recently renovated and boasts some fantastic bars, clothes shops and even a place that has traditional printing presses, but a highlight is Fish Market. A friendly, neighbourhood joint, it has everything you'd expect from a bar like this: TVs blasting out sport; Pabst Blue Ribbon in cans; shots of Jameson poured after every other purchase; and the best god-damn ginger chicken wings you'll ever taste.

✖
111 South Street, New York, NY 10038 +1 212 227 4468
✖
IN THREE WORDS:
Order The Wings!
THE DRINK TO TRY:
Come on...keep it simple and go for a beer and a shot of Jamie.
WE SAY:
A real discovery for the local in you.
PRICE RATING: ✱

LITTLE BRANCH

An unassuming door on a slice of building that juts out violently into the street, as if Le Corbusier himself had designed a bar entrance, on 7th Avenue between the West Village and SoHo. This is Little Branch, a cash-only cocktail haunt that invites you in to find out what secrets are hidden inside. Opened as a follow-up to New York's Milk & Honey, Little Branch is more of a downstairs-candlelit, personal affair but the cocktails are as good as the fantastic service inside. A warm welcome is in stark contrast to the cold austere entrance.

✖
22 7th Avenue, New York, NY 10014 +1 212 929 4360
✖
IN THREE WORDS:
Down The Stairs.
THE DRINK TO TRY:
The Cock and Bull Special is a delight.
THEY SAY:
"It's just the best! I went there for the first time in 2005 and it's still just as perfect."
— ALASTAIR BURGESS, UK
PRICE RATING: ✱✱✱✱

NEW YORK*

MACE

Alphabet City conjures up the idea of a Sesame Street-style suburb, complete with brownstone houses, talking birds and "things" in bins. But the Alphabet City neighbourhood in Manhattan's East Village is so named because of the Avenues A, B, C, and D – the only streets with single-letter names in Manhattan – and is anything but childish, playing serious games with booze at venues such as Mace. An unassuming swinging sign invites you into this sleek, almost industrial-cum-nordic-looking bar. Inside, the walls are "decorated" with jars of botanicals, mirroring the names of the cocktails, which all take their name from a herb or a spice, using incredibly interesting ingredients such as soy-washed Calvados. With such a stunning physical bar, the drinks might be a little overshadowed, but not so here. Well made and beautifully presented, these are some of the best cocktails in the city. Today, your drinks are brought to you by the letters M, A, C and E.

✖
649 East 9th Street, New York, NY 10009 macenewyork.com
✖

IN THREE WORDS:
Nordic Swigging Swagger.
THE DRINK TO TRY:
Try their house-named cocktail, Mace.
THEY SAY:
"The cocktails completely blow me away at this place."
— HANNAH LANFEAR, UK
WE SAY:
Don't miss this one off the list.
PRICE RATING: ✶✶✶✶

MAISON PREMIERE

It is not often that places spring up and establish themselves quite so quickly, and ingratiate themselves with the bartending community quite as fast as Masion Premiere did. When it first flung open the doors of its Williamsburg premises, it offered a unique mix of Paris, New York and New Orleans; and, just a few years on, its style, drinks and food plates remain as much in demand as when it first opened. First and foremost, Maison Premiere is an "Oyster House and Cocktail Den" (and, along with Cull and Pistol, see page 209, is probably the finest place to grab an oyster in New York – they often have over 30 different varieties ready to order) but it is so much more than that. It is a social lubricant, with no table left silent, the chitter-chatter of guests being the most welcome sound in the world. With a focus on absinthe, the cocktails are as good as the oysters and small plates they are designed to accompany (try the awesome Chrysanthemum) and after a few oysters and absinthe (check out their replica of an original fountain that once stood in the Olde Absinthe House of New Orleans, see page 233), you may well see the Green Fairy herself, sitting at your table with you.

✖
298 Bedford Avenue, Brooklyn, New York, NY 11211
+1 347 335 0446
maisonpremiere.com
✖

IN THREE WORDS:
Shucks, It's Great.
THE DRINK TO TRY:
The Inverness is a corker.
THEY SAY:
"A fantastically executed New Orleans-inspired Absinthe house in Williamsburg."
— JACK MCGARRY, USA
WE SAY:
Viva la Green Fairy.
PRICE RATING: ✶✶✶✶

MCSORLEY'S ALE HOUSE ↑ ↗

New York is steeped in history, shaping much of the 19th and 20th century with music, fashion, art, architecture, politics, film and literature. Sitting through all of this, quietly observing, and no doubt having its own small influence, has been the great venue that is McSorley's Ale House. Originally called The Old House at Home, this watering hole first flung open its saloon doors in the mid-1800s, but only to men. In fact, this place only admitted women for the first time after legally being forced to do so in 1970 and is said to have had such luminaries as Abe Lincoln, John Lennon and Hunter S Thompson through its doors– now there's a conversation we'd loved to have overheard.... Even Prohibition couldn't stop this place from serving, and this Grand Old Man of New York keeps going today. A must-visit when you're in Manhattan, this is a true spit-and-sawdust venue that gives only ales, and of course a cheese platter with raw onions.

✖

15 East 7th Street, New York, NY 10003 +1 212 473 9148 mcsorleysoldalehouse.nyc

✖

IN THREE WORDS:
Older Than You!

THE DRINK TO TRY:
Only one: McSorley's Ale.

THEY SAY:
"You can only order two drinks – Light Beer or Dark Beer – which are each served in two tankards.

It is the oldest Irish ale house in New York and is an experience like no other."
— **REBEKKAH DOOLEY, USA/UK**

"A perfect pub environment that exudes a classic character of the city."
— **ALLEN KATZ, USA**

"Sawdust, worn wood, a nude with a parrot, two beers – dark or light – on tap. Ask for one and you get two glasses."
— **DAVE BROOM, UK**

WE SAY:
This is the best place to experience the history of drinking that shaped New Yorkers' thinking.

PRICE RATING: ✱

NEW YORK*

NOMAD BAR

The Nomad Hotel in New York has fast become one of the hottest places to stay in the city and just next door is the brilliant NoMad Bar. A grand space in the truest way, the physical bar is huge, with a mirrored back bar that reaches high into the sky, looking down on the bottles below like an aerial being watching over citizens below. The seating is on two levels giving the whole thing the feel of a Victorian railway station waiting room (First Class, of course), complete with a working fireplace. The bar staff buzz around in a manner that befits such a stylish place. There is food, as there is in so many New York bars, and this includes hot dogs and burgers to help bulk out the drinking, adding to the general atmosphere of the place.

✖

Nomad Hotel, 1170 Broadway & 28th Street, New York, NY 10001 +1 212 796 1500 thenomadhotel.com

✖

IN THREE WORDS:
Never, Ever Lost.

THE DRINK TO TRY:
The Blinker with rye and smoky Scotch whisky.

THEY SAY:
"I went there on a recent visit and it was the perfect experience."
— **MARCIS DZELZAINIS, UK**
"A redefinition of the modern hotel bar."
— **PHILIP DUFF, USA**
"My absolute favourite bar in the world is NoMad Bar. I love everything about this place!"
— **MONICA BERG, NORWAY/UK**

WE SAY:
Not cheap, but worth the price.
PRICE RATING: ✱✱✱✱✱

PDT (PLEASE DON'T TELL) ↑

Hot dogs – surely there isn't a person alive (well, apart from vegetarians) who doesn't like a good hot dog. If you're a fan, then this is the place for you, for Please Don't Tell (or PTD as it is known) is sneakily hidden behind a telephone booth inside the Crif Dogs diner on St Mark's Place, just off 1st Avenue. Simply pick up the phone inside and ask for a table. To call this place an "institution" would be doing it down, as it really was the first place to pioneer the modern "speakeasy" movement, and hide the bar away. No neon signs, no overt marketing, no obvious entrance. News of the place spread by word-of-mouth and there are a plethora of other bars trying to hide away, too (London's Callooh Callay, see page 27, through a wardrobe door; Oji, see page 145, in Shanghai, hidden inside another bar...and the list goes on). Okay, there might be a level of novelty to this idea, but PDT was never going to survive if it didn't have great drinks, and great drinks it has. So much so that you can now purchase a *PDT Cocktail Book*, and have a go at home yourself, as it gives a complete guide to creating your own version of PDT (complete with hot dog tips). Just don't try to crawl into your house through the letterbox, or lose your keys to get the speakeasy vibe.

✖

113 St Mark's Place, New York, NY 10009 +1 212 614 0386
pdtnyc.com

✖

IN THREE WORDS:
Hard To Find.

THE DRINK TO TRY:
Possibly the best Manhattan in Manhattan.

THEY SAY:
"The first time I visited, I remember having a WD50 hot dog, some tater tots and a perfect cocktail in hand, recognizing the city's brilliance in one fell swoop."
— RYAN CHETIYAWARDANA,
AKA MR LYAN, UK

WE SAY:
This is a must-visit for anyone looking to experience one of the greats. And don't forget to have a hot dog when you're there.

PRICE RATING: ✳ ✳ ✳

PEGU CLUB

Few places have the same approach and ethos as the Pegu Club, who pride themselves on detail and "doing the little things well", which includes making their own ginger beer, and even curating and selling a wide range of hard-to-find bitters.

A dark and mysterious interior welcomes you into a bar where the team are clearly dedicated to their art. This is a venue that oozes style and class, themed around an almost Oriental imaginary world, and their cocktails are crafted with care, reflected in the fact that some of the city's finest bartenders have graced the stick at Pegu. Not so much an academy for bartenders, but simply a place that understands ingredients, quality and dedication, on an almost microscopic level.

✖

77 West Houston Street, 2nd floor, New York, NY 10012
+1 212 473 7348 peguclub.com

✖

IN THREE WORDS:
Detail, Detail, Detail.

THE DRINK TO TRY:
The Aviation.

THEY SAY:
"It is a mild understatement to say that [founder] Audrey Saunders's place has been my Manhattan 'living room' since she first opened the doors in 2005."
—ANISTATIA MILLER, UK
"It's where I really cut my teeth in the world of cocktails."
— ALASTAIR BURGESS, UK

PRICE RATING: ✳ ✳ ✳ ✳

SUFFOLK ARMS

Approaching this new bar, it has the feel of a traditional London boozer, and this pretence continues when you enter and see a section of booths, tables and chairs and a classic bar. But then you spot the lovely hand-drawn headshot of New York icons, you pick up the menu and you start to believe.

"This bar is meant to be a celebration of our fair city," they proclaim, meeting their goals of producing a menu that takes three things very seriously: history, service and mixology. That's a good start, and it gets better when you actually order a cocktail from their wonderful list. The Suffolk Arms is worth a try as the closest thing they get to a "house cocktail".

✖

269 East Houston Street, New York, NY 10002 +1 212 475 0400
suffolkarms.com

✖

IN THREE WORDS:
It's The Future.

THE DRINK TO TRY:
Horse Apple, in which you can choose your spirit of choice to be mixed with Granny Smith apple and fresh horseradish.

WE SAY:
A brilliant addition to New York's first-class cocktail lounges.

PRICE RATING: ✳ ✳ ✳ ✳

FEATURE*

A SPIRITED STROLL IN...
BROOKLYN

As you can see from this curated compilation, New York is home to many great bars. Some are renowned for the quality of the drinks, some for their history, but some have both of these qualities and ice their cake (or dust their Big Apple pie) with an extra layer of magic: a simply jaw-dropping view.

The bar at the top of the **Wythe Hotel** ↗ ↘ (see opposite) in the Brooklyn hipster-haven of Williamsburg has the lot. The view from this rooftop modernist masterpiece across the East River and the forest of skyscrapers that makes up Manhattan Island, simply can't be beaten. Add to this its location opposite the new legendary **Brooklyn Brewery** → (brooklynbrewery.com) and you've got one hell of a day out on your hands.

Our advice is take a leisurely stroll from a base in the lower end of Manhattan – you can't go wrong with the redeveloped South Street Seaport – and then head over the Williamsburg Bridge, which acts like a direct line into the heart of one of New York's most happening suburbs.

Stepping off the bridge, you'll find yourself in Williamsburg with the chance to explore some of the excellent boutiques and outlets that make Williamsburg, Bushwick and Greenpoint such a destination for those looking for style, flavour and fashion. In just under a decade, Williamsburg and the surrounding neighbourhoods have risen like a phoenix from down-at-heel to high fashionista, with small, independent boutiques keeping out the big-name chain shops.

After picking up something locally made, be it a leather belt or scented candle, and choosing which of the extensive independent restaurants you want to relax in for lunch, make

When you've finished watching the sunset over Manhattan and the city springs into life for the night shift, head out to explore some of the local bars...

your way up to the Brooklyn Brewery for one of their excellent tours. Before and after you can grab a beer from their extensive range in the "spit-and-sawdust" bar there, adding some real colour and, literally, flavour to their beer-making process.

Just a few doors down on the same block, look out for the bottle shop called simply **The Whiskey Shop Brooklyn** (whiskeyshopbrooklyn.com), which sells a fantastic range of distillates from all over the world, but also the locally produced King's County Bourbon.

After finishing up your allotted ales, simply cross the road to the Wythe Hotel where you might find on busier days a short queue, before you're escorted into an elevator and up to the top floor of the building.

On exiting the lift, you are faced with one of the most stunning panoramic views of the Big Apple, the shimmering East River and the vast, open sky. With seating both inside and

out, you can enjoy the view in any weather, along with a well-made cocktail. We'd recommend their Blood & Sand, made with Cutty Sark Prohibition, a nod to the time when this part of New York would have been all sharp suits and Tommy guns.

When you've finished watching the sunset over Manhattan and the city springs into life for the night shift, head out to explore some of the local bars and you'll find, alongside local ales, a section of pickle juices ready to provide the perfect pickleback, or a wash for a really dirty Martini, in a neighbourhood enjoying a renaissance and living life to the maximum.

✖

80 Wythe Avenue at North 11th Williamsburg, Brooklyn, New York, NY 11249 +1 718 460 8000 wythehotel.com

✖

IN THREE WORDS:
Roof Top Kingpin.

THE DRINK TO TRY:
Blood & Sand – the classic inspired by Rudolph Valentino's 1922 film.

WE SAY:
Get there early for sunset. Stay in Williamsburg until sunrise.

PRICE RATING: ✱✱✱✱

BOSTON & WASHINGTON DC*

J.J. FOLEY'S ↓

A trip to J. J. Foley's, billed as the oldest continuously operating family-owned Irish pub in the USA, will undoubtedly leave you with many happy memories indeed. It was established in 1909 in Boston's South End and has all the hallmarks of a cracking, no-nonsense, straight talkin' Irish pub: a dozen or so draft beers (where the Guinness is consistently great), bartenders

When the world is seemingly heading toward homogenized high streets and chain/theme pubs, say a prayer while sipping your pint and thank the lord for the likes of these fine folks....

in white button-down shirts and ties, a gorgeous slab of mahogany for a bar and a cranked-up jukebox playing the likes of The Clash and Depeche Mode, once the post-work crowd have left. It's clear that family is important to the Foley boys and the lineage still runs deep. Jerry Foley, grandson of the founder Jeremiah J. Foley, still oversees the proceedings on a nightly basis and Jerry's cousin Jimmy runs a second location not far away, which opened in the 1950s. When the world is seemingly heading toward homogenized high streets and chain/theme pubs say a prayer, while sipping your pint and thank the lord for the likes of these fine folks....

117 East Berkeley Street, Boston, MA 02118 +1 617 728 9101 jjfoleyscafe.com
✖

IN THREE WORDS:
Takin' Care of Business.
THE DRINK TO TRY:
A Guinness, followed by a Pabst, followed by a Blue Moon.
THEY SAY:
"I lived in Boston for many years and this was the first place I ever became a regular when I turned legal drinking age."
— LIZA WEISSTUCH, US
PRICE RATING: ✱

COLUMBIA ROOM

Washington cocktail guru Derek Brown is quite the man about town. After moving the original Columbia Room to its new location, this award-winning mixologist has expanded the concept of the bar, which leads the way in inspirational drinks, made with a skill akin to Michelin Star status. The recent incarnation on Blagden Alley now has three distinct areas: a classy, yet contemporary cocktail lounge, which brings together exquisite ingredients, vintage glassware and some of the latest modern techniques in mixed drinks. There's a garden space, dedicated to punches and pre-mixed bottled cocktails and finally – and perhaps most impressively – a tasting room; a veritable library of incredibly vintage spirits, including pre-Prohibition whiskeys, Napoleonic Cognac and other ancient delights. Never standing still, the Columbia Room puts Washington DC right up there on the hallowed list of gastro cocktails not to be missed.

✖

124 Blagden Alley NW, Washington DC 20001 +1 202 316 9396 columbiaroomdc.com

✖

IN THREE WORDS:

Three's the Magic Number.

THEY SAY:

"I remember sitting with Derek at an ungodly hour trying Pre-Prohibition rye and then changing my train to a much later time the next morning…it was quite an introduction to the place."

— **GEORGIE BELL, UK**

PRICE RATING: ✱✱✱✱

JACK ROSE ↑

It was about the time we first discovered *House Of Cards* that we were also introduced to Jack Rose in Washington DC. Naturally intrigued by the locations in the opening credits, we took a trip to Capitol Hill and ended up, jet-lagged and in need of a drink, at the bar with our great friend Darrel Sheehan in his souped-up Ford Mustang. Jack Rose is not a person, but a shining light in the Washington whiskey scene. Yet it would be pointless to mention the bar without introducing you to Harvey Fry, in whose amiable, wonderfully eccentric company we spent a truly unforgettable night. Fry helped set Jack Rose up back in 2011 and has sort of hung around ever since, effectively a customer with his own set of keys. Fry's whiskey knowledge – and insane personal collection of rare bottlings

– is like nothing else we've experienced, and this is reflected in the whisk(e)y list, which at the time of writing, comes to exactly 2,687 bottles. Mesmerizing doesn't even come close.

✖

2007 18th Street NW, Washington, DC 20009 +1 202 588 7388 jackrosediningsaloon.com

✖

IN THREE WORDS:

Walls Of Whisk(e)y.

THE DRINK TO TRY:

Go big: a cask-strength single malt.

WE SAY:

The Capitol Hill of whisky bars, where Harvey Fry is the unofficial Commander-in-Chief.

PRICE RATING: ✱✱✱

PHILADELPHIA, MIAMI, LOUISVILLE & NASHVILLE *

LIBRARY BAR ⬊

Housed in The Rittenhouse Hotel, the Library Bar is a hidden gem in the city centre of Philadelphia. With a distinctly Art Deco feel, it has a menu that features a selection of craft cocktails, beers, wines and the very best rare spirits and beverages, which include a 100- year-old Madeira. The cocktail list itself is not the longest in the world, but the general atmosphere of the bar, the quality of the service and the consistency of drinks from this hotel bar, is what makes this such a great drinking experience.

✖

210 West Rittenhouse Square, Philadelphia, PA 19103
+1 215 546 9000
rittenhousehotel.com

✖

IN THREE WORDS:
Relaxed City Centre.
WE SAY:
This really is a haven in the city to take a break and have a great cocktail.
PRICE RATING: ✱✱✱✱

THE ANDERSON ⬆

Bespoke glassware always makes a bar stand out, and at The Anderson they've taken the humble tumbler and put their wonderfully retro logo across it, making it by far the coolest regular glass we've ever seen. This rock'n'roll joint is a proper neighbourhood bar, cramming in locals to listen to excellent DJs, while sipping on their own unique cocktail creations. This place is part diner, part rock'n'roll club, part cocktail bar. Above all else, it is simply cool! Expect to see people dressed from Teddy Boys to 1980s warehouse party neon ravers. Open till 4am – it just keeps getting better as the night goes on.

✖

709 North East 79th Street, Miami, FL 33138 +1 305 757 3368 theandersonmiami.com

✖

IN THREE WORDS:
Smile, Drink, Dance.

WE SAY:
One of the most fun hangouts in Miami, and that's saying something!

PRICE RATING: ✖✖

PROOF ON MAIN

Ah, Louisville...home of the all-American drink, bourbon, and a great place to drink. To really drink. This is a city filled with interesting bars, but most of them cater to the boiler-maker crowd. However, if you take a walk down Main Street, along from the KFC Yum! Center, the slugger store and the excellent Evan Williams Bourbon Experience, you'll find the wacky "museum hotel", The 21c. The place is rammed with works of art, and it really is "contemporary" in the truest sense of the word. You're as likely to see a cast of someone's genitals hanging on the wall as you are an oil painting. And if you use the men's toilets, you may see even more, as the urinals are see-through!

However, this wackiness is translated at the bar, Proof On Main, where their excellent cocktail list builds on the local spirit. Let's not forget Louisville is a town where the Old Fashioned was "invented" (when a man asked for a cocktail in the "old-fashioned way" at the local Pendennis Club), so you'd be daft not to order one. This is the type of bar where you'll find savvy journalists on a trip to the Blue Grass State, cool designers creating new labels for bourbon brands, master distillers, and band members from major groups who have sold out the KFC Yum! Center just down the road.

✖

700 West Main Street, Louisville, KY 40202 +1 502 217 6360 proofonmain.com

✖

IN THREE WORDS:
100 Percent Proof.

THEY SAY:
"Best hotel bar I can think of: lovely menu of bourbons; exclusive bottlings; bourbon flights!"
— **JEREMY GARA, ARCADE FIRE, CANADA**

WE SAY:
The best place to have a cocktail, post-distillery visits.

PRICE RATING: ✖✖✖✖

Ah, Louisville... home of the all-American drink, bourbon and a great place to drink.

BOOTLEGGERS INN

A proper bar, if bars can ever be "proper", the Bootleggers Inn is home to live music and moonshine. A place for drinkers and spitters, this is a smokers' bar that will offer a haven to anyone looking for an alternative to the clean, new bars that can be found popping up all over America today. The authentic nature of this place hangs from the ceilings with chandeliers made out of mason jars, and plenty of moonshine on the back bar. Not familiar with moonshine? Well, the staff will guide you through the options and help you find one that works best, maybe even in their famous Moonshine Margarita with Jalapeño, or their Blackberry Moonshine from the flavoured moonshine menu.

✖

207 Broadway, Nashville, TN 37201 +1 615 457 3983 bootleggersnashville.com

✖

IN THREE WORDS:
Make Mine Moonshine!

THEY SAY:
"A phenomenal small joint at the end of the main strip."
— **STAFFAN ALEXANDERSSON, NORWAY**

PRICE RATING: ✖✖

CHICAGO*

THE AVIARY/
THE OFFICE ↓

A curiously brilliant venue for drinking, The Aviary is a place where the approach is more akin to one you would find in a high-end restaurant owned by the likes of Heston Blumenthal.

Drinks are made with incredible precision to exacting recipes, all of which can be watched as you wait in their "kitchen" area. Such is their dedication to the art of cocktail making that they even have their own ice creators, dedicated to

making sure that the flavours from the ice, which are imparted to your drink, make the experience better, not as is often the case with ice, much worse. This place takes a lot of cues from its twin establishment, the multi-Michelin-starred restaurant Alinea, where flavour is taken seriously. Their mantra is that the bartenders are trained as chefs, and it works very well indeed. You'll never have more stunning drinks delivered to you.

While you're there, don't forget to ask about The Office, a bar with the same address…shhhhh.

✖

955 West Fulton Market, Chicago, IL 60607 +1 312 226 0868 theaviary.com

✖

IN THREE WORDS:
Molecular Chef-ology Brilliance.

THEY SAY:
"The ambiance is unique!"
— **JOHNNY SCHULER**, PERU

THEY WHISPER:
"Shhhhhh…The Office is almost the antithesis to The Aviary. It's all about classic style where you need a key to get in – it's all invite-only so everyone is connected in some way – but totally not pretentious."
— **HAYLEY FOREST**, USA

PRICE RATING: ✶✶✶✶✶

BORDEL

The good old-time vibes just keep on coming and Bordel has successfully managed to fuse together brilliantly made classic Prohibition-style drinks, vintage decor, tea cups, glassware and cabaret all into an authentic bordello-style joint. It's sexy, opulent, sophisticated but above all else a lot of fun.

✖

1721 West Division Street, Chicago, IL 60622 +1 773 227 8600 bordelchicago.com

✖

IN THREE WORDS:
Old-Time Chic.

THE DRINK TO TRY:
The Ramos Gin Fizz.

WE SAY:
Sipping gin cocktails from a tea cup always brings a smile to our faces.

PRICE RATING: ✶✶✶

DELILAH'S ↑

Opened in 1993 by Mike Miller, this is a true music joint with DJs spinning everything from rock'n'roll to punk rock, which can be accompanied by over 1,000 beer and spirit options, some of them bespoke. This is best seen in a unique limited edition blend produced by artisan Scotch whisky blending house Compass Box, which is designed to be paired with beer and is sold exclusively at the joint. Part art gallery, part rock club, part beer bar, part whiskey watering hole (it has won Best Whiskey Bar in America a number of times), part friend, part foe.

✖
2771 North Lincoln Avenue, Chicago, IL 60614 +1 773 472 2771 delilahschicago.com
✖
IN THREE WORDS:
Rockabilly Whiskey Wonder.
THE DRINK TO TRY:
A Boilermaker.
WE SAY:
Just an outstanding place full of friendly folk, amazing beers and astonishing whiskeys.
PRICE RATING: ✳

GREEN RIVER

Green River is a collaboration between the guys behind Dead Rabbit in New York (see page 212) and catering guru Danny Meyer. It is a very sophisticated, sky-view, fine-dining cocktail bar, the drinks of which take their influence from the Irish-American culture, which has built Chicago into the city it is today. One really nice touch is that the menu is broken down into the base ingredients of each spirit – different grains, apples and grapes, agave, molasses and juniper – so you can trace the lineage of each cocktail and its core ingredient back to the beginning. A simple, yet thought-provoking drinking experience.

✖
259 East Erie Street, Chicago, IL 60611 +1 312 337 0101 greenriverchi.com
✖
IN THREE WORDS:
Jade Tower of Greatness
THEY SAY:
"Stunningly crafted cocktails, created with a simple style."
— LYNDSEY GRAY, UK
PRICE RATING: ✳✳✳✳

LOST LAKE

The tiki bars listed in this book just keep on going, and here we have yet another example of a world-class tiki venue where the Mai Tais keep flowing and the rum punch never ends.

With tiki, you usually know exactly what you are going to get, and Lost Lake in Chicago is no exception to the rule. (However, they do have their own ale, which isn't quite in keeping with the idea of tiki, even if their turquoise coloured, fish-inspired label is.) As they say themselves, "What makes a tiki drink great is half what's in the glass, and half what's happening around the person with the drink in their hand." With tropical drinks to the max, this place is a must-seek haven in the freezing Chicago winter winds, or the warm summer breeze.

✖
3154 West Diversey Avenue, Chicago, IL 60647 +1 773 293 6048 lostlaketiki.com
✖
IN THREE WORDS:
The Tiki City.
THEY SAY:
*"Cos tiki f***ing rocks! One of the few bars in the world I would get a cab straight from the airport to."*
— IAIN GRIFFITH, AUSTRALIA/ UK
PRICE RATING: ✳✳✳

NEW ORLEANS*

BACCHANAL

Bacchanal is something of a phenomenon: essentially a really brilliant wine bar and shop, which also houses a cool jazz music venue and, to cap it off, has a wonderfully shabby chic cocktail bar on the first floor – all located in a slightly dilapidated old house in Bywater. However it was nearly not meant to be. Given the dreadful aftermath of hurricane Katrina, Bacchanal emerged as a pop-up speakeasy and diner, hosting all manner of guest chefs from around the city – until some clever sod from the authorities tried to close it down, because of a lack of legal permission. Fortunately, common sense prevailed and, after a year-long struggle, this undoubted New Orleans gem is here to stay, with both residents and visitors enjoying its celebrated platters of cheese and meat, cracking wines and, above all, truly wonderful service.

✖
600 Poland Avenue, New Orleans, LA 70117 +1 504 948 9111 bacchanalwine.com

✖
IN THREE WORDS:
Baccha' Nacca' Nory!
THEY SAY:
"Not about cocktails this one, but all about the people, good wine, live music, BBQ and a fantastic atmosphere."
— DAVIDE SEGAT, UK/SPAIN
PRICE RATING: ✳ ✳

BEACHBUM BERRY'S LATITUDE 29

With all the exuberance of the tiki movement, and behind the bright colours, ephemera and ridiculousness, lies a burning passion and supreme craftsmanship, which may sometimes appear to take a back seat to the glassware and the garnish in your drink. Under the watchful eye of tiki legend Jeff "Beachbum" Berry, Latitude 29 has gone a step further than most to deliver not just a menu of personality-filled greatness, but one that also borders on genius. Berry, the author of numerous books about the history of tiki drinks culture, has unearthed many a lost classic, and the menu, split into Short Hoists and Long Pulls, is brimming with fun, flavour and supreme skill. From the classic Suffering Bastard to the Sinatra favourite, Navy Grog, and the signature Latitude 29, everything here is utterly charming and served to perfection, with that engaging smile that only tiki can do.

✖
321 North Peters Street, New Orleans, LA 70130 +1 504 609 3811 latitude29nola.com
✖
IN THREE WORDS:
Tiki Lover's Dream.
THE DRINK TO TRY:
The Latitude 29.
THEY SAY:
"The best tiki bar I ever visited!"
MARC ALVAREZ SAFONT, SPAIN
"The obvious choice for any tiki fiend. Crazy fun!"
— STAFFAN ALEXANDERSSON, NORWAY
PRICE RATING: ✳ ✳ ✳

BOMBAY CLUB

A very sophisticated and quiet restaurant bar in the Prince Conti hotel, Bombay Club is part colonial gentlemen's club and part Dickensian library. Here, you'll be able to escape into the comfort of live jazz duos, comfy leather chairs and a cigar menu. From a drinks perspective, the list is outstanding – part history of New Orleans, part history of the cocktail. You'll be spoiled for choice between the classics (the Martini is a speciality) and the thoroughly comprehensive list of whiskeys, sherries, Cognacs and gin.

✖
*830 Conti Street, New Orleans,
LA 70112 +1 504 577 2237
bombayclubneworleans.com*
✖

IN THREE WORDS:
French Quarter Respite.

THE DRINK TO TRY:
The Bombay Club Martini.

THEY SAY:
*"A cool and dark panelled haven
of civilized conversation and
great drinks."*
— NICK MORGAN, UK

PRICE RATING: ✖✖✖✖

ERIN ROSE ↑ ↗

This bar really is a proper
"meeting house". Built as a family
home over 100 years ago, it
became a bar in the mid-1950s.
Home to the drinking habits of
locals, artists, musicians and,
of course, tourists, it offers a
friendly atmosphere, where a
drink can be enjoyed just off
Bourbon Street. The bartenders
are some of the most relaxed
around, happy to chat about their

selection of ales, lager and spirits,
or just about anything in general.
Run by the amiable "Troy and
Angie", they really aim to make
this place a home from home.
The catchphrase is "Local prices.
Local chaos. Local love."
✖
*811 Conti Street, New Orleans,
LA 70112 +1 504-522 3573
erinrosebar.com*
✖

IN THREE WORDS:
The Irish Beauty.

THEY SAY:
*"Got Guinness, made friends and
ended up smashed there more
than one night."*
— STAFFAN ALEXANDERSSON,
NORWAY

PRICE RATING: ✖✖

> **Everything here
> [Latitude 29] is
> utterly charming
> and served to
> perfection, with
> that engaging
> smile that only
> tiki can do.**

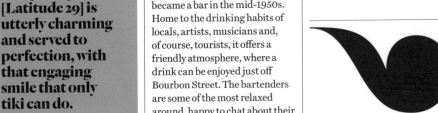

NEW ORLEANS*

FRENCH 75 ↓

There are several other entries in this book where the bar is named after a famous drink (such as Bramble on page 58), and French 75 (itself named after the powerful French 75mm field gun) is an intriguing tale indeed. The bar is based in renowned fine-dining restaurant Arnaud's, and, since 2003, French 75 has been a haunt for those in search of New Orleans's finest vintage classics. Take one look at the bar top, which dates back to the late 1800s, and you'll realize you're almost entering a time capsule of one of the most decadent and elegant times in drinking history. Beautiful wood panelling, vintage glassware and service from a bygone era all create an experience like no other.

✕

813 Bienville Street, New Orleans, LA 70112 +1 504 523 5433 arnaudsrestaurant.com

✕

IN THREE WORDS:
Classic, Decadent Sophistication.

THE DRINK TO TRY:
Arnaud's French 75. →

THEY SAY:
"Evocative of the 1940s, maybe earlier, life at French 75 is an emotional escape, a time capsule."
— ALLEN KATZ, USA

PRICE RATING: ✱✱✱✱

OLD ABSINTHE HOUSE ↑

Some places are steeped in history. In the case of the Olde Absinthe House on Bourbon Street in the New Orleans's French Quarter, the history is definitely there, (the building dates back to 1806), the stories are there (the likes of Sinatra, Mark Twain and Oscar Wilde are reported to have passed through the famous doors), and the walls are no doubt soaked in the pungent, aromatic spirit fumes from high-strength absinthe.

Today, the bar is as much a tourist destination as a place to try a decent drink, but you can't escape the significance it once had on the birth of the cocktail and the notoriety of absinthe in the USA – the original place was destroyed during Prohibition but rose phoenix-like in a flash of green flame once the alcohol ban was lifted.

✖

240 Bourbon Street, New Orleans, LA 70112 +1 504 523 3181 ruebourbon.com/oldabsinthehouse

✖

IN THREE WORDS:
French Quarter Greens.

THE DRINK TO TRY:
An Absinthe Frappe.

WE SAY:
Part of the fabric of the French Quarter, no visit should really be complete without sipping an aromatic frappe in this historical joint.

PRICE RATING: ✱ ✱

THE SAZERAC BAR

This fine hotel bar may not be able to lay claim to being where the classic Sazerac was conceived, but it sure makes a tasty one. A typically grand, wood-panelled affair meets you on arrival, with white-coated bartenders and servers scurrying past Art Deco murals, pouring frothy tins from a great height. This is a perfect introduction to the other classic drink they specialize in, the Ramos Gin Fizz. It's classy, traditional sippin', albeit a little on the pricey side, but delivered with aplomb.

✖

130 Roosevelt Way, New Orleans, LA 70112 +1 504 648 1200 therooseveltneworleans.com

✖

IN THREE WORDS:
Herbaceous Grandeur Guaranteed.

THE DRINK TO TRY:
Either the aforementioned Sazerac or a deliciously frothy Ramos Gin Fizz.

WE SAY:
Like having a Manhattan in Manhattan, a Sazerac in the Sazerac Bar gives you a similar feeling of joy.

PRICE RATING: ✱ ✱ ✱ ✱ ✱

Like the sound of this? Then check out **Bourbon O** (bourbono.com) a few blocks away for a different take on the New Orleans classics.

KANSAS CITY, AUSTIN & DALLAS*

HARRY'S COUNTRY CLUB ↓

As predictable as a great bar may be, there'll always be something to catch you out, when you least expect it. Harry's Country Club is full of little surprises. From the signed photos of the country stars who adorn the walls, your eye is drawn to the huge painting of a naked North American Indian lady hanging in the middle of the bar. Then, when you pick up the menu, it suddenly hits you. With one of the most comprehensive assortments of Scotch whisky in North America, Harry's is something of a rare find…then you turn the pages and see the same thing replicated with American whiskey, world whiskies, Tequila, mezcal and craft beer. "Wow" doesn't even come close. Harry – we salute you.

✖

112 East Missouri Avenue,
Kansas City, MO 64106
+1 816 421 3505
harryscountryclub.com

✖

IN THREE WORDS:
Good Ol' (whisky) Boys.

THE DRINK TO TRY:
Scotch, Tequila and a small batch bourbon.

THEY SAY:
"A mind-blowing single malt selection and a jukebox that isn't connected to the internet."
— LIZA WEISSTUCH, USA

PRICE RATING: ✖✖

With one of the most comprehensive assortments of Scotch whisky in North America, Harry's is something of a rare find…

KING BEE

Austin is one of those cities that, dependent on the time of year you visit, could give you two completely different experiences. A thriving university ensures that there's always stuff going on, but head there mid-March and you'll suddenly find a city in lockdown as thousands of musicians, music industry executives and associated hangers-on head over for the weeklong ~~party~~, sorry, music convention that is South By South West. 6th Street becomes the central focus for the entire place and the scores of dive bars and music venues come alive, where anything goes – and usually does. Up on 12th, you'll find King Bee, once the home of 1960s blues joint The Legendary White Swan. King Bee is a simple but oh-so-awesome premise, where whiskey and mezcal are the order of the day, with owner Billy Hankey and his wife taking regular trips to Mexico to extend their offering. When they turn on the frozen Margarita machine, that's when things ironically hot up and the bar's signature drink, The Bee's Knees, is a chilly, gin-based delight.

✖

1906 East 12th Street, Austin, TX 78702 +1 512 600 6956

✖

IN THREE WORDS:
Absolutely Buzzin' Place.
THE DRINK TO TRY:
A mezcal, or Bee's Knees.
THEY SAY:
"I LOVE THIS BAR. It's just a perfect place, with a perfect vibe."
— HANNAH LANFEAR, UK
PRICE RATING: ✳✳✳

MIDNIGHT RAMBLER ↑

A stunningly designed, dimly lit, chic drinking den in the Joule Hotel, this place has really thought through what it means to be a customer at a bar. A great soundtrack, the lighting just right, staff who really care and a drinks list that is unique to the venue, all create a truly sumptuous hangout. Don't forget, you're in Dallas, and in this stunning place you're really in Dallas. So settle in and let the good times roll.

✖

1530 Main Street, Dallas, TX 75201 +1 214 261 4601
midnightramblerbar.com

✖

IN THREE WORDS:
Vintage Dallas, Baby.
THEY SAY:
"Amazing soundtrack, one-of-a-kind drinks, and attentive service without all the stuffy airs and graces."
— IAIN GRIFFITHS, AUSTRALIA/ UK
PRICE RATING: ✳✳✳✳

PORTLAND & SEATTLE*

MARY'S

This book is all about some of the best, or most memorable, drinking experiences around the world, sourced from our own experience or from professionals in the drinks business, or both. Mary's Bar is one that has been recommended for sheer entertainment value and a night out so good that most of it is lost to the annals of time. Mary's, the oldest strip club in Portland, has a wonderful history. Opened in the 1930s as a traditional piano bar by Mary Duerst Hemming (hence the name), it was purchased in 1954, and the new owner, Roy Kellar, introduced dancing girls to entertain punters between breaks in the piano playing. The sound of ivory being tickled soon faded in favour of the dancing girls, and this has maintained its pole position as a dancing bar ever since.

The bar's neon strip sign is considered a local landmark in the city. The place serves beers and cocktails, with a minimum one drink policy and is certain to

be the fulcrum of many a night out in this most hipster of towns.

✖
129 South West Broadway, Portland, OR 97205
+1 503 227 3023 marysclub.com
✖

IN THREE WORDS:
A Local Landmark.
THEY SAY:
"One of my favourite nights out that I can remember…you just let it happen to you."
— **MICHAEL VACHON, USA/UK**
PRICE RATING: ✳

CANON ↑

If the claim made by the bar owners here is true, this bar has the largest collection of spirits in the western hemisphere (and we'd happily take up the challenge of counting them, if we're allowed to sample too!). That's over 3,500 if you were wondering, making this more of an emporium, a library, a cabinet of curiosity, than a bar.

As you can imagine, with so many bottles, the back bar

reaches high into the sky and there is little need for anything other than shelves with bottles on for decoration, and this, along with the wood and leather interior, means it has a warm and welcoming feel.

It isn't just the huge selection of bottles that makes this bar remarkable; it is also their cocktail list and creations that are off the hook. These cracking concoctions have recently spawned a book called *The Canon Cocktail Book: Recipes From The Award-Winning Bar*, giving a good indication of the quality of these drinks, which range from complex to simple.

✖

928 12th Avenue, Seattle, WA 98122 +1 206 552 9755 canonseattle.com

✖

IN THREE WORDS:
Cocktails And Bottles.

WE SAY:
Don't be overwhelmed by the huge number of bottles on display and ask staff for guidance.

PRICE RATING: ✳ ✳ ✳

RADIATOR WHISKEY ↓

It isn't often you find a whiskey bar that serves direct from the barrel, which makes Radiator such a rare joint. An incredible selection of bottles is built around a large barrel with seven smaller barrels and taps inside. These hide a selection of unique whiskeys, including their own creation, Radiator, made by 2Bar Spirits using only Pacific Northwest grains, then aged in-house in their own lightly charred oak barrels. They also have barrel-aged cocktails on tap.

✖

94 Pike Street, #30, Seattle, WA 98101 +1 206 467 4268 radiatorwhiskey.com

✖

IN THREE WORDS:
Unique, Unique, Unique.

THE DRINK TO TRY:
Have a go at their own whiskey, mixed into an Old Fashioned.

WE SAY:
How many bars have whiskey on tap, let alone their own whiskey on tap?? Exactly!

PRICE RATING: ✳ ✳ ✳

THE WHISKY BAR

The Whisky Bar in Seattle has been an established drinking institution for over 20 years. It started life as a classic dive bar, serving fast and hard with a focus on beer. Now it has one of the largest selections of whisky this side of the country. Located in Belltown, Seattle, they don't just serve whisky, but a range of cocktails (classic and their own creations – a Blood Orange Bellini for those non-whisky drinkers and a Paper Plane for those of you partial to a dram of the mature stuff), beers and some food.

✖

2122 2nd Avenue, Seattle, WA 98121 +1 206 443 4490 thewhiskybar.com

✖

IN THREE WORDS:
Whisky Bar-None.

WE SAY:
Pop in to check out the expertise behind the bar.

PRICE RATING: ✳ ✳

LOS ANGELES*

BIG BAR

Big Bar is a retreat from the onslaught of modern life. Brilliantly crafted cocktails are served in a bespoke bar adjoining sister joint Alcove Cafe & Bakery, which has been a staple for great food and fun in LA over the past few years. This place is less a speakeasy and more a local neighbourhood hangout, with events that bleed onto the Alcove's patio and into their main rooms; the venues work in harmony for a great alfresco drinking experience.

Serving some of the most creative cocktails in town, this is a place to pitch up for brunch, drink some punch and see where the winds of the weekend take you!

✖
1927 Hillhurst Avenue, Los Angeles, CA 90027 +1 323 644 0100 alcovecafe.com/bigbar
✖

IN THREE WORDS:
Relaxed LA Style.

WE SAY:
The perfect place for a brunch cocktail!

PRICE RATING: ✱✱✱

THE BLACK CAT

A charming addition to Silverlake's already super-cool set of gastropubs, diners and bars, The Black Cat, opened in 2012, is the sort of haunt that you can enter at any time and immediately feel at home. With its high-backed leather chesterfield booths and wood panelling, it feels vintage, but not at all dated. The original Black Cat Tavern, based at this site, was a significant LGBT bar back in the 1960s, made famous for the protests after the joint was raided on New Year's Eve in 1967. Today a plaque from 2008 states that the location was the nation's first documented LGBT civil rights demonstration. Inside, you'll find framed newspaper cuttings from the time, reminding patrons of a very different, less tolerant era.

Today though, the bar is a celebration of all things flavour and you'll marvel at the daily punches, the house cocktails and especially the list of different Mules, served in traditional copper mugs – particularly the wonderfully titled Suffering Bastard, a heady mix of bourbon, gin, lime and ginger beer.

✖
3909 Sunset Boulevard, Los Angeles, CA 90029 +1 323 661 6369 theblackcatla.com
✖

IN THREE WORDS:
The Cat's Whiskeys.

THE DRINK TO TRY:
The daily punches are a terrific opening drink – and super value for money too.

THEY SAY:
"Somewhere you can park yourself all night."
— ALEX WOLPERT, UK

PRICE RATING: ✱✱

EVELEIGH ↓

Freshness is a word bandied about a lot in the restaurant world, but one which certainly applies to the Eveleigh. Essentially this is a restaurant experience (bringing together a simple use of traceable ingredients, with a European twist), rather than a bar, but deserves its entry here because the drinks themselves are superbly constructed, fresh and unique. There's a lunchtime cocktail menu (surely a lost

opportunity for restaurants), which sees plenty of fresh juices, herbs and infused spirits.

✖

8752 Sunset Boulevard, Los Angeles, CA 90069 +1 424 239 1630 theeveleigh.com

✖

IN THREE WORDS:
Fresh, Delicate, Balanced.

THE DRINK TO TRY:
The Eveleigh Lemonade.

THEY SAY:
"One of the best restaurant bars I've seen, consistently good from Day One."
— LOUIS ANDERMAN, USA

PRICE RATING: ✱✱✱✱

HARVARD & STONE ↑

Harvard & Stone is, in many ways, the perfect concept for a bar. A fun, good-time, knockabout drinking haven, with an emphasis on craft spirits brands, unusual but strangely familiar twists on classic drinks, and rock'n'roll bands on tap. The industrial revolution decor is part steampunk, part Wild West gold rush, and the whole place gives off a totally unpretentious vibe. The overriding genius at work, however, comes from the concept of the separate R&D

bar, located to the back of the venue. Here, you'll find an almost daily changing of the guard, with a new guest bartender popping by, offering a completely different menu every time. It's experimental, it's unconventional and it's bloody brilliant if you and your palate truly live for the moment. Consider it the highly flavoursome mayfly of the drinks world.

✖

5221 Hollywood Boulevard, Los Angeles, CA 90027 +1 323 466 6063 harvardandstone.com

✖

IN THREE WORDS:
Live The Moment.

THEY SAY:
"It's a great place for bartenders to go wild and try new things."
— LOUIS ANDERMAN, USA

PRICE RATING: ✱✱

MELROSE UMBRELLA CO.

It never rains but it pours… seemingly something many people are destined to say, if they live in climates where a sunny day is treated with an almost apocalyptical display of joy and fear; meaning that nothing ever gets done and the parks overflow with pale bodies, eager to catch

the precious rays while they last. One would imagine that in LA, almost the opposite applies, so it seems ironic that the logo for the Melrose Umbrella Co is that of an umbrella-wielding 90-year-old James Melrose, once the Lord Mayor of York in the north of England – where it rains a lot.

The theme for this achingly cool bar is that its location was one of the first places to drink after Prohibition was lifted, signified by the logo of an umbrella with raindrops coming out of it – promising "many wet days to come". Today, the bar is festooned with vintage umbrellas, apothecary-style drawers, shelves and antique cabinets holding its spirits – all tastefully done to avoid feeling overdone in the historical department. The drinks themselves veer into classic territory but are finely crafted and manage to bring the right level of playfulness.

✖

7465 Melrose Avenue, Los Angeles, CA 90046 +1 323 951 0709 melroseumbrellaco.com

✖

IN THREE WORDS:
Jolly Brolly Dollies.

THE DRINK TO TRY:
Coffee, cocktails and pretty much everything there!

WE SAY:
Style, passion and lots of fun.

PRICE RATING: ✱✱

FOCUS*

STARTENDER
KATIE EMMERSON

Katie Emmerson is an award-winning bartender whose talents have taken the Omakase-inspired **Walker Inn** cocktail experience (see page 244) to great acclaim globally. Her latest project is helping to develop the cocktail menu at **Gwen** (gwenla. com), one of LA's most recent

fine-dining experiences, as well as educating the bartending community on delivering greater levels of service.

Where do you drink when you're off duty?
Mignon (mignonla.com) – a wonderful little wine bar in downtown Los Angeles. It has everything I want – great wine, cheese, charcuterie and lovely people all around me.
You're marooned on a desert island...assuming you have the ingredients, what's your favourite drink of all time?

The Paper Plane, by Sam Ross from **Attaboy** in New York (see page 208); equal parts bourbon, Amaro Nonino, Aperol and lemon juice, shaken and served up. I know I'm supposed to say simple things like a Daquiri, Negroni, Manhattan, etc., but the Paper Plane has been my favourite drink for as long as I can remember loving cocktails. For my palate, it is just perfect in every way.
What is your favourite city in the world to go drinking in?
The city I loved most recently (that also surprised me) was

Stockholm. Obviously New York, London, San Francisco are all great and have some of the greatest variety of talent. Stockholm had zero pretence and some of the best and most creative drinks I've had in a long time. Everyone was incredibly warm, the food is unbelievable – I can't wait to go back!

What do you think is the most underrated cocktail of all time and why?

The Piña Colada. People are starting to come around, but I still get so many eye rolls when I say this is an underrated cocktail. Even if it's a terrible one, I'm still definitely having a great time if I have a Piña Colada in my hand.

The concept of Omakase drinking is really growing outside of Japan now. Explain exactly what this means in the bar world and what have you learned from the style of serve?

First, to be clear, Cocktail Omakase is different to "Bartender's Choice", though I do believe the development of one led into the other. When I first started bartending, I couldn't get anyone to drink anything other than vodka. Then people started to pay attention to what they were drinking and became curious. As our guests got curious, we started educating ourselves more and our guests started to trust us with Bartender's Choice – "I like bourbon and citrus; what can you make me?" That grew into some being able to completely let us take the reins, saying, "I trust you completely with whatever journey you want to take me on." What a time to be alive!

KATIE'S TOP HANGOUTS:

✖

Attaboy, New York (see page 208) ↑

The owners have taken what we all loved so much about Milk & Honey and really elevated it and made it their own. There's a million bars opening in New York, but I always make sure to end my night there.

✖

Eastern Standard, Boston (easternstandardboston.com)

The epitome of hospitality in every way and a Boston staple. Everyone is welcome, everyone is included and everyone feels special – even during a post-Red Sox game crush. That's hard to pull off.

✖

Trick Dog, San Francisco (trickdogbar.com)

Creative and ambitious, yet comfortable and kind. What more do you want in a bar?

✖

Ling Long, Stockholm (ling-long.se)

Like most cocktail bars in Stockholm, the people are warm and the atmosphere is just right – you'd never know you're also about to get one of the best drinks you've had in a long time.

LOS ANGELES*

OLD LIGHTNING AT SCOPA ITALIAN ROOTS

On first glance, this fine Italian restaurant/gastropub in Marina Del Rey, Venice, has all the hallmarks of a great place to eat: plates of tasty cold cuts, antipasti, a solid Italian wine selection. But all is not as it appears. Rumours circulate. Looks are exchanged. Knowing nods here and there. The reason is Old Lightning. Old Lightning is the Fight Club of the booze world. Not quite a secret, but not something anyone seemingly wants to shout about. It is essentially a speakeasy hiding in plain sight. The masterstroke is that once you have secured your booking, you're escorted to an unmarked door, asked politely to check your phone in and then are free to enter. Yes, that's right. You are separated from your worldly contacts, social media, camera and all the things that make a great bar experience... utterly rubbish. This stance is brilliantly admirable. It means you focus implicitly on your companion, the surroundings and, more importantly, the drinks. To say "the bar menu is life-affirming" is an understatement. The scarcity and rarity of the whiskeys, Tequilas and mezcals on show here is utterly breathtaking.

✖

2905 West Washington Boulevard, Venice, CA 90292
+1 310 821 1100
scopaitalianroots.com

✖

IN THREE WORDS:
Don't Phone Home.

THE DRINK TO TRY:
Google the menu and just weep.

WE SAY:
A hidden gem of booze wonderment.

PRICE RATING: ✦✦✦✦

SEVEN GRAND ↘

One of the bars that undoubtedly signalled the resurgence of the fine-drinking scene in LA, Seven Grand – a whiskey bar of some distinction – was opened in 2007, to a mini fanfare across the industry. The concept is not simply to show off an insanely detailed list of whiskies, but to guide drinkers through the entire category, demystifying the spirit and, ultimately making it more accessible. In 2014, a separate Japanese whisky-focused bar, with room for just 18 guests, was opened up – again gauging the trend toward the spirit really before it had had a chance to become mainstream. Inside, Seven Grand could be perceived as being a little "themed", with its hunting lodge taxidermy and tartan carpets, but this is merely a reflection on the fascination of all things Scottish and when it comes to the things that matter – the whisky list itself and knowledge of the bar staff – both are exceptional.

✖

2nd Floor, 515 West 7th Street, Los Angeles, CA 90014 +1 213 614 0736 213dthospitality.com

✖

IN THREE WORDS:
Highlander In LA.

THEY SAY:
"LA's first whiskey temple."
— **LOUIS ANDERMAN, USA**

PRICE RATING: ✦✦✦✦

TIKI TI

There's a well known saying that goes something like "less is more…" Yeah, right. Try telling that to father and son Michael and Mike Buhen who run the glorious Tiki Ti, something of a bartending institution for well over half a century now. This tiny place may have just 12 seats at the bar, but there's so much tiki ephemera behind the bar, hanging off the walls, ceiling and pretty much everywhere, like brightly coloured Christmas decorations, that there's really only room for that many patrons at any one time. You'll spend your first 10 minutes simply gazing around wondering at just where all this stuff came from, before you realize you should really be ordering one of the 100+ drinks on offer. Apparently, some of the tiki mugs were donated to the bar by customers, so we imagine that the collection is actually a shrine to the tiki gods, to keep bestowing drink-making brilliance upon the Buhens. If it is, it's certainly working!

✖

4427 Sunset Boulevard,
Los Angeles, CA 90027
+1 323 669 9381 tiki-ti.com

✖

IN THREE WORDS:
High Priests of Tiki.

THE DRINK TO TRY:
Spin the Tiki Wheel and put
your palate in the hands of the
tiki gods!

THEY SAY:
"It's a true institution with boozy
tiki drinks."
— **THOMAS ASKE, UK**

PRICE RATING: ✱✱

THE VARNISH ↑

Having spent some time exploring the extensive network of speakeasy bars in Tokyo (see pages 132–9) you'd probably expect us to be a little jaded by the whole affair. You know, finding the "secret" door, learning the handshake, rolling up the trouser leg and affecting the "knowing look". So when it came to exploring the trend in the USA, our guard was raised a little. Needless to say, one drink in The Varnish changed all that. The bar is accessed through a door at the back of Cole's Diner in Downtown LA and you know what's coming next: a dimly lit atmosphere, an immaculate back bar and a plethora of boutique spirits brands, vermouths and bitters. Here's where it gets exciting – the service is at the top of its game and the menu is as simple as it can be. Order yourself something along the lines of an Improved Whiskey Cocktail (an invention of the Victorian era bartending god "Professor" Jerry Thomas, see page 122) and marvel at how only a few simple ingredients can reinvent the way you look at American whiskey. Stunning stuff.

✖

118 East 6th Street, Los Angeles,
CA 90014 +1 213 265 7089
thevarnishbar.com

✖

IN THREE WORDS:
Slick, Stylized Speakeasy.

THE DRINK TO TRY:
A Bartender's Choice.

THEY SAY:
"One of the first bars in LA to
bring back well crafted classics."
— **LOUIS ANDERMAN, USA**

PRICE RATING: ✱✱✱

LOS ANGELES*

WALKER INN ↓

There's a word that crops up in several places in this book, which you may not be familiar with: "Omakase". The emphasis is on the extreme culinary skills of the chef to pinpoint exactly what makes you tick. This trend has shifted over to the bartending community and Omakase-style bars are widespread across Japan. They're also making an impression in America, and LA's Walker Inn, a not-so-secret

hidden bar found inside the Hotel Normandie, is perhaps the finest example you will find on the West Coast – and maybe anywhere in the world, for that matter. The menu is unpredictable and rotates on a six to eight-week average, ensuring that you're always going to be given a unique experience. And experience is the operative word here. You're treated to a mini flight of either two or three drinks, where the only indication of the spectacular result is from the questions your bartender asked you to begin with: Any allergies? Style of drink, i.e. very boozy or a little lighter? Sweet or more herbaceous? Smoke will emanate from your glass. Strange infusions will be

used. You'll be drinking from very unpredictable glassware. The scant detail will eventually serve as your best friend and the experience will be a deeply memorable, personal affair, truly worthy of the Omakase ethic. Mind. Blown.

✖

3612 West 6th Street, Los Angeles, CA 90005 +1 213 263 2709
thewalkerinnla.com

✖

IN THREE WORDS:
Unpredictable Omakase Magic.
THE DRINK TO TRY:
Put your trust in the bar and be prepared to be amazed.
THEY SAY:
"Amazing. You may not know it, but that perfect pour may have taken three days of work behind the scenes."
— **LOUIS ANDERMAN, USA**
"The degree to which this is executed really demonstrates just how special a bar experience can be."
— **IAN GRIFFITHS, UK**
"The best drinks I've ever had."
— **JARED BROWN, UK**
PRICE RATING: ✶ ✶ ✶ ✶ ✶

SAN FRANCISCO*

ABV

San Francisco is a city that's always had the cocktail at its heart and it's fantastic to see ABV giving back to the city some of the best cocktails found coast-to-coast. It is the brainchild of some seriously experienced bartenders and hospitality experts, who have produced a light and airy bar, with a focus on great liquors, mixers and cocktails.

With the expertise of experience behind the cocktail list, this place really is a mirror to the influence that San Francisco has had over the recent years and should be one of the main reasons to head out drinking in the city. Think of ABV as a "best of" compilation of the West Coast bartending talent, presented in a beautifully simple yet visually stunning cocktail list. The food here is also worth noting; with its simple-to-eat ethos, it means there is time to carry on drinking, even if you get the munchies.

✖
3174 16th Street, San Francisco,
CA 94103 +1 415 400 4748
abvsf.com

✖
IN THREE WORDS:
Alcohol By (ad)Venture.
WE SAY:
Take a trip here for the best of the best in San Francisco.
PRICE RATING: ✱✱✱✱

BAR AGRICOLE →

This award-winning bar and restaurant has taken many plaudits for its food, drinks and physical space in which their wonderful brand of hospitality is played out. A contemporary space that wouldn't be out of place in Oslo, Copenhagen or Berlin, it has a naturally easy vibe that immediately makes you feel both relaxed and comfortably stylish at the same time, living up to their own evaluation of the place as a "contemporary tavern".

The drinks are strong twists on classics that almost demand to be paired with some of the excellent food on offer, and have a focus on using "craft" spirits, or "farmhouse distillates". This gives each drink a twist and you can almost feel the hands of the artisans who created the spirit serving you the drink themselves. Of course, natural, local wines are also served and the knowledgeable staff will walk you through the bottles on offer to make sure the correct flavours meet your palate.

✖
355 11th Street (between Folsom and Harrison), San Francisco, CA 94103 +1 415-355-9400
baragricole.co
✖
IN THREE WORDS:
Farm To Glass.
THEY SAY:
"They only source spirits with ethics that are sustainable and well made."
— **MICHAEL VACHON** USA/UK
PRICE RATING: ✱✱✱✱

FEATURE*

A DAY DRINKING IN...
SAN FRANCISCO

We spoke to **Haley Forest**, a New York-based spirits and cocktails writer (who is also a dab hand behind the bar) about her ideal day drinking in San Francisco. You can follow Haley at @HCForest.

San Francisco is one of those small big cities where everyone kind of knows everyone, and while there is an expensive-ish residential area most of the actual culture (read: watering holes) is contained within very specific areas. While these areas can become overrun with the Bridge & Tunnel crowds on the weekends, head in on a Sunday to Wednesday and you'll be sure to find old locals, industry workers and plenty of creatives propping up the bars, knocking back expertly made craft cocktails and boilermakers in equal measure.

Start off your day at the much acclaimed **Trick Dog** (trickdogbar.com) in The Mission. Founded by Scott Baird and Josh Harris of the **Bon Vivants** (bonvivants.com), this spot is known for their cocktails, crazy menus and changing themes, but

the food is also something you can't miss out on. Why not snag a table on the mezzanine and give yourself a good layer of delicious chow while eyeing up their considerable drinks menu?

From there, take a short cab ride up to 19th and Lexington to **Wildhawk ↑** (wildhawksf.com). Housed on the site of San Francisco's last amazing lesbian

bar, this place is sultry with monochrome prints, emerald green velvet, and a vermouth-heavy menu. It's only a quick walk over to one of the classic Dive bars here: **Dalva** (dalvasf.com). Loaded with a heavy beer selection (many local brews), plus an epic jukebox, it's a great place to escape the hipster invasion that has become much of The Mission district. Be sure to also stick your head into their hidden, red-lit cocktail bar in the back, **The Hideout**. This cash-only micro bar is all leather booths and classics, but sometimes that's exactly what you need.

Amble across the street and give Ryan Fitzgerald a visit at **ABV** (see page 245). This high-ceilinged agave-fuelled wonderland is bright and breezy with some serious talent behind

the stick and a near constant stream of off-duty bartenders and dedicated regulars passing through for a one-and-done. Everything is delicious, plus they serve food till 1am.

Next up, you're going to want to cab it over to the modern speakeasy that really kicked off the whole rebirth: **Bourbon & Branch** ← (see page 248). Housed in the Tenderloin, an area known historically for junkies and crime rates, this place really took a gamble opening up here back in 2006, but they heralded some great ideas. You'll have to reserve a space and receive a password to enter, but once inside you'll find five bars tucked away, each with their own slight theme and feel, so be sure to take a good look around. Their menu is like an opus of liquid delights so get reading and drinking.

From there, why not stroll around the corner to **Rye on Geary** at Leavenworth (ryeontheroad.com)? This neighbourhood favourite has long been holding the torch for easy drinking in a tough area, where you can get a good drink, but no one will judge you for downing shots and beers either. Order a Negroni or a beer, sit back and people watch.

If you find yourself still at odds after this, and before 1:30am, grab a taxi to **15 Romolo** ↑ ← in North Beach (15romolo.com). While the surrounding area is filled with strip clubs (and consequently the people who frequent them), this spot is tucked on a quiet side street and is loaded with a killer sherry collection, delicious late-night food and a jukebox that will provide the perfect soundtrack every damn time. The guys behind the stick like to have a good time, but also really know their stuff, so let them talk you into something new. You never know what you'll discover.

SAN FRANCISCO & ELEUTHERA*

BOURBON & BRANCH

The Prohibition era of the 1920s has provided the bar community with a wealth of cocktails, literature and overall bar direction in the last decade or so. We are sure this wasn't the plan when the Great Experiment was introduced, that nearly 100 years later bars would be happily trading off the back of it, in the new golden age of the cocktail! One bar that draws on this era perfectly is Bourbon & Branch in San Francisco, where you'll experience the ambiance of that time in an actual speakeasy that operated illegally at this location from 1921 to 1933. The address that is listed in the San Francisco Telephone Directory of the day is "The Ipswitch – A Beverage Parlour". Operating as a bar during Prohibition, under the guise of "JJ Russell's Cigar Shop", the booze would have likely been shipped in by bootleggers from Canada.

Along with the dark lighting, a set of house rules helps maintain the feel of Prohibition drinking, and the drinks rotate around

whiskey, bourbon, rums and Tequilas. Well worth a visit.

✖
501 Jones St, San Francisco, CA 94102 +1 415 346 1735
bourbonandbranch.com
✖
IN THREE WORDS:
Speak Easy, Friend.
WE SAY:
The perfect Prohibition Parlour.
PRICE RATING: ✱✱✱

Atmosphere-wise, this place [Hard Water] has a clean, retro, mid-century feel to it, halfway between a 1960s airline lounge and a modern-day Oslo apartment, making it one of the most stylish places in San Francisco to drink whiskey.

HARD WATER

This "project" is a curios spot down by the waterfront in San Francisco. With only seats at the bar and some other communal seating in a horseshoe shape, Cajun food is served. You don't come here for the food, however, but for the whiskies. Their selection of bourbons is unique and dates back past Prohibition. Such is their selection, that a ladder is required to reach the uppermost bottles on their shelves. Atmosphere-wise, this place has a clean, retro, mid-century feel to it, halfway between a 1960s airline lounge and a modern-day Oslo apartment, making it one of the most stylish places in San Francisco to drink whiskey, from any era.

✖
Pier 3, The Embarcadero, San Francisco, CA 94105
+1 415 392 3021
hardwaterbar.com
✖
IN THREE WORDS:
Stylish Whiskey Selection.
THE DRINK TO TRY:
Their bespoke single barrel Four Roses bourbon.
THEY SAY:
"An epic whiskey selection."
— ALEX WOLPERT, UK
PRICE RATING: ✱✱✱

SMUGGLER'S COVE ↑

One of two bars named Smuggler's Cove in this book (see page 51 for the other, just a 14-hour flight away in Liverpool, United Kingdom), it won't be difficult to guess that this venue has a certain pirate, tiki, seaside feel to it. Opening back in 2009, this West Coast Smuggler's Cove has established itself as one of the best rum bars in the world, delivering cocktails that are as exotic as its surroundings. The bar draws heavily on what its owners claim is the largest rum selection existing in the United States for their range of interesting cocktails, with an overview of historical rums thrown in for good measure. There is probably no better place to learn about the fun of rum, than here.

✖

650 Gough Street, San Francisco, CA 94102 +1 415 869 1900 smugglerscovesf.com

✖

IN THREE WORDS:
Tot, Tot, Tot.

WE SAY:
Head here for a truly immersive rum experience.
PRICE RATING: ✱✱✱

THE COVE

Eleuthera. "Where?" we hear you ask. This is probably the most remote bar in the book, but we'll bet you it is the prettiest. Situated in a "W" shaped cove on the island of Eleuthera in the Bahamas, The Cove is a hotel-cum-resort-cum-hangout on one of the most easterly islands in the archipelago. Completely rebuilt after a devastating storm in the early 2000s, it nestles between pristine white beaches, which provide the perfect backdrop for a drink at their outdoor bar.

It is the intimacy and sheer awesomeness of the location that make this place so special. Try their local rum punch with a conch fritter just as the sun is setting and gaze out at the perfect horizon.

✖

Queens Highway, BS, Gregory Town 1548, Bahamas +1 242 335 5141 thecoveeleuthera.com

✖

IN THREE WORDS:
White Sand Heaven.
THE DRINK TO TRY:
It has to be the rum punch.
WE SAY:
The most remote bar in the book, and all the better for it.
PRICE RATING: ✱✱✱✱✱

TORONTO*

CIVIL LIBERTIES ↓

Democracy in a cocktail bar is a strange concept. One could say that there are three types of customer (and we're not limiting the experience to simply these three): 1. those who wander in bereft of any idea of what to drink; 2. those who know their tastes, but are prepared to experiment; and 3. those who are fairly militant in the type of supping they like to engage in.

Should these three be on a night out together, the concept of Civil Liberties would have a hugely profound effect on each of them – in different ways.

The motto of the bar is "night after night, freedom comes in a glass." This freedom is delivered by the lack of a menu and the experience of the bartenders to choose what they feel is right for the customer to drink. Give them a vehicle (your choice of spirit, be it bourbon, gin, rum) and they'll take you to a destination that you will not only want to Instagram, but will probably want to move to, buy an apartment and settle down, content that your palate is in completely safe hands. Skilful, artful and daring, Civil Liberties

are experts in reading your taste buds like a book.

✖

878 Bloor Street West, Toronto, ON M6J 1M2 +1 416 546 5634 civillibertiesbar.com

✖

IN THREE WORDS:
Life, Liberty, Mixology.

THE DRINK TO TRY:
Your choice, squire. But do have a Civil Liberties toasted sandwich with your drink. They're excellent.

WE SAY:
Toronto's perfect answer to the "Bartender's Choice" conundrum? Quite possibly.

PRICE RATING: ✱✱✱

THE LOCKHART ↗

Ever heard the saying that, when a butterfly flaps its wings in one location, a tsunami occurs in another? This can be applied to The Lockhart. When the place opened back in late 2015, word started to trickle through to the world's media that a Harry Potter vibed-up bar had appeared – almost in a puff of smoke. Things got out of hand and Potter fans descended on the place – which, to be fair, *is* "influenced" by the famous films, but is certainly not anything like the theme-bar nonsense that you can read online. Instead, you'll find well-made drinks on a menu that includes occasional nods to

Potter (the Gin Weasley being one) but alongside the infusions and potions, what we have is a solid and skillful team having a bit of fun. The place is small and doesn't like standing customers, so getting in may be tricky, but when you do, let there be magic.

✖

1479 Dundas Street West, Toronto, ON M6J 1Y8
+1 647 748 4434 thelockhart.ca

✖

IN THREE WORDS:
Cocktailarium Extra-Ordinaria!

THE DRINK TO TRY:
The Big Bad Wolf, with bacon-infused bourbon and walnut bitters.

WE SAY:
Hype is a dangerous game, but in the case of The Lockhart, they just manage to stay the right side of skilful.

PRICE RATING: ✱✱✱

PHARMACY

Housed in a former pharmacy in the Parkdale district of Toronto (the signage is still nicely preserved for posterity), this place is one of those drinking dens that locals covet and visitors either never manage to find or simply pass on by, because it lacks the gravitas of a "premium", associated with great bars. But great it is. The selection of craft beers is fresh, innovative and constantly revolving, and Chris Harper, the creator/owner and, one could say, curator, clearly knows what he likes – and his customers love. The appeal is very simple here– great beer, simple decor, quiet vibes. Soulful sippin' indeed.

✖

1318 King Street West, Toronto, ON M6K 1G8

✖

IN THREE WORDS:
Medication for The Soul.

THE DRINK TO TRY:
Whatever new draft brew is on tap.

WE SAY:
"Curated" is a current buzz word, but Pharmacy feels decidedly curated, while being free of any pretence. Some places spend a lot of money and time trying to perfect this vibe...and still fail.

PRICE RATING: ✱✱

FEATURE*

A DAY DRINKING IN...
TORONTO

Depending on when you're planning to visit, be prepared for extremes. Toronto's bar scene is one of the most vibrant and diverse you'll ever experience, rather like the city's notorious weather. If like us, you happen to be visiting in November, wrap up warm and admire Toronto's imposing, cinematic skyline, the CN Tower set back against the brooding cloud cover. In fact, if you want cinematic, then start your day over at the Distillery District – originally the site of the former Canadian whisky distillery Gooderham & Worts, also famous for allegedly being the rundown location for a number of scenes in the 1987 classic action film, *Robocop*. The once imposing buildings have now been modernized into a complex of artisan cafés, restaurants and brewpubs.

After enjoying a Tankhouse pale ale at the **Mill Street Brewery** (millstreetbrewery.com), take a cab over to another regenerated hub of activity – Queen Street West. Here you'll find **BYOB Cocktail Emporium →**

> For the perfect nightcap you have a difficult decision on your hands: whisky or craft beer – not that either is going to leave you any way other than giggling with delight.

(cocktailemporium.ca – see page 254) which, for us, completely embodies the enthusiasm for all things cocktail in the city. Choose the most random flavour of cocktail bitters you can find (Ms Piggy Peppercorn Bacon Bitters, anyone?) then wander down to one of the area's best-known landmarks, **The Drake Hotel** (thedrakehotel.ca) with its **Sky Yard ↗** rooftop patio. Here you'll find a mix of slightly twisted classics, the highlights of which must include the ridiculously moreish Brown Butter Maple Old Fashioned (artfully combining butter-washed bourbon, cigar tincture, maple syrup and mole bitters – not the animal, but a take on the classic Mexican mole sauce.

If you're struggling for choice on what to drink, let the bartenders do the work and decide for you. Head to **Civil Liberties** (see page 250) where you give the guys behind the stick an idea of the spirit you like and they'll do the rest.

Now, head to **Burdock Brewery** (burdockto.com). You'll find amazing decor and atmosphere, with plenty of interesting beers and food as well as an excellent bottle shop.

For a perfect nightcap you have a difficult decision on your hands: whisky or craft beer – not that either is going to leave you any way other than giggling with delight.

If it's the whisky route, then you could go full Canadian at **Char No.5** (charfive.com), or Scottish at **The Caledonian** (thecaledonian.ca) on College Street, run by the Wolffs – a dynamic husband and wife team – which has more than a smoky whiff of the Highlands about it with 250 whiskies to stay late into the wee hours working out which you prefer.

The Canadian craft brewing scene has exploded over the last decade and the trend toward brewpubs, modest in production size, but anything but in terms of innovation in flavour is showing no real sign of slowing down. With a motto "to never run out of beer", **Bellwoods Brewery** ← (bellwoodsbrewery.com) on Ossington Avenue is almost issuing a challenge to those with a penchant for brilliantly made pale ales and saisons. Handily, there's a takeaway

bottle shop if you happen to be defeated in one session.

Although the **Lansdowne** (lansdownebrewery.com) is a little way out of the centre of town, on the seemingly endless Lansdowne Avenue, the number of great beers on tap is well worth the visit. This craft-sized brewpub housed in an old warehouse unit regularly hosts nights based around different styles of beer, many produced by other local craft breweries, as well as cider makers. Think some seriously bizarre offerings including Tepache, a traditional Mexican "cider", made using fermented pineapple, which sits alongside Darjeeling tea and honeysuckle-infused cider.

Ta Ta, Toronto – you've brought a big smile to our faces.

FEATURE*

A DRINK WITH...
KRISTEN VOISEY

Kristen Voisey is the founder of BYOB Cocktail Emporium (cocktailemporium.ca), a shop like no other, which exemplifies Toronto's growing love for all things *cocktail*. From exotic and vintage glassware and tiki punchbowls to arguably the greatest selection of different bitters in the world, BYOB demands more than a few minutes of your time. In fact, write the afternoon off and clear some room in your suitcase....

What was the motivation behind setting up BYOB?
To tell you the truth, I loved cocktails and vintage glassware. I had a large collection and that was a large part of the store when we opened. I got the idea to open a cocktail-themed store when I was in LA and came across a store called Bar Keeper that sold bar tools, vintage glassware...and actual booze – which I don't see us being able to do anytime soon due to Ontario's weird liquor laws!
Why is the Toronto drinks scene so vibrant at the moment?

Toronto has an amazing tight-knit bartending community. There are very passionate bartenders who, through this dedication, have created quite the scene here. I think because of the enthusiasm behind the bars, it has spread out to the general public, which has created a demand and desire for great cocktails and bars throughout the city. We are an A-class city with an A-class bar scene.
Tough question, but what's your all-time favourite drink and who made it?

My all-time favourite drink changes by the day! When I think back about my favourite cocktails I mostly remember the experience. Some stand-out memories have been the presentation of the cocktails at **Hemingway Bar** in Prague (see page 115), tropical cocktails by the pool at **The Broken Shaker** in Miami (freehandhotels.com), classics such as the Sazerac and Ramos Gin Fizz at **The Roosevelt Hotel** in New Orleans (+1 504 648 1200), the perfection of the cocktails at **Bar Tender Ginza** in Tokyo (see page 134) and **The Savoy** in London (see page 22).

The craft beer scene seems to be booming in Toronto. What's your favourite brewery in the city?

Yes, there are *a lot* of breweries here! I love the **Bellwoods Brewery** (bellwoodsbrewery. com) – the space and location are perfect.

I think because of the passion beind the bars, it has spread out to the general public, which has created a demand and desire for great cocktails and bars throughout the city.

KRISTEN'S OTHER FAVOURITE TORONTO HANGOUTS...IN UNDER 140 CHARACTERS:

✖
Bar Alo (alorestaurant.com)
Gorgeous bar and outstanding cocktails and hospitality.

✖
Peoples Eatery (peopleseatery.com)
Amazing bar in Chinatown. Super great staff, decor, food and cocktails. Good vibes.

✖
Cocktail Bar (hoofcocktailbar.com)
Best cocktails, amazing patio and great staff. Classic.

✖
Black Dice Café (blackdicecafe.com)
A tiny Japanese biker dive bar with great Japanese draft beers and sake.

✖
Gaslight (thegaslightto.com)
Nicest people and most relaxing vibes. Great cocktails and beers!

✖
Edulis (edulisrestaurant.com)
Best atmosphere for a meal and wine pairing. The wine and food pairing is mind blowing.

✖
Imanishi (imanishi.ca)
Delicious Japanese food and great sake selection.

✖
Wildflower (lovesusnot.com)
Best spot for a beer and nachos. Wonderful decor. Cosy and relaxing. Cheap.

MONTREAL*

ISLE DE GARDE

This super-friendly brewpub and European-style restaurant was one of the most pleasant surprises on a recent trip to Montreal. The clear dedication to the beers they curate is there to be seen and the revolving list is really quite something: cask specials from local breweries, as well as – at the time of writing – over 25 different draft beers, including some gluten-free options. Add to this a strong whisky menu and some decent French and New World wines and you have the makings of a perfect little home-from-home – somewhere we'll be returning to in a heartbeat.

✖

1039 Rue Beaubien East, Montreal, QC H2S 1T3 +1 514 303 1661 isledegarde.com

✖

IN THREE WORDS:
Isle De Great.

WE SAY:
One of the definitive highlights of the craft brewpub scene in Montreal.

PRICE RATING: ✱✱

LE LAB ↓

Bartenders, eh. What's in a title. The word "mixologist" seems to bring a mixture of both admiration and loathing across the bartending community and now we have a new one, courtesy of the founder of Le Lab, one of Montreal's undisputed bartending success stories, Fabien Maillard. Under his tenure of over 15 years creating incredible cocktails, he goes under the moniker of Labtender. Some may regard this as a little pretentious, but when you see just what he has achieved at Le Lab the title is wholly justified. After training for a degree in Culinary Arts, Fabian began his bartending career in Paris and has travelled extensively to gain his unique grasp on flavour. The results are absolutely outstanding. The menu is largely split into flavour groups (Powerful and Elegant/Fruity and Inebriating/Prestigious and Decadent), alongside the "Lab's Legends", which are perennial signature drinks. On top of this, the bar team – sorry, Labtenders – have blackboards, which explore a new spirit they have just discovered and also a number of drinks revolving around a certain ingredient not usually associated with cocktails at all.

✖
1351 Rue Rachel East, Montreal,
QC H2J 2K2 +1 514 544 1333
barlelab.com
✖

IN THREE WORDS:
The Dream Factory.
THE DRINK TO TRY:
Fabien's signature drink,
El Commandante.
WE SAY:
At the top of their game, Le Lab
isn't just a great Montreal bar, it's
undoubtedly a world class one.
PRICE RATING: ✱✱✱

LARRY'S

A smart, new addition to the
stylish Mile End area of the
city, Larry's is the next piece of
the puzzle from the owners of
the highly regarded Lawrence
restaurant, delivering a
meticulous selection of over
60 wines, a fine list of local
craft beers and a dozen or so
highly original cocktails – all to
accompany the sumptuous small
plate cuisine. There's a complete
dedication to the craft of serving
on display here – whether you
come in for a morning coffee or
a late-night sharper.
✖
9 Avenue Fairmount East,
Montreal, QC H2T larrys.website
✖

IN THREE WORDS:
Stylish, Creative, Seductive.
THEY SAY:
"A wine/cocktail/small plates
bar – little brother to Lawrence
restaurant (a favourite). Small
but thoughtful selection of
boozes, creative cocktails,
great atmosphere."
— JEREMY GARA, CANADA
PRICE RATING: ✱✱✱

THE SPARROW ↑

A smart split-level restaurant
bar, The Sparrow demonstrates
a move away from a high volume
drinks culture and showcases
a deep understanding of
craftsmanship behind the
bar. Coupled with the modern
European-style cuisine with a
distinct spice running through
many of the dishes, the drinks
list is as classic as can be.
Perennials like the Manhattan,
Old Fashioned and Negroni
meet the likes of The Last Word

**There's a complete
dedication to the
craft of serving on
display here.**

(an undervalued drink, in our
opinion) alongside some decent
house specials – the Basil Gimlet
is a fine choice. Nothing flighty
about this Sparrow.
✖
5322 Boulevard Saint-Laurent,
Montreal, QC H2T 1A5 +1 514 507
1642 sparrow-lemoineau.com
✖

IN THREE WORDS:
Cocktail of A Feather.
WE SAY:
Perfect spot for some brunch,
which could very easily turn into
a night-time return, given the
skill behind the bar.
PRICE RATING: ✱✱

VANCOUVER & CALGARY*

THE KEEFER BAR ↓

The Keefer Bar was established before Vancouver's Chinatown was a hot destination to visit, and it embraces its surroundings by using ingredients from the Chinese shops around it. It also takes aesthetic inspiration from the area: done up like a Chinese apothecary, it welcomes you with a huge, high-rise back bar, which gives the team here a great palate of flavours to play with when making cocktails.

✖

135 Keefer Street, Vancouver, BC V6A 1X3 +1 604 688 1961 thekeeferbar.com

✖

IN THREE WORDS:
Prescriptions, Not Cocktails.

> **The tiki bar is almost an international language. No good city is complete without one, and in Vancouver [Shameful Tiki] is one of the finest tiki bars around.**

WE SAY:
This is one of the coolest hangouts in town.
PRICE RATING: ✱✱✱

SHAMEFUL TIKI

The tiki bar is almost an international language. No good city is complete without one, and in Vancouver this is one of the finest tiki bars around.

The key to a good tiki bar is to start with the decor, and Shameful Tiki has been curated brilliantly, all but bringing the beach hut indoors – which is quite some feat in the cold Canadian winter!

In their Vancouver venue (they also have a site in Toronto) the door is almost hidden from the street, but inside is considerably warmer. Black and white TVs from the 1950s play beach movies, fishing nets hang from the walls and ceiling and there is tiki paraphernalia everywhere. To top it off, they have a fog machine (just to keep the seaside theme real), and of course damn good tiki drinks like the Zombie, Jet Pilot and Mai Tai. Live music can be anything from a surf band through to someone playing a ukulele. Prepare yourself for a true experience.

✖

4362 Main Street, Vancouver, BC V5V 3P9 +1 604 999 5684 shamefultikiroom.com

✖

IN THREE WORDS:
No Shame, None!
THE DRINK TO TRY:
Go for the Grog!
THEY SAY:
"This bar is escapism at its finest and the drinks are awesome."
— **KELSEY RAMAGE, CANADA/ UK**
PRICE RATING: ✱✱✱

SHEBEEN WHISK(E)Y HOUSE ↑

Home to one of the largest selections of Scotch whiskies and American and Irish whiskeys in Canada, this place lists somewhere in the region of 200 different expressions. This is a bar that has a huge following and curates their list for the whisky lovers of Vancouver. Housed in the beautiful heritage building in Gastown, it is simply a wonderful place to while away the hours, for both experts and novices alike.

✖
212 Carrall Street, Vancouver, BC V6B 2J2 +1 604 688 9779
shebeen.ca
✖

IN THREE WORDS:
Whisky And Whiskey.

WE SAY:
A classic hangout in a classic space where you can enjoy a classic Scotch.
PRICE RATING: ✱✱✱

BUCHANAN'S

Buchanan's, a steak and seafood house, doesn't do just burgers and lobster but whisky too. Decked out in classic mahogany and brass with atmospheric school house lights, this intimate bar is home to one of the best whisky lists in North America. Aside from the bottles on display, the rest of the bar is decked out like a proper old-school drinking establishment; part London gin parlour, part classic American bar, this is the perfect spot for anyone in Calgary who is wanting to learn more about the art of drinking whisky.

✖
738 3rd Avenue SW, Calgary, AB T2P 0G7 +1 403 261 4646
buchanans.ca
✖

IN THREE WORDS:
Whisky Winter Wonderland.
WE SAY:
The perfect place to kick back with a flight of Scotch and a great burger.
PRICE RATING: ✱✱✱

FOCUS*

STARTENDER
KELSEY RAMAGE

Canadian-born StarTender Kelsey Ramage was one of the key bartenders at London's **Dandelyan** (see page 31) and has launched a groundbreaking side project with Iain Griffiths – also of Dandelyan fame – called **Trash Tiki** (trashtikisucks. com), a travelling, waste-free, punk pop-up bar that uses spent ingredients from bars and restaurants from all around the world to create delicious tiki drinks with zero-waste.

We caught up with Kelsey over a few drinks to talk about the joys of a Sherry Cobbler and how sustainability will be the word on every bartender's lips for the next few years.

Where do you drink when you're off duty?
The **Sun Tavern**, Bethnal Green (see page 48). This place used to be my local and was one of the first bars I drank at in London, on a recommendation from another bartender. They have really good local brews on tap, paired up with the biggest selection of Irish whiskey I've

> I hope we will continue to strive to create new flavours, use fermentation and preservation and look to chefs for inspiration.

seen outside of Ireland. The bartenders are knowledgable and will suggest something tasty or just pour the usual Green Spot I'll have when I'm there. They are usually good for a laugh or a story about some shenanigans they got up to over the weekend.
Your favourite drink of all time...?
It changes constantly. I have been drinking the Martinez lately, but I love a good Tommy's Margarita.
Where is your favourite city in the world to go drinking in?

I still love Vancouver. The Gastown neighbourhood holds some really excellent cocktail bars, and now there are a few opening up outside of the Gastown core. Some of the best beer is made there too, and many breweries are within biking distance of each other. I also love a good dive bar, and some of the best are in Vancouver.

What do you think is the most underrated cocktail of all time and why?

I love a Sherry Cobbler. They don't get ordered maybe because they don't have a base of whisky or gin and are fairly low ABV. They also don't need many ingredients to be damn delicious either.

What's the most exciting trend in the drinks industry right now?

Sustainability has become a major subject in bars recently. While it can be a bit of an industrial word, I think it will be those bars who really find creative ways to reuse ingredients and create new, interesting flavours with things that previously would have only had one use. Bars have been following restaurants recently and I think we are now where the restaurant industry was five years ago. I hope we will continue to strive to create new flavours, use fermentation and preservation and look to chefs for inspiration in the coming years.

KELSEY'S TOP FIVE, ALL-STAR GLOBAL BARS:

✖
The Lucky Liquor Co, Edinburgh (see page 59)

This bar is so incredibly creative. Opened by the guys from Bramble (see page 58), they bring in 13 different spirits for each menu and only showcase those 13 spirits for the duration of the menu, nothing else. Each time I've been I have had a great cocktail and have been met by staff who are so knowledgable and make what could be a really challenging concept easy, unpretentious and a lot of fun.

✖
The Bar with No Name AKA 69 Colebrooke Row, London (see page 18)

Each outstanding drink has roots in the classics but with a really great twist and such attention to detail. The "dry" Martini is what blew me away. It's a wet-style Martini that uses a grape-seed tincture to introduce tannin into the drink – this is what gives you the dry sensation in red wine.

✖
The Connaught Bar, London (see page 30) ↑

Everything in this bar is absolutely seamless every time I go. The service is completely outstanding, from the front door to your table, the bartenders and servers...everything.

✖
White Lyan, London (whitelyan.com)

Every time I go here there is another drink on the menu that blows me away. Wine without grapes; a Daiquiri without citrus – plus it's always a fun vibe in the room. I think they throw away maybe one bag of waste per week?! More bars need to look to them as inspiration – I am inspired every time I go in.

✖
Shameful Tiki, Vancouver (see page 258)

This bar is escapism at its finest – tiki paraphernalia everywhere, a fog machine, and damn good tiki drinks.

CENTRAL & SOUTH AMERICA*

Countries

INTRO*

With some of the most unforgettable hospitality in the world, it's likely that a visit to any of the bars we have listed here is going to end up as a truly memorable experience.

Mexico's bars in particular are among the most diverse of these,

ranging from sophisticated flavour-led, high art, award-winning mixology, to the most endearing, engaging and downright colourful cantinas, serving incredible Tequilas and mezcals, where you'll make new friends and develop your thirst for agave spirits.

A special mention must go to the wonderful **Café No Sé ↓** (see page 271) in Antigua, Guatemala, and its owner, the charismatic John Rexer (read about his exploits as a mezcal smuggler on page 272), both of which completely embody the ethos of this book and the genuine soulful caress that a great bar can give you.

Lima's growing importance on the international cuisine scene is also to be underestimated at your peril: the rest of the world is seemingly becoming entangled in the sweet, creamy genius of the Pisco Sour and we talk to one of its biggest advocates, the celebrated chef Martin Morales on page 279 about his love for both the city of Lima and this wonderful spirit.

Finally onward to Cuba, a true melting pot of cultures and a place undergoing intense change. The old ways of Havana and its customs are still very much what makes drinking in the city such an awe-inspiring experience. We managed to catch up with one of the true legends of the business, Alejandro Bolívar Rodríguez (see page 275), bartender for the last 25 years at the iconic **El Floridita** (see page 274), which was patronized by Ernest Hemingway.

MEXICO CITY*

BALTRA

Possibly the only bar in the world to take its name and inspiration from one of the Galapagos Islands, Baltra draws on a truly unique influence for its theme, attire and cocktails. Sitting proudly in the Condesa district of Mexico City, the place is surrounded by maps and the odd piece of taxidermy, and has Charles Darwin as its unlikely hero. This is Darwin, however, who lived his life for discovery, and not a fantasy figure such as Phileas Fogg (see Mr Fogg's Residence on page 41), so everything here makes sense, including the excellent cocktails, which change with the seasons. Here it isn't about survival of the fittest, but relaxing with your friends until sunrise.

✖

Iztaccíhuatl 36D, Cuauhtemoc, Condesa, 06100 Mexico City +52 55 5264 1279 baltra.bar

✖

IN THREE WORDS:
Awesome Evolutionary Drinking.

THE DRINK TO TRY:
It's a seasonal menu, so just ask for the bartender's best.
THEY SAY:
"One we love to visit."
— ADRIAN BORGARO,
MEXICO CITY
PRICE RATING: ✳ ✳ ✳

FIFTY MILS

Situated in the Four Seasons Hotel, this bar takes its name from one of the standard tools of the bartenders' trade: the 50ml (2fl oz) jigger, used for measuring out spirits into cocktails.

Here [at Baltra] it isn't about survival of the fittest, but relaxing with your friends until the sun comes back up once again.

Since opening in 2016, it has established itself as one of the best bars in Mexico City, serving not just the international hotel guests but those locals who are looking for the ultimate drinking experience too. A clash of British and Mexican culture, the surroundings are reminiscent of a sumptuous mansion house, with plush furniture, sofas and a lighting regime that bathes the whole place in a subtle lighting. Created by Mica Rousseau, the menu features 10 classic cocktails and 10 newly developed creations, which can be enjoyed either in the relaxing indoor surroundings, or sipped outside in the bar's equally lush open-air section.

✖

The Four Seasons Hotel, Paseo de la Reforma 500, Juarez, 06600 Mexico City +52 (55) 5230-1818 fourseasons.com

✖

IN THREE WORDS:
Pour Me More.
THE DRINK TO TRY:
The Bugs Bunny.
THEY SAY:
"I know Mica and he does everything so well."
— ADRIAN BORGARO,
MEXICO CITY
PRICE RATING: ✳ ✳ ✳ ✳ ✳

LICORERÍA LIMANTOUR ↑ ↓

Limantour has become somewhat of a brand in Mexico City, originally opening in 2011 and gaining such a strong reputation for their cocktails, service and all-round hospitality that the team opened a second venue in the city to cope with demand. The first site, in the ultra-cool district of Roma, was joined by Limantour Polanco, and both sites have become destination bars in the city, setting the standard for cocktails in Mexico as a whole. With an incredible team, there is a passionate drive to deliver great drinks, wrapped in a great drinking experience, from one of the most diligent groups in hospitality. If you find yourself in Mexico City, the original, Roma venue is a must visit for a wonderful cocktail and a truly classic and classy experience.

✖

Avenue Alvaro Obregón, 106
Roma Norte, 06700 Mexico City
+52 55 5264 4122 limantour.tv

✖

IN THREE WORDS:
World Class Cocktails.

THE DRINK TO TRY:
The gin-based Tony Ten is a winner.

WE SAY:
A must when visiting Mexico City.

THEY SAY:
"Amazing mentality from the Mexican bartenders and Tequila cocktails from another dimension."
— ARIS CHATZIANTONIOU, GREECE

PRICE RATING: ✳✳✳

"For my night out in Mexico City I would start at Licoreria Limantour before heading to Baltra, which is a little bit more of a classic bar, and then I would move on to the Fifty Mils bar at the Four Seasons Hotel. Right now it is one of my favourite bars. The bartenders there really focus on hospitality and try to do the best possible things all the time. It really is a fantastic place to have a drink."
– Adrian Borgaro, Limantour, Mexico City

FEATURE*

MEXICO: A DRINKING CULTURE
LIKE NO OTHER...

H ere's a swift round-up of some of Guadalajara's best places to visit, according to our friend, Matt Sykes, Tequila ambassador for Patron – and all-round agave travelling man.

FOR AWESOME COCKTAILS:

✖
Fat Charlie, Guadalajara (+52 33 3615 8513) ↓
A speakeasy bar where the owner is one of the best mixologists in Guadalajara. A real mix of cocktails and music – from DJs to rock to live jazz.

✖
Oliveria, Guadalajara (+52 33 1992 3030)
A nice cocktail bar where all the bartenders and mixologists in Guadalajara hang out. One of the key bars in the Guadalajara cocktail scene.

FOR A MODERN TAKE ON THE CANTINA CONCEPT:

✖
Reyes Salón Cantina, Jalisco (Real de Acueducto 360)
A younger clientele with more tourists, so the focus of the place is to transform the custom of the cantinas into a more contemporary thing.

FOR THE HIGH-END MEXICAN HOTEL BAR EXPERIENCE:

✖
Hotel Demetria, Guadalajara (hoteldemetria.com)
The bar at the Demetria has a a very modern design concept behind it, and its mixologists are always looking to create new cocktails to appeal to the taste of demanding consumers.

FOR THE TRUE CONNOISSEUR SIPPIN' EXPERIENCE:

✖
Pare de Sufrir, Guadalajara (+52 33 3826 1041)
This classic bar is definitely the place of reference for the advocates of the wider agave spirits culture (Tequila, mezcal, Bacanora, raicilla and so on). They really aim to focus on less common Tequilas and mezcal in the marketplace. Highly recommended.

GUADALAJARA*

CANTINA LA FUENTE

"Old School" is a phrase that is overused in modern times, but in the case of Cantina La Fuente, nothing else will do. The place was founded in 1921 and is one of the oldest and most traditional cantinas in the city, bringing with it a unique charm. Don't expect hotel-level service, this is the real deal. Simple drinks, a raucous atmosphere. Everything about it screams Guadalajara like nothing else.

✖

Calle Pino Suárez 78, Zona Centro, Guadalajara

✖

IN THREE WORDS:
Cantina Good Times.

THE DRINK TO TRY:
Whatever your host is having... cerveza, a shot of Tequila...it all tastes good.

WE SAY:
Sometimes it's easy to lose sight of what makes a truly great bar experience. La Fuente is a proper leveller – somewhere that everyone looking for a good time will fit in just fine.

PRICE RATING: ✷

LOS FAMOSOS EQUIPALES

Looking like part of the set from *Fistful Of Dollars*, this cantina is another of Guadalajara's life-changers.

A good number of the pictures on the walls feature a football team, and legend has it that, back in the time when it was okay for footballers to have a quick swig on match day, the team would come here for a little ring-a-ding-ding to liven them up. Today, little has changed. Plonk yourself down in one of the red leather *equipales* (from which the bar takes its name) and order a Tequila – the back bar has plenty of decent ones – or the house speciality, *Nalgas Alegres* (if you can keep a straight face when ordering it...it means Happy Butt).

✖

Calle Juan Álvarez 704, Artesanos, 44200 Guadalajara +52 33 3614 1500

✖

IN THREE WORDS...
Performance Enhancing Fun.

THE DRINK TO TRY:
The Happy Butt: a lurid, bright orange drink, served in a pint glass, consisting of a shot of white rum, one of gin, one of red wine, and lemon juice, topped up with orange crush soda. Not so Happy Butt, more totally Bad Ass.

WE SAY:
Get there in the right frame of mind and you'll have an absolute ball.

PRICE RATING: ✷

ORIENTAL MASCUSIA

Another of Guadalajara's not-to-be-missed cantinas, where the Tequila is free flowing and the beer is always cold. Serving simple but delicious food, the vibe is busy, bustling and highly entertaining. Just make absolutely sure you go there both sober and hungry...you certainly won't leave in the same state.

✖

Avenue Francisco Javier Mina 336, San Juan de Dios, 44360 Guadalajara +52 33 3617 3508

✖

IN THREE WORDS:
Mexican Soul Food.

THEY SAY:
"The idea behind it is the more you drink, the more they feed you, something I think is a fantastic concept, so you drink buckets of beer and bottles of Tequila."
— JON ANDES BORCHGREVINK FJELDSRUD, NORWAY

PRICE RATING: ✷✷

TEQUILA, BOGOTÁ & ANTIGUA*

LA CAPILLA

A hugely popular bar with our esteemed panel of contributors, where the very soul of Tequila runs deep within its ancient walls. One of the oldest cantinas in the town, La Capilla is also run by one of the most charismatic gents you'll find in the business of Tequila – Don Javier, a man with a remarkable twinkle in his eye, renowned the world over not only for his extraordinary hosting skills (he's been doing the job for a *very* long time) but also for his creation – the Batanga. Yes, you could order any number of the great Tequilas Don Javier keeps, but it is the Batanga (ask him how he came up with the name and he'll give you a potted history dating back to the 1960s) that keeps everyone coming back for more. A true legend – in personality and in spirit.

✖
Hidalgo, 46400 Tequila, Jalisco
✖

IN THREE WORDS:
Spirit Of Tequila.

THE DRINK TO TRY:
The Batanga: an explosive long drink over ice, with a hellish amount of silver Tequila, and the juice of one lime, topped up with Coke and stirred with a big knife.

THEY SAY:
"This bar is pure magic."
— **MEGS MILLER, USA/UK**
"The welcome you'll get here is one of the warmest of any bars in the world. Don Javier is a true gent and perfect host."
— **LAURA FOSTER, UK**
"Don Javier is the Buddha of bartenders."
— **AGOSTINO PERRONE, ITALY/UK**

PRICE RATING: ✱✱

BLACK BEAR ↓

Bogotá is undergoing something of a cocktail renaissance, with a few bars picking up the American and European idea of high-end service and cocktail creation. One of the key leaders of the scene is Black Bear. Housed in a beautifully designed room, the well-dressed and presented bartenders want to encourage local drinkers to expand their flavours and are willing to let you try different cocktails, if you don't like the first. Here, it is all about the escape, the enjoyment and the service. When the room is full, the place comes to life and

the staff always wear a smile. Wonderfully stylish, the menu is easy to read and the drinks very well curated.

✖
Carrera 11a #89-06, Bogotá, +57 1 6447766
blackbear.com.co
✖

IN THREE WORDS:
New World Order.

WE SAY:
A stunning bar that wouldn't be out of place in London or New York.

PRICE RATING: ✳✳✳✳

THE UGLY AMERICAN

You might think this a strange name for a joint, but this restaurant-cum-diner focuses on all-American food and drinks, such as burgers and waffles, with an excellent selection of cocktails. You'll be drawn in by the homely environment and then you'll discover their cocktails, such as the Bogotá Donkey, made with vodka, house ginger beer and blackberry syrup. The concept behind the bar was to present cocktails that complement the food, and it works very well indeed. There is a focus on natural ingredients and authentic flavours which work brilliantly.

✖
Calle 81, #9–12, Bogotá
+57 1 644 7766 uglyamerican.co
✖

IN THREE WORDS:
Really Very Pretty.

WE SAY:
They've nailed the concept of an American-style joint in Bogotá. Pop in for food and drink.

PRICE RATING: ✳✳✳✳

CAFÉ NO SÉ ↑

If there's one thing that's influenced the DNA of this book, it's that genuinely extraordinary first impression that places like Café No Sé instantly instil in the soul. Located in the colonial capital of Antigua in Guatemala, this dark, ramshackle bar brings more light, life and sheer experience to the drinker than most gleaming hotel bars could ever dream of. It's the sort of place that time forgot, suddenly remembered, then chose to forget about again, for fear that any contemporary intervention would ruin the unique vibe for an eternity. Inside, the space is split into three zones: a live music area leads into a buzzing little back bar, where cocktails are thrown with abandon. It is in here that you'll notice a small fridge door – this leads into the mezcal shot bar, which is really where the evening gets started. Mezcal may not be for everyone, but in here, it tastes like the finest nectar to pass your lips and the more you have will somewhat ironically reinforce the stories – and memories – that you tell about the place for years to come. Truly remarkable.

✖
1a Avenida Sur, Antigua, Guatemala +502 5501 2680
cafenose.com
✖

IN THREE WORDS:
I Don't Know.

THE DRINK TO TRY:
Unquestionably two shots of Ilegal Joven mezcal: 100% agave, Oaxacan sun, water and time.

THEY SAY:
"A truly unforgettable location and a bar that edges on just the right side of dangerous in many ways."
— **THOMAS ASKE, UK**
"The best bit about this place is the secret mezcal bar."
— **ALEX KAMMERLING, UK**

PRICE RATING: ✳

271

FOCUS*

STARTENDER
JOHN REXER

As the owner of the truly wondrous Café No Sé, John Rexer is effectively the host to clients he describes as "a funky petri dish" of visitors. He's also one of the men who first bought mezcal into the country, albeit illegally, giving birth to his brand Ilegal Mezcal, which you'll find cropping up in some of the coolest joints all over the world.

Where do you drink when you're off duty?

When home in Guatemala I go to **El Paso**, a family-owned cantina on 7th Avenida Norte, where everyone drinks the local aguardiente, Quetzalteca. It costs about a buck for a very generous measure. With each drink you get a small plate of food. I go there because it's a bar where I can hide, throw up my feet, and escape into another world to erase a few unwanted thoughts.

How did you start your journey into mezcal and what was the motivation behind Ilegal?

I was living in Mexico in the late 1990s and had spent a good deal of time in Oaxaca. I fell in love

with the countryside, the rough landscape, the food, the ever-changing light, the markets, the beautiful buzz from drinking mezcal, and especially the warmth of the people. In 2003, I opened Café No Sé. I wanted to have mezcal in my bar, but there was one big problem: at the time mezcal was not legal for export. It was pretty easy to cross the border into Guatemala with a few bottles – but in a quantity enough to stock a small bar for a few months, well, that was tricky. We had to get creative. On rafts made of wood slats and tyres, under cover of night, we crossed the river that separates Mexico from Guatemala. Hence the name Ilegal. It took until

2006 to get our first bottles legally into Guatemala, and until 2009 to bring a small quantity to the USA.

What is your favourite city in the world to go drinking in?

Probably Prague. I was only there for a few days, but have to say it is my favourite city for drinking. The city has so many layers of history. Romanticism and nihilism walk hand in hand. The architecture – Baroque, Gothic, Renaissance standing side by side. The city is food for the soul. Drink goes well with that food. I don't remember a single name of the many bars I stumbled into and out of. I just have one ecstatic, swimming, vague memory. That's a good sign.

Why do you think Café No Sé has become such a memorable destination for people to visit?

When I first started the place I had no idea what I was doing. I was just trying to put most of my vices under one roof and hoped people would show up. Thankfully they did. I don't know if it is memorable – our first T-shirt used to read, *Café No Sé... For a Night You Won't Remember.*

Take us on a great day/night bar crawl drinking in the town of Antigua: where would you start and ultimately end up?

Hmmm. So let's say the night before was rough. Around noon

I would wander over to **Panza Verde** (panzaverde.com), an old-world boutique hotel. There I would sit in the bar near reception and order a Bull Shot – a mix of warm beef bouillon and joven mezcal. I'd have one or two of those to cut through the fog. From there I'd make my way east to **The Snug** (+502 5838 5390) and get a shot of Jameson and a beer. Then I'd probably have another shot and beer and walk out forgetting to pay. Then I'd hit **Hugo's Ceviches**, (+502 7832 9354) and have a mixed ceviche and a couple of Micheladas.

From there it's a short walk to my bar, where I'd be greeted with a mezcal. After one or two, I'd head off to **El Paso** where we'd drink Quetzalteca and Coke while eating strange pieces of deep-fried meat, chopped hot dogs and mini bean tostadas. By then it would be about 6pm and God only knows what the evening holds in store.

When I first started the place, I had no idea what I was doing. I was just trying to put most of my vices under one roof and hoped people would show up.

JOHN'S ALL-STAR WORLDWIDE FAVOURITE BARS:

✖
Smalls, New York (smallslive.com) *The jazz musicians' jazz bar. It's a tiny, seedy, dark basement bar from heaven. The place has soul. I've been going there on and off for 20 years. Great drinks, best jazz in the city. Always feel at home.*

✖
Barbès, Brooklyn, New York (barbesbrooklyn.com) ↑ *In the front is a no-nonsense bar. Music or films every night in a small room in the back. Eclectic and magical. On one night you might find Mexican banda, on another blues, on another Slavic soul, and on and on. I love this place.*

✖
Los Cocos, Oaxaca, Mexico (+52 951 516 5889) *Cocos is a real Mexican cantina. Closes early, because by then passions are running high and things are sideways and perfectly out of control. The owner, Pepe, has seen it all, and like all great barkeeps he quietly commands respect and takes it all in his stride.*

✖
Harvard & Stone, Los Angeles (see page 239) *Shots, canned beer, and cocktails served without pretentiousness.*

Great music venue with a line-up ranging from punk to hippy country – sometimes on the same night.

✖
Ducks Eatery, New York (duckseatery.com) *If a bar was ever about the staff then this is it...they make the place. Genuine smart attitude, but with a sense of humour and good fun. If you go for "one drink" forget about it, you'll end up there for the better part of the night.*

✖
Chelsea Pub, Atlantic City (chelseapubandinn.com) *This place is beyond seedy. It is open 24 hours a day and has not closed one day in 40 years. The ceiling is so low that there is no back bar, all the booze is under the bar. Every interesting walk of low-life comes in this place. If a bar has bar stories, this is it.*

HAVANA*

FÁBRICA DE ARTE CUBANO (FAC)

FAC is a multi-use arts space/ project in an old peanut oil factory. Each floor houses something different: a bar, a cinema, a live music venue, dance classes, an art installation, a gallery collection…you name it, it's going on. So much vibrancy in one place, it's as if Mitte in Berlin, Williamsburg in New York and Shoreditch in London have all been distilled into one premises. The tall chimney will guide you into this building and if you head up the spiral staircase you'll find El Cocinero, an astonishingly good restaurant and rooftop bar, which is the ideal place to go for a cocktail before you enter the brilliant madness of FAC.

✖

Calle 26, Esquina 11, Vedado, Havana +53 7 8382260 fac.cu

✖

IN THREE WORDS:
Fun. Arts. CUBA!
WE SAY:
Just one of the best places to go drinking in the world.
PRICE RATING: ✳ ✳ ✳

EL FLORIDITA →

With the current spirits world dominated by perfectly polished smiling faces, extolling their latest product, it's easy to become jaded by celebrity endorsees. So cast your mind back to some of the greatest thinking/drinking celebrities of the past and, in particular, Ernest Hemingway. By sheer coincidence, several drinking dens around the world have gained his patronage, long after he departed the earth. It's easy to be cynical about such things, but when visiting Havana it's almost impossible to escape the influence of his presence on the culture of the city. Propping up the side bar at El Floridita is a full-sized bronze statue of the man in question and it's easy to see why Old Papa was such a fan of the place. El Floridita may well be a hugely popular tourist destination, but it remains a fine example of how important the Daiquiri is to Cuban culture. Here, they're largely served frozen, by gentlemen in red bartending jackets, while in the background a laid-back band of Cuban musicians lays down the perfect drinking soundtrack. It sounds as corny as can be, but it's not. Do this anywhere else and it would stink to high heaven of pastiche. But here you live, breathe and sip Cuban life,

the memories of which you will never, ever forget.

✖

Obispo No. 557 esq. a Monserrate, Havana 10100 +53 7 8671299 floridita-cuba.com

✖

IN THREE WORDS:
Papa Knows Best.
THE DRINK TO TRY:
The Frozen Daiquiri.
THEY SAY:
"What bars should be about: fun; music; elegance. Hemingway knew where to drink…it's a fact!"
— MARIAN BEKE, SLOVAKIA/UK
"A historical bar and a Mecca for the Daiquiri lover."
— KRISZTIÁN CSIGÓ, BUDAPEST
PRICE RATING: ✳ ✳ ✳

FOCUS*

STARTENDER
ALEJANDRO BOLÍVAR RODRÍGUEZ

Arguably one of the most famous drinking locations anywhere in the world, El Floridita has captured the hearts and palates of those visiting with its timeless feel, hypnotic Cuban music and ice-cold Daiquiris, to which the bar has given its own inimitable twist. Overseeing their preparation for nearly 25 years is head bartender Alejandro Bolívar Rodríguez, a man in possession of one of the finest smiles in the business and an intimate knowledge of one of Cuba's finest cocktails.

Tell us about your favourite places to drink around the world...

When I'm back in Cuba, I like to drink at home, where I have my own bar. I live near the beach so it's a perfect place to enjoy a nice drink! When it comes to travelling, in New Orleans there is **French 75** (see page 232), which I really like. When I'm in London, it has to be the **Connaught Bar** (see page 30). When it comes to Paris, the Ritz bar [the **Hemingway Bar**] (ritzparis.com) is a great place to have a drink.

What would you say is your all-time favourite drink?

I love drinking an Old Fashioned, but Cuba-style, made with a dark rum. I like it with a good Cuban cigar.

Pssst...the secret is out! After a little persuasion, Alejandro has given us the recipe to the Daiquiri Floridita, so stick one of Buena Vista Social Club's finest on the stereo, grab some ice and break out the rum. Summer's here...wherever you are.

DAIQUIRI FLORIDITA
✖
1 teaspoon white sugar
juice of ½ a lime
5 drops of maraschino liqueur
40ml Havana Club 3-year-old
    light rum
125g crushed ice

Whizz all the ingredients in a blender for about 30 seconds and serve in a Martini glass.

FEATURE*

A DAY DRINKING IN...
HAVANA

Havana is city that is starting to change, but thankfully not very quickly. With the easing of the once-tense relationship with their near neighbour America, there will soon be a steady flow of Cuban cigars and rum into the USA, giving yet another opportunity for the country's most famous products to find new fans.

Of course, this is bound to have an impact upon the numbers of visitors looking for a trip to Havana and a classic Cuban drinking experience, and quite rightly so, as Havana has some of the most interesting drinking spots around: from classic bars through to rooftop hang-outs, Havana is a great place to share a cocktail...and a cigar!

Yes it's clichéd, but it's essential to take a ride in one of the classic Cadillac-style cars that roam the streets. Couple this with a visit to a cigar factory such as the **Partagas Facility** (+53 7 338060) and you'll be feeling the Cuban beats before lunch. If you have some time, take in the **Museo del Ron Havana Club** (+54 11 4413 7126) where you

Havana has some of the most interesting drinking spots around: from classic bars through to rooftop hang-outs.

can have a tour of the history of rum, and how it has taken root in Cuba. At the end you can pillage the shop for a bottle of rum, or simply relax with a Cuba Libre, with the local soft drink TuKola.

The next stop on a proper drinking tour of Havana would be at one of Hemingway's locals, **Bodeguita del Medio ↑** (+53 7 571375). Bodeguita is situated in one of the streets leading into the Plaza de la Catedral where the stunning Catedral de San Cristóbal sits, and the tiny place churns out Mojitos non-stop. Make sure you have a marker pen with you to sign the walls of the bar.

Next up, head over to **Sloppy Joe's →** (+53 7 8667157), the legendary bar that welcomed

tourists from America during the days of Prohibition. It also featured in the film *Our Man In Havana* when the bustling bar hosted Alec Guinness.

Heading back on the Hemingway trail, do not fail to visit **El Floridita** (see page 274) before grabbing a drink at **Siá Kará** (+53 78 67 40 84). A bohemian bar in style with the vibe of someone's front room, it is the hangout for hipsters and those-in-the-know, with seriously well made, seriously cheap cocktails.

Finally, finish your night on the spectacular rooftop bar, **La Guarida** ↑ (laguarida.com). The entrance to this restaurant and bar demands that you enter what looks like a disused building, with a sweeping staircase that looks as if it has been taken from an abandoned 1920s film set. The food here is simply wonderful and once you climb the stairs to the roof terrace, you'll have the perfect end to your evening. Enjoy the stunning views across the city, while you relax with another cigar and a choice of any of the great cocktails from the impressive list.

LIMA*

THE ENGLISH BAR AT THE COUNTRY CLUB HOTEL →

Quite an eccentric gem inside the traditional 1920s splendour of this wonderful fine-dining boutique hotel, the English Bar, or Bar Inglés as it is known, is built to resemble a traditional English pub, complete with wood panelling and an impressive back bar mirror. While it's not the sort of place you're used to seeing these days in London (they've mostly gone gastro), the vibe is perfect. But rather than warm pints of nut brown ale, the Pisco Sour is the order of the day...and what an order it is. Arguably one of the finest in Lima, this simple (but often maligned) drink is served strong but balanced, and is deliciously quaffable. *Salud!*

✖
Calle Los Eucaliptos 590,
San Isidro, Lima 15076
+51 1 611 9000 hotelcountry.com
✖

IN THREE WORDS:
Pour Blimey, Guvnor!

But rather than warm pints of nut brown ale, the Pisco Sour is the order of the day...and what an order it is.

THE DRINK TO TRY:
While the gin and whisky selection is outstanding, you would be remiss not to enjoy the country's national drink here – it's a cracker.

THEY SAY:
"This is the place for a great Pisco Sour."
— JOHNNY SCHULER, PERU

PRICE RATING: ★★★★★

FEATURE*

IN THE KNOW...
MARTIN MORALES

Peruvian chef, former record company executive and pisco connoisseur Martin Morales, founder of London's Ceviche (see page 27), speaks about his favourite drinking hangouts in Lima.

✖

I love **Bar Piselli** (28 De Julio 297, Barranco 15063) to have a great beer with friends, **Bar Victoria** (Pedro de Osma, Barranco 15063) if I'm hanging out with artists or musicians, and **Ayahuasca Bar** (ayahuascarestobar.com) if I'm taking tourist guests. All in Barranco – the neighbourhood that inspired Ceviche Soho in its design and vibe – a neighbourhood full of life, bohemians, musicians, artists and great food and drinks.

If I want to be really old-skool I go to **Bar Cordano** (restaurantecordano.com) in downtown Lima. It inspired Ceviche Old St. and is a colonial period bar, with dark wood, granite tables and great food and drinks.

MARTIN'S TOP FIVE AROUND THE WORLD:

✖

Ceviche Old St, London [strictly speaking you shouldn't select your own bar, but...oh, go on then!] (cevicheuk.com) *Because it is gorgeous, witty, innovative and has the warmest and most fascinating bar staff. And because I spend half of my life there!*

✖

Bar Juanito, Lima (Av. Almte. Miguel Grau 270, Distrito de Lima) *Because it inspired Ceviche Soho and was the legendary bar favourite of Allen Ginsberg and many great poets, writers and musicians. They know me, welcome me and there's always someone fun to talk to there.*

✖

Dead Rabbit, New York (see page 212) *Because they do unpretentious food and drinks, have great beer, cocktails and their concept menus are world class.*

✖

La Boca Del Lobo, Madrid (labocadellobo.com) *I DJed there 15 years ago, then took Miley Cyrus there 8 years ago and I always pop in every time I'm in Madrid.*

✖

Nightjar, London (see page 43) *Perfect for taking out-of-towners on a night out. It's like seeing a show like Cirque du Soleil, but in cocktail form.*

✖

Also check out Lima's **Malabar** *(malabar.com.pe), which lays claim to yet more excellence with both pisco and the Pisco Sour.*

BUENOS AIRES, BRASÍLIA, FLORIANÓPOLIS & RIO*

THE HARRISON SPEAKEASY

The Harrison Speakeasy, apart from being brilliantly named (if you're a Harrison), is one of the leading bars in the region, making "proper" cocktails that take a twist on classic numbers, with a healthy dose of creative flair on the side. The venue itself is a relaxing haunt, which is hidden away behind a sushi shop. Membership to this hidden bar helps, but then so does a smile and a kind word to your waiter, if you're dining at the front restaurant. It has a sister venue, Frank's Bar (see right), which requires a password to enter through a telephone booth. Both these venues will take you on a real journey.

✖

Malabia 1764, Buenos Aires C1414DMJ CABA
+54 11 4831 0519
nicky-harrison.com

✖

IN THREE WORDS:
Properly Hidden Cocktails.
WE SAY:
Try whatever you can to get in.
PRICE RATING: ✶✶✶✶

FRANK'S BAR

The concept of the speakeasy bar is something we've explored throughout this book, and without question Frank's Bar (which is about as far removed in geographical terms as possible from the other Frank's we've included – in London, see page 33) ticks all the right boxes. Classic discreet signage on the street? Check. False door? Check. (This time, a phone box.) Secret password to get in? Check. Sex shop also included? Check... What??! Wait! Yes, this is where Frank's perhaps differs from most. But although prudish visitors might worry about where they're being taken as they pass by a few interesting "toys", rest assured – once inside, the glamour, timeless elegance of the decor (think Roaring Twenties) and, of course, the outstanding drinks will transport you well and truly to the hedonistic era that has clearly influenced the place. Just don't forget to bring the password with you...cryptic clues on their Facebook page will help you here.

✖

Arévalo 1443, Buenos Aires, C1414CQC CABA
+54 11 4777 6541

✖

IN THREE WORDS:
Calling The Shots.

THEY SAY:
"Unashamedly theatrical, with cracking cocktails to back it up."
—**MATT SYKES, UK**
PRICE RATING: ✶✶✶✶

PARADISO CINE BAR

Rather like Zoetrope in Tokyo (see page 139), Paradiso Cine Bar pays homage to the moving image – albeit in a slightly more modern fashion. As you descend the staircase into this fine establishment you'll find all manner of images taken largely from cult US films (*Pulp Fiction*, *Kill Bill* and so on) and this cinematic theme remains throughout the menu of cocktails and food. But a gimmick it is not: the drinks range from the classically styled Godfather (American whiskey and Amaretto), through to the Jack Sparrow – a novel take on the Mojito, served up in "caviar" form.

✖

SHCS 306, Bloco B, Loja 4, Asa Sul, Brasília +55 61 3526 8072
paradisobar.com.br

✖

IN THREE WORDS:
Lights: Camera: Cocktails.
WE SAY:
A fun, unpretentious drinking experience.
PRICE RATING: ✶✶✶

BOOKS & BEERS

For anyone fortunate enough to visit Santa Catarina, to the southwest of the mainland, the beaches, nightlife and vibe are the main attraction. However, if, like us, you happen to visit during the rainy season you'll want to find yourself a table at Books & Beers, which has an impressive offering of draft and bottled beers, showcasing Brazil's penchant for brewing. Alongside the freshly made ceviche-style food, there's a library to grab a book from (largely in Portuguese though!) and the whole place is perfect to relax in while the storm outside passes by.

✖

Rua Senador Ivo D'Aquino, 103
Florianópolis 88062-050
+55 48 3206 6664
booksbeers.com

✖

IN THREE WORDS:
Read all About It!

WE SAY:
Great beers, great atmosphere – simple pleasures done brilliantly.

PRICE RATING: ✷ ✷ ✷

CAVERNA

This place is a must for anyone who is a fan of hard music and hard liquor. The cocktails are paired with great tunes. A sneak peek of the playlist on offer is given away by the giant neon sign, which simply reads "Highway To Hell" and quotes from songs hidden around the venue. Yes, indeed!

The Hard Rock Cafe this isn't; true and trusted, it is. Expect your cocktails to use the kind of booze found on a band's rider: rum, bourbon and vodka, but served up with real style and paired well with American-inspired food. Fancy a shot? They have a special menu for these too...now that's rock'n'roll, and we like it.

✖

Rua Assis Bueno, 26 Loja
Botafogo, Rio de Janeiro
+55 21 3507 5600
espacocaverna.com

✖

IN THREE WORDS:
R. O. CK!

WE SAY:
Highway to Hell? Stairway to Heaven, more like.

PRICE RATING: ✷ ✷ ✷

ACADEMIA DA CACHAÇA ↑

It is said that the Academia da Cachaça "tastes like Brazil", and there's probably no better way to sum up this place, which is decked out with the iconic colours of green and yellow (the walls and also their drinks. Cachaça, of course, takes centre stage both neat and in cocktails, with one creation using flavoured ice, which brilliantly changes the drink as it melts. This is the level of creativity here and long may it continue. Oh, and don't forget the food!

✖

Rua Conde de Bernadotte,
26 - Leblon, Rio de Janeiro
+55 21 2239 1542
academiadacachaca.co.br

✖

IN THREE WORDS:
Cachaça Me Up!

WE SAY:
Brilliantly Brazilian – a must visit.

PRICE RATING: ✷ ✷

CONTRIBUTORS*

OUR SINCERE THANKS, SALUTATIONS & CHEERS...

Behind many of the suggested establishments featured in this book is an array of creative minds, brilliant palates and ultimately the people we love enjoying a drink with most. You'll see their comments all the way through the book and, if you'd like to learn more about them, we've included their websites, Twitter and/or Instagram feeds below. So check them out. Thanks, guys. Raising a glass of something extra-special to each and every one of you.

Helmut Adam (Germany)
Founder, Bar Convent Berlin
barconvent.com, @HelmutAdam

Karina Aggarwal (India)
Beverage commentator and founder
gigglewater411.com, @Giggle_water

Staffan Alexandersson (Sweden)
Bartender, The Tasting Room, Bergen
thetastingroom.no

Marc Alvarez Safont (Spain)
Group bar manager, @sir_negroni

Louis Anderman (USA)
Owner, Miracle Mile Bitters Co.
miraclemilebitters.com, @MMBitters

Jon Anders Borchgrevink Fjeldsrud (Norway)
Brand champion, Amathus Drinks
amathusdrinks.com, @AmathusJon

Mark Andrew (UK)
Co-founder, *Noble Rot* magazine
noblerot.co.uk

Sandeep Arora (India)
Whisky Expert, spiritualluxuryliving.com

Thomas Aske (UK)
Director, Fluid Movement; Owner,
Whistling Shop, Black Rock and Surfside
fluid-movement.com; @Taske1

Marian Beke (Slovakia)
Bartender and director, The Gibson
thegibsonbar.london, @marianbeke

Georgie Bell (UK)
Global malts ambassador, Bacardi
@BellesWhisky

Monica Berg (Norway)
Bartender, Himkok; Founder member of
(P)Our, pourdrink.org; @Monicasuh

Stephan Berg (Germany)
Co-founder, The Bitter Truth GmbH
the-bitter-truth.com, @yourbittertruth

Alejandro Bolivar Rodriguez (Cuba)
Bartender, Floridita, Havana
floridita-cuba.com

Adrian Borgano (Mexico)
Bartender, limatour.tv

James Bowker (UK)
Head bartender, Edgbaston Hotel
theedgbaston.co.uk @jhbowker

Dave Broom (UK)
Drinks writer, scotchwhisky.com
@davebroomwhisky

Jared Brown (UK, via USA)
Drinks historian and distiller, Sipsmith
Distillery, sipsmith.com, mixellany.com,
@mixellany

Alastair Burgess (UK)
Bar owner, Happiness Forgets, Original Sin
and Petit Pois Bistro
happinessforgets.com @AliLovesADrink

Sam Bygrave (Australia)
Editor, *Australian Bartender*
australianbartender.com.au, @sambygrave

Derek Chang (China)
Marketing director, Whisky L, whiskyl.com

Aris Chatziantoniou (Greece)
Bar owner, MoMix, momixbar.gr

Helen Chesshire (UK)
Founder, distiller, Brighton Gin
brightongin.com, @thechesshireset

Ryan Chetiyawardana (UK)
Bartender, aka Mr Lyan
mrlyan.com, @RyanCheti

Tony Conigliaro (UK)
Bartender, author and founder, Drink
Factory, thedrinkfactory.com

Tash Conte (Australia)
Bartender and owner, The Black Pearl,
Melbourne, blackpearlbar.com.au

Devin Cross (South Africa)
Bartender and whisky expert,
@DevinCross

Krisztián Csigó (Hungary)
Bartender, Boutiq'Bar, @krisztian_csigo

Alex Davies (UK)
Head Distiller, The Kyoto Distillery, Japan
kyotodistillery.jp, @Alexjfdavies

Raissa de Haas (Netherlands)
Co-founder and CEO, Double Dutch Drinks
doubledutchdrinks.com

Javier de las Muelas (Spain)
Bartender and owner, Dry Martini
Organisation, drymartiniorg.com,
@DryMartiniJDLM

Megs DeMeulenaere (Canada)
House of Tequila ambassador, Pernod
Ricard UK, @megsmiller

Gregg Donovan (Australia)
Artist manager and whisky enthusiast

Rebekkah Dooley (UK)
Events, marketing and PR Director,
The Dead Rabbit and BlackTail, NYC
@RebekkahDooley

Peter Dorelli (UK, via Italy)
Bartender and educator

Philip Duff (Republic of Ireland)
Spirits educator, Tales of the Cocktail
talesofthecocktail.com, @philipduff

Marcis Dzelzainis (UK)
Director, Abacus Drinks Ltd
Drink maker, Sager + Wilde
sagerandwilde.com, @mr_marcis

Katie Emmerson (USA)
Bartender, @katiejean36

Lizzy Evdokimova (Russia)
Bartender, Garden and Twins, Shanghai

Haley Forest (USA)
Connector of dots, hospitality consultant,
freelance writer
@HCForest

Laura Foster (UK)
Drinks journalist
laurafoster.net, @LauFoster

Jeremy Gara (Canada)
Musician, Arcade Fire, @metajeremy

Amanda Garnham (UK)
Attachée de Presse for Armagnac; Founder
of glamourandgumboots.com
@ArmagnacManiac

Eduardo Gomez (Mexico)
Founder and director, Tequila & Mezcal Fest
tequilafest.co.uk

Gal Granov (Israel)
Founder and editor, Whisky Israel
whiskyisrael.co.il, @whiskyIsrael

Lyndsey Gray (UK)
Quaich Bar manager at The Craigellachie
Hotel, @thecraigellachie dramsandscran.
wordpress.com, @lyndsey_gray

Ken Grier (UK)
Creative director, The Macallan
themacallan.com

Iain Griffiths (Australia)
Creative and development manager for
Mr Lyan Ltd; Co-founder, Trash Tiki
trashtikisucks.com, @trashtiki
@iaingriffiths_

Daryl Haldane (UK)
Drinks expert, @DarylHaldane

Aaron Hayden (Ireland)
General manager, Peruke & Periwig, Dublin
peruke.ie

Jon Hillgren (Sweden)
Founder and master distiller, Hernö Gin
hernogin.com, @HernoGin

Rogerio Igarashi Vaz (Japan)
Bartender and co-owner, Bar Trench
small-axe.net, @Rogemadruga

Alex Kammerling (UK)
Founder and director, Kamm & Sons
kammandsons.com, @KammAndSons

Sarunas Karalius (Lithuania)
Owner, King & Mouse Whisky Bar
kingandmouse.lt

Allen Katz (USA)
Co-founder, New York Distilling Company
nydistilling.com, @nydistilleryman

Hiroyasu Kayama (Japan)
Bartender and owner, Benfiddich, Tokyo

Dan Keeling (UK)
Co-founder, *Noble Rot* magazine
noblerot.co.uk

Alex Kratena (Czech Republic)
Bartender and co-founder,
(P)Our Foundation
alexkratena.com, @Alex_Kratena

Vasilis Kyritsis (Greece)
Bartender and co-founder, The Clumsies,
Athens, theclumsies.gr

Yangdup Lama (India)
Mixologist and owner, Cocktails and
Dreams Speakeasy, Delhi
cndspeakeasy.com, @YangdupLama

Hannah Lanfear (UK)
International Brand Ambassador/Director
of Sales, Jensen's Gin, jensensgin.com,
@jensensgin, @hannahlanfear

Sandrae Lawrence (UK)
Editor, The Cocktail Lovers
thecocktaillovers.com, @cocktaillovers

Oron Lerner (Israel)
Owner, operator, bartender and dishwasher
French57 bar, Tel Aviv
french57.com @French57

Steven Lin (Taiwan)
General manager, THAI-YU Co. Ltd
facebook.com/whiskymaster

Yao Lu (USA)
Bartender and co-owner of Union Trading
Company, Shanghai, @uniontradingco

Stuart McCluskey (UK)
Bar owner, The Bon Vivant, Edinburgh
bonvivantedinburgh.co.uk, @StuMcCluskey

Jack McGarry (Ireland)
Managing partner, The Dead Rabbit NYC
deadrabbitnyc.com, @JackMcGarry1

Joe McGirr (Ireland)
Founder and CEO, The Boatyard Distillery,
Northern Ireland
boatyarddistillery.com, @Whiskywingsuit

Joerg Meyer (Germany)
Bartender and founder, Le Lion
lelion.net, @joergmeyer

Kieran Middleton (UK)
Brewer and business development manager,
Bellfield Brewery, bellfieldbrewery.com,
@Kieranmiddleton

Anistatia Miller (UK, via USA)
Director of Mixellany Limited
mixellany.com, @mixellany

Martin Morales (Peru)
Founder, chef, Ceviche and Andina
cevicheuk.com, andinalondon.com,
@martinceviche

Nick Morgan (UK)
Head of Whisky Outreach, Diageo
@nicholasjmorgan

Eddie Nara (Hong Kong)
Whisk(e)y consultant, @eNaraWhisky

Laura Nissinen (Finland)
Head bartender, A21 Decades
a21.fi/en/decades

Stephen Notman (UK)
Drinks expert, founder Whisky L
whiskyl.com, @Whiskyasia

Jane Overeem (Australia)
Brand ambassador, Overeem Whisky; Sales
and marketing manager, Lark Distillery
overeemwhisky.com, larkdistillery.com
@janeovereemwhisky

Jane Parkinson (UK)
Wine writer, author and broadcaster
janeparkinson.com, @jane_parkinson

Agostino Perrone (Italy)
Director of mixology, The Connaught
the-connaught.co.uk

Tess Posthumus (Holland)
Bartender and hospitality professional
tesspostumus.com, @tessposthumus

Keshav Prakash (India)
Founder and chief curator, The Vault
vaultfinespirits.com, @vaultspirits

Kelsey Ramage (Canada)
Bartender and co-founder, Trash Tiki
trashtikisucks.com, @trashtiki,
@KelseyRamage

Jon Rexer (USA)
Owner, Café No Sé and founder, Ilegal
Mezcal, Guatemala cafenose.com, @
IlegalMezcal

Tim Ridley (New Zealand)
Barista, @TimRidley

Joan Samia (Kenya)
Head bartender, Artcaffe Coffee & Bakery,
Kenya, artcaffe.co.ke, @samia_joan

Remy Savage (France)
Head bartender at Little Red Door
lrdparis.com @LRDparis, @RemypSavage

Bernhard Schäfer (Germany)
Spirits expert
@silberohr25

Johnny Schuler (Peru)
Master distiller Destileria La Caravedo,
Pisco Portón and Pisco La Caravedo, Peru
piscoporton.com, lacaravedo.com
@piscojohnny

Davide Segat (Italy)
Bar manager, the Punch Room at
The London EDITION
@davidesegat

Andy Shannon (UK)
Head of bar operations at The London
EDITION, editionhotels.com/london

Dima Sokolov (Russia)
Bartender and owner, Mr Help, Moscow
mrhelpbar.ru

Matthew Sykes (UK)
Director of international marketing,
Patrón Tequila, patrontequila.com,
@mcwsykes

Karl Too (Malaysia)
Bartender and co-owner,
Omakase + Appreciate
facebook.com/omakaseappreciate

Michael Vachon (USA)
Head of brand development, Maverick
Drinks, maverickdrinks.com,
@MaverickDrinks

Alain Vervoort (Belgium)
Bartender trainer, BarConnector
@Barconnector

Kristen Voisey (Canada)
Owner, Cocktail Emporium,
cocktailemporium.ca, @cocktailemporium

Josh Wang (China)
Whisky and spirits writer; Founder,
Spirits Magazine

Liza Weisstuch (USA)
Freelance writer, editor and spirits judge
lizaweisstuch.com, @livingtheproof

Sadie Whitelocks (UK)
Lifestyle writer and intrepid barfly
@isleofsadie

Alex Wolpert (UK)
Founder, East London Liquor Company
eastlondonliquorcompany.com
@eastlondonliquorcompany

INDEX*

MAJOR PAGE REFERENCES ARE IN BOLD

PICTURE CREDITS*